Feminist Art Criticism

An Anthology

Studies in the Fine Arts: Criticism, No. 27

Donald B. Kuspit, Series Editor

Professor of Art History
State University of New York at Stony Brook

Other Titles in This Series

Feminist Art Criticism
An Anthology

Edited by
Arlene Raven
Cassandra L. Langer
and
Joanna Frueh

U·M·I Research Press
Ann Arbor / London

Produced and distributed by
UMI Research Press
an imprint of
University Microfilms Inc.
Ann Arbor, Michigan 48106

Library of Congress Cataloging in Publication Data

Feminist art criticism.

   (Studies in fine arts. Criticism ; no. 27)
   Includes bibliographies and index.
   1. Feminism and art—United States. 2. Feminist
art criticism—United States. 3. Women artists—
United States—Biography—History and criticism.
I. Raven, Arlene. II. Langer, Cassandra. III. Frueh,
Joanna. IV. Series: Studies in the fine arts.
Criticism ; no. 27.
N72.F45F445 1988   701'.03   88-4800
ISBN 0-8357-1878-6 (alk. paper)

British Library CIP data is available.

For all the women
who have made this book possible
especially
Doris Month Langer
and
Ricki Levenson

Contents

Foreword

These essays take us back to a kind of golden age of feminist thinking—it was not long ago—in which the communication of information was not separate from the communication of emotion, in which the analysis of art was informed by intense advocacy. They give a new meaning and cutting edge to Baudelaire's famous call for a criticism that is "passionate, partisan, political." The authors offer a corrective reading of the art scene, and call for a larger-than-art psychosocial revolution—as part of the same critical practice. This is altogether novel for art criticism, which supposedly ought to be impersonal and limit itself to art, itself supposedly impersonal ("autonomous"). What we have, in other words, are activist essays, which deny conventional notions of art and art criticism—which refuse to read and value art in codified formalist terms and mood. They do not accept their inevitable, self-evident rightness. They make no pretense of neutrality. They do not stand on the ceremony and civility of aesthetic consciousness. They cannot tell us about the art without telling us about its role in the feminist revolution. They cannot wait for art history to catch up with the art; they show it making social history. They refuse the division between cultural and social history. They cannot describe without being dramatic, because the art, and the context of its creation, are themselves dramatic. Today, when feminism seems to have receded into the background of society, when it does not seem to be as newsworthy as it was in the 1970s, when it has become more identifiable as an area of academic studies than an indictment of society's betrayal of woman's possibility, it is important to recall that feminism once meant not only the "rehabilitation" of woman but the total transformation of capitalist American society, with its exploitive, patriarchal use of body and psyche. This underlying thrust is vividly felt in these often militant, sardonic essays, full of the vigor of feminist self-consciousness. They are communal—missionary—as well as personal in spirit, revolutionary as well as revelatory in intention. They are often written with the air of self-discovery as well as discovery of the art.

The essays fall into two broad categories: accounts of different female artists, and efforts to formulate a female art criticism. Some of them involve reconsiderations, from a feminist perspective, of past art, as in Carol Duncan's essay, while others examine the effort of feminist artists to revive myths of superior female significance, as in Gloria Orenstein's essay. What is often thought of as marginal—not only woman's art, but art made by Chicana and black women artists, as in the essays of Shifra Goldman and Lowery S. Sims—is presented as central, without apology. None of the authors think there is any need for the art to justify itself in terms of the mainstream's notion of the central. The 1970s, in fact, and the female art examined in these essays, represents the collapse—the increasing unintelligibility—of the notion of mainstream centrality. It is not simply that all art will henceforth speak its significance for itself, but that through the female (and generally political) art movements of the 1970s, the 1960s version of mainstream centrality in art was decisively challenged and overcome. In a sense, it was a pushover because of its self-fetishization and amoral commercialism.

The so-called mainstream has now caught up to much of this art, and is utilizing feminist ideas, such as gender deconstruction and forbidden sensuality. As Arlene Raven writes, "conceptual and sensual feminist perspectives coexisted in the 1960s and 1970s, and both continue to be created," and to be appropriated by art that is not clearly feminist in orientation for their provocative potential. Does this mean that provocation itself has become empty, an end-in-itself? Perhaps, but in these essays it remains tied to a cause whose legitimation has not meant its success. It seems all the more important that these essays be published together, as, in Raven's words, the "national reversal of circumstances" that has occurred "since the turn of this decade and the inauguration of the Reagan administration," is coming to an end. Hopefully these essays signal the end of the "misogynist attitudes" that accompanied that reversal—a revolutionary reversal of that reactionary one. It is not nostalgic to publish them, for they still have a claim on the future. They represent an incomplete revolution.

Donald Kuspit

Preface

Feminist Art Criticism begins with Maryse Holder's blunt and lush language analyzing and interpreting the significance of female sexuality as a ground of freedom. "Another Cuntree: At Last, a Mainstream Female Art Movement" exemplifies the tone and developing theory—often more implicit than explicit—of the early 1970s, when the Women's Movement, having seeded the art world since the late 1960s, was bearing rich fruit.

Holder asserts the primacy of women's experience. Her exuberant belief in the body, her stunning consciousness regarding sexuality and her use of "dirty" words all belong to a feminist effort in art to show connections between art and social, human, and individual experience. Holder, along with many women artists, was engaged in what has been called reclaiming. This process has involved the use of words, subjects, and images that many feminists consider potent and authentic for women despite the devolution of such language into "inappropriateness." Affirming the feminist maxim that "the personal is political," Holder and others have known that the exploration of intimate arenas can reveal both the private and public power of woman.

Holder's passionate voice may not sound theoretical, but it is, for theory is not simply academic intellectualization written in neutral(ized) language; and a quintessential part of feminist theory lives in the writing of women who, having responded passionately to circumstances in their own and other women's lives, have analyzed and abstracted from those particulars without losing the passion.

The essays in *Feminist Art Criticism* are theoretical, and we selected them for several reasons. First, they show a diversity of concerns. These include spirituality, sexuality, the representation of woman in art, the necessary interrelationship of theory and action, women as artmakers, ethnicity, language itself, so-called postfeminism and critiques of the art world, the discipline of art history and the practice of art criticism. Second, the contributors' work has not been either widely disseminated or readily available. Third, the essays, especially arranged as they are (chronologically), demonstrate a continuous feminist discourse in art from the early 1970s through the present, a discourse that is neither monolithic nor intellectually trendy but that rather exhibits many elements, the polemical, Marxist, lyrical, and poststructuralist being only a few.

Viewed chronologically, the discourse is clearly a process. A dialectic emerges as some critics focus negatively on male-dominant culture, some positively discuss woman-centered art and criticism and others do both. The process involves continually rethinking the conditions of the art world and the status of women and feminist art criticism within that sphere. Thus the authors in *Feminist Art Criticism* state accomplishments as well as offer critiques of the theory and practice of feminists in art.

This display of a desire for movement and change and their consequent creation are perhaps feminist art criticism's greatest powers. For in its presentation of alternatives to the powers that be, feminist criticism offers ways not only to reshape the art world but also to extend its values into the world at large. In these new forms of feminist criticism woman has presence. The fact that Maryse Holder's essay remains riveting is, on one hand, a tribute to her literary gifts. On the other hand, however, her essay's pertinence suggests that the power it embraces has yet to be fully realized.

Arlene Raven, Cassandra L. Langer, and Joanna Frueh

Another Cuntree:
At Last, a Mainstream Female Art Movement

Maryse Holder

Let us record an amazing phenomenon before some old gent in Boise puts on the clamps: these days, as if by some spontaneous combustion, women all over the country and in all media are describing unprecedentedly explicit sexual content. Henry Miller and Norman Mailer must be dismayed at women's not only redeeming their cunts from male pawn shops, but appropriating the entire matter of human sexuality as well. All those years of doodling (not to mention diddling) our own anatomy has given rise to a great sexual blossom. Among writers this expresses itself in novels which describe oral sex (written by women one would have described as staid), in an increase, so I hear, of pornography written by women, and in any number of sexual primers, from the Cosmopolitanesque to the exhortatory and political. Very recent women's films are direct, exposed or lush. Niki de Saint Phalle's *Daddy* shows women masturbating or being masturbated in the most frontal and clinical way. Silvianna Goldsmith's beautiful and romantic *Orpheus Underground* depicts rape from a woman's angle of vision, and renders female orgasm as a bursting forth of pomegranate seeds—blood jewels—from the cunt. In videotape, women lift transsexual skirts, upping Warhol's ante. At the NOW conference on Female Sexuality, Betty Dodson demonstrated five kinds of vibrators. In private conversation, it is not unusual for two relative strangers to begin discussing orgasm. Whereas male sexuality is a cliché—Lawrence's dated pedagogy, Mailer's posturings, and Roth's broad, predictable joke—female sexuality is uncharted and a matter of the freshest curiosity. A recent round of visits to shows and studios convinced me that female sexuality is especially visible in the fine arts.

This article originally appeared in *off our backs,* September 1973.

This article began, I suppose, in April 1972, when I heard Judy Chicago speak at Cornell's ''Festival of Women in the Arts.'' A page turned in my mind. Using numerous slides of her own work and that of Georgia O'Keeffe, Louise Bourgeois, and Miriam Schapiro, among others, she pointed out four patterns she had observed over and over again in women's art. As I remember them, they were: *Repeating forms* (cylinders for instance); *Circular forms* (deriving from the breast, perhaps); *Organic forms* (she called these ''biomorphic,'' examples would be plants, genitalia, gardens). The one I could never forget was the central *aperture*, the representation of an opening in the center of a painting. These openings could appear as the hearts of flowers, as tunnels or portals leading to a mysterious infinity beyond, in O'Keeffe, or as chasms, rifts, cracks, deep central edges. Too often to be coincidental, the compositions of numerous female artists converged on a dark, inner space.

This thesis was hotly debated for days: Chicago had after all selected work that proved it. Some women felt her thesis limited women. A general objection to Chicago's thesis was that women's work might show these differences, but that these were sociological rather than biological in origin. But beyond the signaling of specific patterns in women's art—the greatest excitement of the thesis was that it established a different, women's, metaphysics and aesthetics. No longer pale echoes of men, women were seen to be generating from the deepest levels of the unconscious, a different universe.

Not the least valuable gift I took with me that night was exposure to women artists I'd never known or barely heard of before, but it wasn't until a year and a book on O'Keeffe later that I had a chance to pursue my curiosity. Several things happened in rapid succession for someone over thirty: the Gallery of Modern Art was successfully pressured into presenting the ''Women Choose Women'' exhibition; the Women's Interart Center had a show called ''The Erotic Garden,'' and *off our backs* was asked to review a mostly women's show at the Erotic Art Gallery. Anne Sharp, who works at the E.A.G., put me in touch with some of the artists and in that process I came to interview, in their studios, women who belonged to the ''Fight Censorship Group.'' Thus Chicago and New York met: the unique sensibility, it surprised me to discover, in women was their bold treatment of sex. Even more satisfying was the representation of sexuality from a woman's perspective.

Metaphorical Cunts & Measured Cocks

The frecuncy, the fecuntitty, of cuntassy. The most striking and uniform aspect of the two shows I saw at the Erotic Art Gallery was the metaphoric treatment of women's anatomy. Cunts appeared as fruit, primarily, or leaves, park swings, elements of landscape.

Shelly Lowell's *You Don't Have to Be Jewish* is a parody of the Levy's Bread poster. A grinning Indian is about to bite into a peach whose core is glistening pink inner and outer lips. In her large *Apple,* the core is cunt again. In Kiki Kogelnik's subtle *Swing in Central Park* widely spread legs are park swings. Sara d'Allesandro's *Cunt Tree,* is a ten-inch-high painted and fired terra cotta piece. A brown tree's branches end in cunts, apple-green on the outside, pink inside.

The best cunt work I saw was not at the Gallery but at the Women's Interart Center show. Instead of deriving cunt *from* object, its point of departure is the sexual organ itself. Marge Helenchild's *Vulva Hammock* is a hammock in the form, texture and color of a cunt. Four different colors of fabric are used to delineate outer from inner lips from entrance to the vagina from at last—the clitoris. The fabrics go from dark brown on the outside to brilliant red textured silk or acetate for the inside. The clitoris is a round pillow, done to scale, at the head of the hammock, protruding from under the head of the inner lips. This is a stunning work in its witty realistic imitation, its size, its metaphoric functionalism (a cunt is to rest in, it is a womb, it is the shape of a hammock without strain), lastly, in its simplicity. Certainly one of the reactions we have to brilliant art is: it's so simple; why hasn't anyone thought of it before?—it's "right," a form waiting to have been discovered.

Breasts were also played with. Shelly Lowell did a witty mixed media work: a black mohair coat stiffened with polyester resin, with pink plaster nipples for buttons. In another, *Slice of Life,* a small Oldenburg-like plaster pie, the meringue peaks are nipples. In her dadaist painting *Don't Make Any Noise, the Cake Will Fall,* a meticulously photo-realist cool grey oven houses a crudely painted breast in a cake pan. The cake is tautly risen: the breast is a metaphor for fragile sexual arousal overwhelmed by a clinical environment. We are afraid it will collapse momentarily.

Other, nonanalogical breast works existed as well. Helenchild's mammoth *Breast Wall* (shown at the Interart show) is an imposing wall-sized piece of breast sets. Various subtly distinct shades of pink and tan nylon form substantial sacs enclosing different kinds of foam fill. The breasts vary not only in texture but in size. They are hung directly from the wall and overlap to create a dense, full environment. The day I visited the show, a young girl was rolling down the wall with manifest pleasure.

Louise Bourgeois did a beautiful semiabstract piece called *Trani Episode.* In white plaster, it consists of two breast forms, one folded over the other, roughly one and a half feet long. The breasts are elliptical in shape and the one on top is collapsed over the one beneath it, a kind of soft football. There is an exciting contrast between the softness of the shape and the hardness of the material.

I found some of the cunt works doctrinaire and in danger of establishing new banalities: I foresee a decade of fruity cunts. In some work there was, rather than O'Keeffe's seductive "R" glamour, an "X" literalness. In Lowell's *Apple,* however, there are two different things that never come together. Suggestion, with its stirring mystery, has been reduced to predetermined comparison. We get glib studied effect, rather than discovered connection. This literalness

Louise Bourgeois, *Trani Episode,* ca. 1971–72
Hydrocal and latex, 16½″ × 23″ × 23¼″.
(*Photo by Allan Finkelman; courtesy Robert Miller Gallery, New York*)

is perhaps intended, a blunt exposure of what had been considered our wound, which, coopted by ourselves (and incidentally removed from the realm of smut, deobscenified), becomes our strength. This aggressive presentation of the cunt is a first step at self-definition. Analogous to saying "cunt," or "clit," it is a hard jab at reality, a parting of the mists of both shame and lyricism, a forcing into contact with matter—our own, at that.

Some of the sexual comparisons were evocative, however. Anne Sharp's *Nude with Peaches* is a small (16 by 17 inches) pastel in colors reminiscent of Bonnard. A lush female torso, headless and armless, for some reason, all firm orbicular forms, reposes, legs wide apart amid flowery and striped cloths in front of the weathered siding of a house and beneath an overhanging peach tree branch. One of the fruit has been cut away and the coral mauve and green colors of its interior correspond to those of the woman's. Her nipples are brilliant coral. The skin and light in the drawing seems impregnated with late afternoon summer sun. Everything suggests summer ripeness and a still waiting for pleasure. The cunt really seems like a peach, all summery warmth. Her *Garden of Eden* is a pen and ink drawing which similarly blends sexual and landscape imagery. Very subtly and quietly hillocks derive from breasts, cunts form coral banks, pricks bend in clumped masses.

At the same time that the artists were extending the significance (in sometimes forced ways) of their own anatomy, they were constricting the significance of the prick. Agnes Denes's *Napoleonic Series I and II* is an ink print of different size pricks inked onto graph paper. The caption reads: "Program title: Investigation of World Rulers; chart title: Napoleon Overlooking the Elba." This witty feminist work is precisely ironic. Judith Bernstein did a funny grafitto of a flying male figure who sports an erection twice his size. His cape floating behind him identifies him as *Superzipper.* Her *Fun Gun* is a diagram of the lower male bod seen in profile, with the slightly bloated belly of anatomy-book land. The erect "ejector rod" emits the links one sees in cheap key chains.

My favorite of this genre was Anita Steckel's *Feminist Peep Show,* a wall piece consisting of thirty-nine separate cigar boxes, above which are old sepia portraits of Victorian men. Inside the shallow boxes Steckel continues the portraits with line drawings of naked bodies, each with a unique and revealing penis. One plump body ends in a prick which spells "Mom." Another is attached to a jock's clublike prick. There is a double prick, a prick like a tree, one that is long vines that wrap around the body, a prick like a tail, a forked prick, a prick which gives birth to another prick, a winged prick, a broccoli prick. One figure has no prick, but a bow ties his balls into a pretty gift. Though there is certainly metaphoric elaboration here, what we predominantly get in this playful game of correspondances is measurement, an astute appraisal of phallic personae.

There were several other works which were interesting either for their original use of sexual "material" or for their delineation of a kind of tragic sexuality.

Patsy Norvell does "landscapes" in hair, a great deal of it pubic. She uses different colors which she pastes onto clear plastic. One called *Hairpiece* is a quiltlike piece of nine squares, each different, with a deep fringe all around. Norvell also did some sculptures using diaphragms and condoms.

Arlene Love's *Crucifixion* is a life-sized painted plexiglass sculpture which substitutes a faded woman in tawdry underwear for Christ. The woman is in her forties, wearing a hairdo and clothes from that same decade. She has on a black garter belt, a dingy cotton brassiere, panties, and black stockings, while a plastic handbag dangles from one hand. The sculpture reminds one of the drabness and constriction age and their sex condemned our mothers to. The woman is crucified by her underwear and her obscenity in it. Sara d'Allesandro's small clay *Prayer Boxes* are similarly somber. They resemble mediterranean street altars. In them women and men enact a baleful sexual passion.

There was an extraordinary silkscreen by Chicago in the Erotic Arts Show which was in a class by itself. Called *Red Flag,* it is an extreme close-up in monochromatic pink, red, white, and black of part of a hand, an edge of thigh, and a dark pubic shadow. These are the setting for what at first sight appears to be the birthing of a startlingly bright red and white prick but reveals itself to be, on second examination, a Tampax. There is perfect control in the tough, tight composition and the content could not be more dramatic. What we see of the posture suggests assertive stance, staunch bloodletting; it makes taking out a Tampax a warrior's act. This print breaks not only the menstrual taboo but suggests that any revelation, if handled confidently, is possible. Too, Chicago subjects her content to rigorous aesthetic control. In no way does she subordinate formal values to political message. She is confident enough to let the content dictate the form.

When I talked with Anne Sharp she told me that the reason so much work in this gallery—owned by a man—was done by women was that women were doing the best work in this area. Two of the gallery's shows were, in fact, entirely devoted to women.

Giant Women in New York

I liked most of both shows I saw at the Gallery but found they had, often, a flavor of brilliant amateurism. This partly derived from the sloppy, unprofessional presentation of the works and also from there being only one or two works of an individual artist to look at at a time. For years I have been most impressed by one-artist shows: those of Oldenburg, Lichtenstein, and Arbus had lasting impact. I think group shows (or film or video festivals) are particularly dangerous to women. Instead of gearing one to the differences among artists, they force one to reduce a great deal of diverse work to a single statement about "the woman's point of view." Further, a group show relegates all women to a category equivalent to a single male artist: women=Oldenburg. Lastly, it has an insidious sexist effect. An amorphous notion of "women's art" substitutes for a vigorous, precise experience of an artist who *starts* from being a woman and ends in a rich, unique vision in which gender, if present, is experienced in infinitely various ways.

Actually, even in terms of insights about female perspectives, I was far more enlightened by the examination of a *single* woman's work. Survey courses are fun but the real training in apprehending works of art is in the ever more subtle consideration of the distinctions present in an artist's work, at least for me. Not surprisingly, then, I found the studio visits more exciting.

The "Fight Censorship Group" comprises an epic dozen women artists banded together to accomplish roughly two goals: to remove sexual subject matter from the "closet of the fine arts," as Anita Steckel, who founded the group, states in a press release, and also to "uncover the male" as much as the woman traditionally has been. My compulsiveness somewhat tempered by other commitments, I visited about half of the group. These women are united by a common content but their approaches are vastly different. Nothing could better illustrate the appropriateness of getting sex out of the closet or the stupidity of the label "women's art" or even "sexual art."

Bodies, Beasts, Blood

Juanita McNeely is a "painterly" painter whose forceful, primitive forms, bold composition, raw, brilliant colors, and interest in creating original, symbolic milieu shows an inheritance traceable from post-Impressionism through Expressionism. I love the style, so from that standpoint alone I loved McNeely's work. The excitement was multiplied by her content. For one, she paints the female nude as active agent, so that one can finally identify with it.

The Yellow Table shows a robust woman on her stomach tautly stretching on a table, under spotlights that look like giant, ominous eyes. The woman's flesh is green and mauve, the table yellow, the lamps are brown, casting bright green-yellow arcs of light against a brilliant blue background. The painting in these large blocs of simple yet unexpected color (that startling green-mauve flesh). It is the tense line of a substantial female body whose every muscle is taut in a pose that rises to meet a searching examination. The athleticism and movement of the female figure is absolutely new. Finally, it is the mysterious symbolism of those slanted eye-lamps, cats' eyes third-degrees exposing the woman in a way that only *suggests* a traditional relation: woman as object, under scrutiny. The body's tight upward arching certainly suggests, also, an erotic tropism. In *Chameleon*, done in brilliant, mostly primary colors of blue, red, and green, a similarly angular and contorted muscular body "lies" on a table, the face turned round, with cunning, slanted eyes. If these women are sexual, they are so from their own perspectives, in states of alert animal arousal, as aware as cats.

McNeely's sexuality is very free, seeming to take place in a primitive time when the connection between human beings and animals had not yet been severed.

Juanita McNeely, *Yellow Table,* 1972
Oil, 74″ × 72″.
(*Photo courtesy of the artist*)

Her Egyptianesque *Ripples in the Red,* which I liked best, shows two women lying with dogs in unexplicit but clearly sensual ways. A large painting again, it is a stunning, hotly colored composition. At the top is a band of light green sky on which a semicircle of red-edged green rests: the sun. This sun, which is also a spotlight and an eye, throws down a wide pyramid of light. The arc of light, suggesting pyramid, defines the blood-red ground as vast. In it are two female figures: one, painted earth-brown, lies on her back as straight and serene as the stone figures on Egyptian sarcophagi. A black dog lies on her. Beneath her, a larger female figure sits up, one knee raised. In the cradle, her body forms a large green animal of tortuous outline—it looks like a crocodile, but McNeely says it's a dog—cranes up toward the woman's face, its muzzle stretched up as if to kiss her. The relationship between the women and the animals is companionable and natural. With its big space, and intense, elemental colors, the painting creates a mythic place and time when blood and nature were not such discreet entities.

McNeely, like many other "sexualist" painters, is involved in the creation of myth. *Woman's Psyche* is a large work in four panels in raw primary colors and dark browns and blacks representing women, strange beasts, and biomorphic phalluses engaged in disturbing sexual rites. Black wolves lick a stretched woman's nipples, a woman strangles birds, in one panel, while beasties group below. In another, a squatting woman wearing a bird mask bleeds and birds crouch on the back of a nearby wolverine with prominent teats who looks somehow tender, a beneficent spirit of femaleness sympathetically attending the woman's bloodletting. In yet another, large black phalluses arch like palms over a woman's bloated belly. Symbolic interpretation of this work, which is as dark and atavistic as dreams, is left up to the viewer. McNeely, all of whose work speaks of the unfathomable depths of the female experience, restores to the trivialized woman that sense of herself as cosmic protagonist, an Everywoman deep with primal mysteries.

McNeely is very interested in blood and birth. She did a series on abortion in which women are transmogrified into examined objects on slabs, amongst cruel metallic stirrups and lamps like claws. Her shocking *The Tearing* (84 by 64 inches) has the force of medieval allegory. Three, perhaps four figures are involved in a birth which is simultaneously a death. A female figure whose upper torso is entirely skeletal is dangled, by hands holding onto the ribbons of flesh covering her rib cage, in front of an enormous yawning vagina. Ribbons of blood-red hair, a seaweed top-knot, trail from her skull which grins in rigor mortis anguish. Below this figure, another, on her knees, her ass high in the air, is holding her face in agony. It is deep red inside the vagina and blood flows from the skeleton-woman's cunt, forming a dark pool in which the prostrate woman suffers in a dire inheritance. More neatly symbolic than McNeely's other work, it suggests, at least on one level, that a woman is born dead, perhaps because she is regarded as a hole. It is in painting the equivalent of de Beauvoir's tragic vision of woman.

The Primal Scene

If blood is mythic for McNeely, it is the sexual act which is so for Joan Semmel, who does large paintings (six to nine feet) of monumental female-male couples, interlocked in sexual connection in a flat, limitless space. Her style is hard-edged photo-realism done in colors thinned with turpentine to a pastel, almost sherbert, transluscence. In one (there are no titles) a massive grey female body is hunched over a pink male figure further back, most of which is obscured in a luminous orange space. The line of the strong female body is beautiful—sinuously intricate. (Semmel has an Oriental genius for interesting line.) The body, especially the thigh, is mountainous. As with a telefoto lens there is interesting spacial distortion as well: the female thigh is huge in relation to other parts of both bodies in Semmel's simultaneously intimate and distant angle of vision.

The larger-than-life figures loom forward from the ground. Semmel is interested in their "being in the room with you," in "forcing a confrontation." In another painting, a male figure, seen frontally, fucks a female figure upsidedown but facing forward. I try to visualize where the camera would be if there were one but can't, just as I can't describe the positions. The male figure, midnight blue, is cut off just before the shoulders at top-frame; the female, chartreuse, is cut off at the breasts, at bottom frame and at mid-calf on the right. The male torso describes a powerful, thrusting arc; the female torso is compressed and back. One feels the conjunction of vectors. The focus of the painting is the boundary-less funnel shape of genital connection. Often there are dark inner shadows where, presumably, the mystery happens, shrouded in darkness. In this, as in her other work, there are no faces.

Semmel's paintings have a "2001" quality: extraordinary angles of vision; gods fucking in free fall in the total silent concentration of empty space. The giant bodies are cut off at unexpected points: a knee, a heel, the top of a rib cage. This makes not only for extremely dramatic composition but suggests an inexhaustible mystery of sexuality. What we do see is so charged and interesting, so rich already, yet there is even more. Too, the cropping and the angles recharge sex by focusing our attention on unexpected bodily configurations, points of contact and sensations. The facelessness makes the mystery reside in the body and creates an intimacy all the greater for being impersonal. Semmel is interested in the odd configurations two interlocking bodies make. Representing couples making love, she says, is not so much thematically interesting as an opportunity to be released from the cliché of the single and posed studio nude. Complexity of composition (and line) increases by geometric proportion from the single to the double nude.

Semmel says that it's logical and natural for eroticism to have been taken up now, especially by women. Women weren't permitted to paint the male nude until the late nineteenth century. Also, when males posed nude, they wore jock straps until very recently, so women are curious. Semmel cites de Beauvoir's idea that because a man's sex organ is outside, he is divorced from his sexuality.

Joan Semmel, *Untitled* (from "Second Erotic Series"), 1972
Oil on canvas, 70″ × 70″.
(*Photo courtesy of the artist*)

Certainly, too, the refusal to show their penises in films or paintings argues male arrogance: the penis was not for the public consumption, but for the private exclusive enjoyment of men. Nor, of course, were men to be sexually defined—in that regard, as in all others, they were the see-ers, not the seen.

Women are unprecedentedly interested in self-definition which necessarily involves a judgment of the "other," to use de Beauvoir's term, who is, finally, the opposite sex—man. (This judgment can be positive: Semmel paints beautiful male bodies: tightly sucked-in buttocks, drum-hard stomachs.) Sex, too, is more important for women who have been simultaneously labeled sexual and sexually repressed. Certainly the sole transcendence allowed them has been love; love, or sex, then, is bound to be more allegorical for them than for men, who are distracted by a thousand more prosaic acts and modes of feeling. Women are the natural mystics of sex. Repression also plays its part in the new sexualism of women: we are finally allowed not to feel like freaks for being sexual. As the afternoon waned, Semmel's paintings began to glow in the darkening studio and the high suspended drama of Olympian coupling, sexual space myth burned into the mind.

Fleshcycle

Martha Edelheit is another painter of large works (one work, three panels, is 17 by 8 ft. 3 inches). More conventionally psychological, somewhat "pop," her work has the exciting contemporaneity of recognized activities and faces, moods, bodies, and locales. She, too, is a bold artist who extends the range of female vision in several distinct ways: by portraying imperfect female bodies, showing women in aspects previously ignored, and by observing the male nude with a detached, objective eye.

Her marvelous *Fleshcycle* shows a middle-aged woman on a scooter, repeated in diagonal symmetry but different colors. Both scooters are poised on a diagonal cleft of cloud-filled sky which divides the painting. The woman, nude except for a bike helmet, is pale blue, her vizor-goggles a deep blue-grey; the cycle is flesh-pink with breast headlights. Upside-down she is grey, with brilliant red goggles on a tawny brown and tan bike. Her body is lumpy—but there she is, in a position of toughness and power. Edelheit was asked by male artists why she didn't paint a young woman on the bike and she answered that the model used to come to every session on that—her—bike. What Edelheit, who is acutely attuned to her models, was doing in the act of her painting was letting the women's life define her—her existence was her essence. One of Edelheit's talents is to offer a portrait of a personality through the body. She removes the female from the abstract realm of current female flesh fashions to show us familiar bodies.

Her wall-large (17 by 8 ft. 3 inches) *Women in Landscape* is a three-panel study of three women, each one repeated in different poses per panel. There is a young white woman with oval breasts, a black woman with a short muscular

Martha Edelheit, *Fleshcycle,* 1969
Acrylic on canvas, 84″ × 68″.
(Photo by Henry Edelheit, M.D.)

body, and a fair woman in her thirties who is slightly overweight. Each face is seen in several moods: neutral, dreamy, etc.

Edelheit does new male nudes. In her double male nude *D X2* (68 by 42 inches, acrylic on canvas), a repeated male figure sits and lies amid lustrous, convoluted drapery. He has a good body and a fair-sized penis which droops in an indolent, half-erect arc which is the focus of the lying pose. The male nude here is not synonymous with heroism, strength or brave "human" striving; nor is it even a symbol of beauty (though it is not unattractive) as it is in Greek art. It simply is; another element of Edelheit's still life, like the cloth. Her neutral eye has bothered men, she said, who are not used to being treated so indifferently, or only literally. Certainly a straightforwardly presented penis must disturb them too: mere viewing is a kind of judgment.

Suggestive Form

Louise Bourgeois is a sculptor who came to New York from France in the thirties and who has been producing abstract "sexualist" sculpture for years. She is the most recognized artist in the group, internationally known. She works in many materials: marble, plaster, wood, and plastic, in forms ranging from the directly figurative to the abstract and associative. One group of pieces called *Innards* represents sexual organs. At the Erotic Art Gallery I saw a suspended bronze double prick, two polished sausages emerging from a rough, Rodinesque base. In Bourgeois's cellar there was a striking two-foot-long penis sculpture titled *Filette*. It is done in moist-looking pliable latex and hangs from a meathook. Nothing could be blunter than this shocking viscera. The penis is raw muscle meat—disembodied and vulnerable, a symbol reduced to matter. Bourgeois also did a female genital, much less effective, which is a round latex ball with a kind of pouch slit in the center. The male organ is much more readily detachable and its translation into meat more natural and desirable, a deserved cruelty at female hands. She also did an interesting group of sculptures called *Les Femmes-Couteaux—Knife-Women*—in which the female figure gradually evolves almost completely into a knife.

Another of Bourgeois's favorite forms is the ball. A pencil drawing called *Study for Cumulus* of simple, undulating lines, suggesting clouds, is a preparation for her *Cumulus No. 1*. A white marble piece recently purchased by the Museum of Modern Art in Paris, it is an awesome, almost religious artifact. It is a series of highly polished balls pushing through or emerging from under a smooth, substantial cloth. Its figurative associations are multiple: breasts, more abstractly—female forms, pates. It looked to me like a troop of fulsome nuns. The states it suggests are simultaneously repression and emergence, and grouped solitude. Bourgeois's work involves the polarity of intimacy and aggression, female and male. Like other female artists, she is deeply curious about sexual relations and describes them in archetypal terms.

Louise Bourgeois, *Filette,* 1968
Latex, 23½".
(Photo by Allan Finkelman; courtesy Robert Miller Gallery, New York)

Anita Slavin Arkin Steckel

Anita Slavin Arkin Steckel is a breakthrough genius who fuses various elements of popular "culture" and contemporary concern in an original and revolutionary manner. Her form, as well as her content, is new.

She recently had a one-woman show at a gallery in Westbeth, an artists' residence, where she showed two series of works.

The "New York Skyline" series is a group of six-foot by nine-foot photomontages of a photographic view of New York, one she considers archetypal, a "stamp" or icon (one sees the East River in the foreground and the U.N. and Chrysler building, among others, in the background). This photograph is transferred onto canvas and Steckel paints and draws on it with oil, acrylic, and pencil. She paints giant nude bodies, mostly women who loll among skyscrapers they dwarf, amidst graffiti doodles and ethnic references. In *Skyline No. 5,* her most recent, and a masterpiece, the giant figures, indolently splayed out against the sky, take their ease. A prick which extends the Chrysler building spire spurts semen which a relatively tiny Jewish mother spoon-feeds to her mammoth Olympian son; underneath, the slogan: "Eat your power honey, before it gets cold." He sports a "Lenny Bruce lives" tattoo. The sky is tattooed with other graffiti: "Coney Island lives." "Genet lives 382."

The cityscape is overlaid with a swampy greenish-brown wash, the water and air a sombre atmosphere which corresponds somehow to the depth of unconscious experience: pollution as dream-inducing murky memory. Brilliant yellow-pink clouds, heavily painted, break through the figures here and there, filling them with sunsets of sudden illumination.

A sitting woman, as tall as five Chryslers if she stood, holds up a platter, waitresslike, on which a small female figure rebounds from a somersault. Flower scribbles take off from and arm-hinting that doodles are both cause and effect of an absolutely unfettered, democratic imagination. Jewish star doodles dot the sky, while below, in the river, gefilte fish, mere ovals, swim in magic pools of three, each pool labelled, with "smile button" faces, heading perhaps south to spawn in Miami-land.

This description by no means exhausts the painting; her name on the bottom: Anita Slavin Arkin Steckel—first, mother's maiden, her maiden, and her married name—makes clear the intention: a complete mythic and psychological history of Steckel's life, which is also ours.

Steckel's work is irresistible. The form, combining as it does photography and painting (in a kind of plastic equivalent of Mailer's autobiographical journalism), and combining personal, ethnic and urban motifs—graffiti, doodles, references to the artist's religion, etc.—into an epic mode touches the contemporary nerve and synthesizes more elements of daily experience into a transcendent imagery than one could have imagined possible. Steckel's is the new art, more than anything I've seen since pop (call it "mom"?) art.

Anita Steckel, *Rodeo* ("Giant Women in New York"), 1973
Montage, 8′ × 10′. The series "Giant Women in New York," of which this
is a part, is a representation of woman triumphant and wholly creative. The
paintbrush and the woman straddling the Empire State Building represent an
embodiment of freedom.

(Photo courtesy of the artist)

Her series "Giant Women in New York" is part of a group of works representing nude women painted onto photographs of New York and bearing Steckel's own photographic face. Steckel started out with a photograph, then came to grafting in a fantasy image, and then decided to superimpose her real self on the fantasy image. These montages are "medium," about four by three.

In *Rodeo* a woman straddles the Empire State Building, holding on with one hand and wielding a lasso that resembles a whip with the other. She is in command of the bronco that is the city and the phallus. Her expression is one of manifest contentment as she rides alone in the city, large, beautiful, elemental, free. The montage speaks to women's fantasies of power and mastery. In *Coney Island* a lush odalisk Steckel reclines on the beach on the other side of a boardwalk where *balabustas* sit on benches. Another liberated, female aspect, in somewhat discordant union with the kerchiefed women, Steckel stares at the viewer quasi defiantly.

In *Last Supper,* Steckel is spread out on a long table at a male banquet in an abstract landscape of dark, bleak land and sky and in *Embarrassment* Steckel is torn up the middle with a deep fissure in the presence of oblivious construction workers. Her impassive face lets fall unnoticed stylized tears; she is a building being wrecked. Perhaps because the face is never enraged, that is, because the pain is not *signalized* but *symbolized,* Steckel's description of it is impossible to dismiss.

Her haunting *Women Impaled on New York* represents foggy skyscraper tops on which a tribe of women, infinitely extending—Steckel one—have taken up stalwart residence. The building spires impale the women—the truth about the city—but the truth is also their spectral presence. Luminous vampires, they have come out when the city is silent to reclaim possession.

The Steckel persona that emerges from this series is wry, beautiful, ironic, taking pleasure in shedding her inhibitions, like her clothes, in a city which is a dark river she secretly goes skinny-dipping in, at night, alone.

Similar to "Giant Women" are a group of montages where Steckel draws herself to scale. In *On the Subway,* the Steckel character, her breasts and crotch exposed, sits between a young and an old man on a train. One hand is under the old man's, while another lies loosely between her legs. (It is important that the protagonist is always Steckel—it says that *every* woman has the entire range of experiences Steckel describes.)

Steckel renders female experience in a way which makes pain undeniable, but also presence, fantasy, power, sexuality. Most significant, her tone is *epic:* nothing but the largest arena, the most far-reaching resonances for women.

What Is and What Could Be

Women respect matter more than men do; anyone who has observed men working in an apartment can verify this. Women are more interested in sex and in

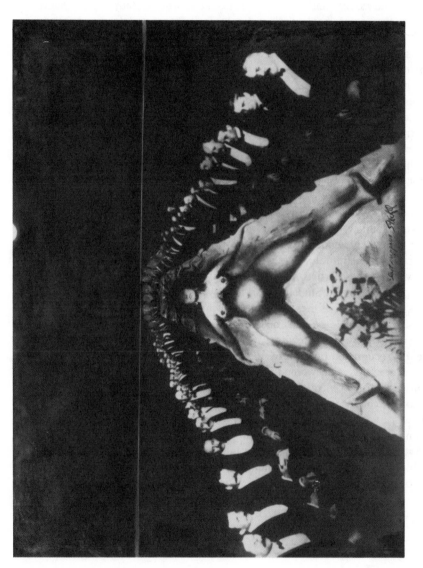

Anita Steckel, *The Last Supper*, 1973

Montage, 8' × 10'. The title of this work refers to a Jewish Last Supper. The work itself is a statement against brutality and represents the idea that a woman's body—a person—will never again be used as a man-made artifact.
(Photo courtesy of the artist)

sexual relationships. And women are discovering themselves. It is therefore not surprising to find that their work is often biomorphic, sexual, narcissistic, and mythic. The work I saw was also representational in the main. I think this a corrollary of self-discovery and the respect for matter, what already exists, reality. Unlike men, women are not lost in a technologically prompted dead-end abstraction.

The sexualist work I saw (and some related ''organic'' work) struck me as being art that women as a group were for the first time not copying from men. A record of female experience, it offered a completely different view of reality. And it was imaginative, often brilliant work about an area of human experience that had not been dealt with before, or even now, by men. ''Sexualism,'' then, to use a more accurate term than ''Eroticism,'' is exciting. It is new and it is a movement. Women can crash into the art world, into the general consciousness, with this work. It could be their work one would be seeing, and reading about, for the next ten or twenty years, without having it referred to as ''women's art,'' as Impressionism was not alluded to as ''French'' art. Women are ushering out pop; women have the new energy, imagination, and coherence. What it will take to launch the movement is an enormous expenditure of pressure and publicity; ultimately, enough confidence on the part of women to establish a separate cultural institution. This work inspires that confidence.

Up to now, these artists have been receiving Red Cross work rather than the red carpets they merit. Students in art history must begin writing theses, monographs, books, on *each* of these women, who must be viewed as having general significance, while male art must be taken as sex-limited. Certainly the male establishment has proven its steadfast resistance to genuine female talent. It has traditionally recognized only a few mediocre women whom it mock-venerates as if to say: see, this is all women are capable of. Too, men's sexist quotas will continually establish women as a limited instance of the total ''human'' experience.

A word of caution: galleries which exhibit women must begin showing respect for their work with slick, professional presentation. I saw titles typed or handwritten on worn tags falling off the walls and drably painted rooms in both the Erotic Art Gallery and in the Women's Interart Center. Surroundings must be impeccable, imaginative, and as glamorous as possible. Diamonds in rough settings are only rhinestones in our society. That is the simple reality of marketing.

Fine Arts and Feminism:
The Awakening Consciousness

Lise Vogel

If she cannot be preached to from the texts of her own bitter experience, then she cannot be awakened at all.
W. Holman Hunt, on the deportment of
Annie Miller, his mistress and model

The very hem of the girl's dress, which the painter has laboured so closely, thread by thread, has a story in it, if we think how soon its pure whiteness may be soiled with the dust and rain, her outcast feet failing in the street.
John Ruskin, on Hunt's *The Awakening Conscience*,
a painting for which Annie Miller posed

In the past decade the women's liberation movement has explored issues touching on virtually all areas of human experience. Why then do we hear so little about art? Why has art, perhaps more than any other field, lagged so far behind the general movement for change initiated by modern feminism? Specifically: Where are the books, articles, or collections of essays presenting a feminist critique of art? Why are there no monographs and virtually no articles on women artists written from a feminist perspective? Where are the reproductions and slides of the work of women artists? Why can't one find syllabi and bibliographies covering issues of women, art, and feminism? What is the meaning of the almost complete lack of feminist studio and art history courses in the schools? Why are there so few feminist art historians and critics? What are women artists today doing? And what are those women artists who consider themselves feminists doing and why?

This article is reprinted from *Feminist Studies* 2.1 (1974): 3–37, by permission of the publisher, Feminist Studies, Inc., c/o Women's Studies Program, University of Maryland, College Park, Maryland 20742.

What *should* a feminist artist, critic, or art historian do? What *is* a feminist point of view in the visual arts?

Only in the last few years have women artists, critics, art historians, and museum workers begun to organize in response to the second wave of feminism. These efforts have centered mainly around such equal rights issues as job discrimination, unequal wages and advancement, lack of opportunity for women artists to show their work, and the like. Vital and important though these problems are, action on them corresponds to a quite moderate position within the women's liberation movement taken as a whole. The wide spectrum of feminist politics is not yet represented among women concerned with art.

To understand fully the issue of women, art, and feminism, it must be considered from several points of view. In what follows I can only begin to outline the questions that must be raised in order to develop the critique I believe necessary. First I will briefly argue that the apparent backwardness of the art world with respect to all social issues including that of feminism is no accident, and that the relative timidity of the feminist art movement reflects the reality of this art world. I will then go on to evaluate the book *Woman as Sex Object;* this collection of essays, published early in 1973, is the first book purporting to deal with the issue of women and art and as such deserves a careful and thorough review. This discussion will lead, finally, into a consideration of the directions in which I think a truly feminist involvement of women with art should be developed.

Introduction: Problems, Past and Present

The complex of persons, objects, and relationships called the art world is well known for a number of peculiar characteristics. Perhaps most striking is the emphatic isolation both of the art world as a social entity and of art as an object for study and experience. Entry into any sector of the art world is difficult: requirements for a passport vary, and may include certain kinds of expertise, talent or taste, sexual, ethnic, or class identity, the right sorts of social graces and tact, or the possession of personal wealth. An art work must also pass a series of entrance examinations, based mainly on its attributes as an object in social and so-called aesthetic isolation. Within the art world, initiates are prone to experience, discuss, create, and present art as if it existed in a sphere essentially distinct from and above the ordinary life and consciousness of most people.

The inhabitants of the art world frequently treat art as a faithful mirroring of reality: the image of a thing is assumed to be identical with, and perhaps more "true" to, its actual being. Thus art is often presented as not only autonomous but also somehow more real than the social experience it is supposed to portray. The possibility that a gap might exist between the image of something in art and the way it is or was in its full social context is occasionally admitted, but rarely explored.

This double isolation—of a pure and lofty art world from some other real but presumably more sordid world, and of the images from the social reality in which they were produced—can result in a diluted and warped response to art. The most severe distortions occur when strains and contradictions within a given society manifest themselves in its art. The issues of class, sex, and race, for instance, represent urgent struggles reverberating throughout modern society, and they extend directly into its art. The apparent isolation of an art world from society should thus be seen as simply a historical phenomenon, a specific consequence of the changed class relations, with the rise of capitalism, between artist, art, and audience. Most interestingly, "woman" has become the chief subject of art in capitalist society, and changes in the relationships between the sexes are explicitly expressed. Moreover, the depiction of women tends to involve not only issues of sex but of class and sometimes of race as well.

The art world has traditionally ignored the issues of sex, class, and race, at most acknowledging them as background or context. Moreover, it ordinarily assumes that a single human norm exists, one that is universal, ahistorical, and without sex, class, or race identity, although in fact it is quite clearly male, upper-class, and white.[1] In this way the art world once again pushes the complexity, difficulties, and contradictions within modern society outside its perimeters, and reinforces the false division between art and social experience.

The kind of radical sociological criticism that has been levelled at most major cultural institutions in the United States for more than a decade has touched the art world only quite recently. The reasons for its late arrival are easy to locate in the special characteristics of the art world's unusually closed social structure. First, today's art world is firmly grounded in wealth, pretension to status, and a certain sensibility cultivated as a badge of class position. Second, it is extremely small. And third, the very existence and maintenance of the art world rely largely on *private* riches and *personal* contact. By contrast, the interests standing behind most other research, teaching, and writing tend to be big business, government, and foundations which represent wealth in a collective or abstract form, and have an essentially impersonal character.

The art world's exceptionally elite social basis manifests itself in its well-known ideological insularity. No area is so fetishized as art through its mystique as a "high" form of commodity worship, nor so totally isolated from its more popularized versions. Compare the "higher" or "purer" levels of most humanistic or even social science fields, which simply represent one end of a long spectrum of possibilities. Even "serious" music, to some a more obscure and unapproachable field than art, has itself a larger audience and in addition a whole range of intermediate and popular counterparts, some of them with a long tradition of being taken quite seriously (jazz, blues, folk). Moreover, music itself cannot be materially possessed in the way an art object can.

The task of trying to project the norms of a fetishized and isolated "high" art onto the lives of art students, museum-goers, art buyers, and the so-called general public falls to the artists, critics, art historians, museum personnel, dealers, and others who can be grouped under the term "art workers." Because these art workers are usually also quite personally involved in meeting the needs of the tiny class that provides the money to run the art world, they internalize its values. It is no wonder, then, that so few art workers have been able to see clearly the reality of their situation, much less speak out or act on it, nor that the art world has been able to remain tight, closed, and relatively immune to criticism.

This description of the only slightly hidden interests behind the seemingly pure world of art and beauty should surprise no one outside the art world. Within it, however, only a very few have tried to explore the consequences of extreme dependence on private, upper-class, status-oriented wealth. Several art historians have articulated particular aspects of the necessary analysis. Some attempts have been made to organize radical and women's caucuses within the profession. Those who are more vulnerable—in particular, artists—have tended to demonstrate, caucus, establish cooperative galleries and publications, speak out on panels, and in general express their more pressing urgency with organization and action.[2]

Where does all this leave the question of women, art and feminism? First, surprisingly few women seriously concerned with art participated actively in the women's liberation movement of the 1960s. Around 1970 movements of women *artists* began tentatively to form. By 1972 more women artists (and a few other women art workers) were willing to call themselves feminists, but even now the women's art movement is notable for its almost total focus on simple reform, for its tendency to assume that its demands can be achieved well within the structure of advanced capitalism, and for its general failure to raise the issue of what a feminist art or art criticism might be. Among art historians the situation seems to me to be worse, and the few art historians who consider themselves feminists have been forced to work largely on their own. In the past year [1973] the picture has improved somewhat, but women art historians on the whole still share with the movement of women artists a moderate and limited approach to the issues of women's liberation. Only a few artists, critics, and art historians have attempted more radical critiques of the questions involved when one approaches art as a feminist.

The major source of this rather depressing atmosphere of timidity and relative conservatism has of course been the dependence and isolation characteristic of the art world in general. At the same time, the existence of a general movement toward women's liberation in the country as a whole is a spectre, as it were, that looms over the art world and creates a real and important context of support for the efforts being made by individual feminists from within. The concrete consequences of this situation are not yet entirely clear, but it does seem that despite the mood of caution things are beginning to move. Already it is possible to list a number of developments indicating the increasing impact made by feminism.

Perhaps the most obvious manifestation of the growing force of feminism is the small but increasing number of exhibitions devoted to women artists, both past and present. Attempts have also been made to mount exhibits of "the image of woman" in art, although these shows have tended so far to range from incoherence to outright sexism. Articles on women artists and on the feminist art movement are beginning to appear in the more established art magazines. Several new publications have been started: *Women and Art, Feminist Art Journal, Womanspace Journal.* Cooperative galleries of various sorts have been founded. A handful of "women and art" courses have been offered as part of the women's studies movement. One or two women's studio programs are in existence. Several conferences have been held, and the College Art Association now dutifully allots several sessions to the topic of "women and art" at its annual meetings. Within art scholarship, the growing commitment over the last decade to seeing art in its social context has converged with the rise of feminism, often with quite useful results. Finally, a very few artists, critics, and art historians are attempting to explore the extremely difficult question of what a feminist point of view might mean for the creation of art and for cultural criticism and history.

All this is hopeful, and I am confident that the art world will never be the same again. Still, the real obstacle remains. Again and again the central question is *who is the audience:* for art, for art criticism, for art history, and for the teaching of art. So long as art workers are forced to depend on the art world as it is currently organized—in particular, so long as artists can find no alternative audience—the issues we can effectively raise and act on will continue to be severely limited.

Woman as Sex Object

For those of us who are attempting to teach courses that relate art to women's liberation, the lack of slides, articles, books, syllabi, bibliographies, and so on is a constant problem. For example, the few relevant articles that have one way or another managed to achieve publication are scattered in a wide variety of books, periodicals, and newspapers. Apparently publishers are not optimistic that a sufficiently large market exists for books dealing with women and art. And, as a sort of last straw, the relatively late arrival of feminism to the art world has meant that available bibliographies and syllabi in women's studies have not included those in art history.[3]

Erotica, the Academy, and Art Publishing

The quite prosaic history of the collection of twelve short essays, *Woman as Sex Object,*[4] is more a model of commercial opportunism than of either feminist or art-historical scholarship. All but one of the essays were originally presented as part of a session at the January 1972 meetings of the College Art Association entitled, "Eroticism and Female Imagery in the Art of the 19th Century." Although it ordinarily takes two to five years for an art-historical study to make it into print, this group of papers was made up into a Christmas package in the form of the 1973 *ARTnews Annual*. The rather scholarly and clearly descriptive title of the CAA symposium was converted into the come-on: *Woman as Sex Object*. At the same time the subtitle promised a detailed and dedicated endeavor: *Studies in Erotic Art, 1730–1970*. (One can only speculate on the function of this subtitle. Was it to reassure those who might be puzzled or put off by the title? Or was it perhaps a campy attempt to participate in that convention of literary pornography which creates a provocative atmosphere of repressed sexuality through the use of a pseudo-academic pedantry?) Some of the original titles of the individual talks were also quite marvelously reworked to suggest a more erotically charged content.[5]

Advertisements for *Woman as Sex Object* began to appear in the fall of 1972. An ad published in the September 1972 *ARTnews* featured a quartet of illustrations from the book (a Betty Grable pinup, Ingres's *Grande Odalisque*, a nineteenth-century pornographic photo, and a satirical etching based on a sado-masochistic theme) framing the book's cover—a disquietingly blown-up detail of female hands and breasts and body entanglements taken from Ingres's *Turkish Bath*. The promises implicit in the illustrations were made blatantly explicit in the long text of the ad, written in a sort of caricatural academic porn which presented the book as a rare example of high-class erotica:

> The 1973 *ARTnews Annual*, WOMAN AS SEX OBJECT, explores the lively and controversial topic of the female as portrayed in 18th–20th century erotica. Reflecting the sexual repressions of the age, man's images of her ranged from edifying moralization to ribald perversion. In every art form she was made the embodiment of personal visions of domesticity, lust—even terror.
>
> . . . .
>
> Over a hundred examples of erotic art, 24 in full color, illustrate the essays. Here is Woman—as Manet, Ingres, Courbet, Renoir, Picasso, de Kooning, Klimt, Fuseli and others saw her—in works that run the gamut from outright sensualism to masterpieces of subconscious sexuality.

At the same time, the brazen proposition of the visual layout and the above paragraphs was carefully tempered by a more scholarly tone:

> The authors have brought together a series of enlightening, probing essays on the erotic elements of Woman in the arts: the influence of popular pornographic photography on Manet's *Olympia* . . . the corset as fad and fetish . . . the recurrent themes of the maid, the mistress, and the prostitute . . . Fuseli's *Nightmare* revealed as a "masterpiece of psycho-sexual projection" . . . male chauvinist Renoir . . . the "fair sex" in the role of femme fatale, vampire, and virgin . . . the pinup as a modern icon.
>
> . . . .
>
> The fascinating, intelligent essays alone would delight any art lover. The volume's exquisitely

reproduced illustrations, and handsome binding make WOMAN AS SEX OBJECT a valuable and enjoyable addition to any fine artbook collection—for reference as well as pleasure.

Apparently this ad did not sufficiently express the appropriate dialectic between open titillation and semi-serious reassurance of academic validity, for in the *Art News* of subsequent months, the message was clarified. Huge letters over a photo of the book (prominently displaying its cover) proclaimed that "FOR ONLY $7.95 YOU CAN GET A BOOK FULL OF THE BEST EROTIC AND SENSUAL ART PICASSO, RENOIR, MANET, RUBENS, COURBET, INGRES AND GAUGUIN EVER DID." Below, a short section in tiny print reassured the timid with the more academic sections of the first ad, culminating in the suggestive promise that "It's not just another art-book you buy to keep on the shelves for your friends to see, it's a book you'll enjoy reading cover-to-cover." In short, this was surely to be an experience that would revive and inspire even the most discouraged of confused Portnoys.

With these ads, which appeared also in such magazines as *Playboy,* one begins to wonder what audience was assumed for the book. The sexploitation market? Then why bother with the frequently straight and often boring text? The coffee-table art world? Then why the stress on art history? Art historians? Then why the relative thinness and even mediocrity of so many of the essays? The women's liberation movement? Then why include only one mildly feminist article? It seems clear, in fact, that a rather confused and contradictory attempt was made to exploit all these markets. Indeed, *Woman as Sex Object* has quite rightly been termed "a truly dirty book" and is probably a commercial as well as an art-historical dud.[6] Almost in spite of itself, however, it poses a number of feminist questions, while its many omissions suggest others. In order to make these issues and questions explicit, a critical review of the book is necessary.

Overview

The scope of *Woman as Sex Object* is decidedly peculiar from several points of view. Despite the aggressively sexual advertising and the overall erotic-to-pornographic physical presence of the book, it is essentially a quite conventional art-historical undertaking. The authors are trained art historians, and they employ a variety of traditional approaches—with, of course, widely varying levels of competence, eloquence, humor, and sexism. The main structural weakness of the book, as with so many such collections, is its utter lack of bearings or coherence; it fails even to maintain its commitment to the exploration of "erotic art." Above all, *Woman as Sex Object* is not a collection of feminist essays on art.

The chronological range covered by the book is uneven. The subtitle promises 1730 to 1970, but in fact the majority of the essays focus on the nineteenth century. The twentieth century is awkwardly represented by two articles on contemporary painting. Here again one senses a desire to produce a "relevant"—that is, saleable—commodity, at the expense of coherence.

The orientation of the essays is very clearly toward "high" art. Popular imagery, contemporary social and sexual practices, and other aspects of social context are invoked in about half the selections, but the assumptions remain those of traditional art history. Moreover, because the collection focuses on the sexual objectification of women, it is inevitable that virtually all the artists discussed are men. The few attempts to explore the association of the art works to human experience are thus in fact investigations of *male* experience, usually erotic. In short, the impact of the modern women's liberation movement on the art world has resulted in a book that ignores women artists of the recognized calibre of Cassatt or Kollwitz, while including a great number of the most marginal of male artists. The responsibility for this stress in *Woman as Sex Object* on the image of women in "high" art produced by men must remain with the editors, and indeed with the art-historical profession as a whole.

The twelve essays in *Woman as Sex Object* can be grouped into three categories. First, a number of studies of a quite traditional sort, with virtually no usefulness for developing a feminist approach to the topics they cover. Second, a group of essays which, while not explicitly feminist, provide a number of insights and a good deal of useful material that should form part of the necessary foundation for the making of a feminist art history and criticism. And finally, the article by Linda Nochlin, the one piece in the entire book that might fall into the small but growing category of feminist art writing.

The Autonomous Image

An article on Ingres's *Antiochus and Stratonice* (1840) by John L. Connolly, Jr., typifies in almost caricatural fashion the essays in *Woman as Sex Object* that might just as well have appeared elsewhere (or perhaps not at all). Connolly's goal is to prove that the painting is an allegorical representation of its patron and his wife, and as such is somehow "the quintessential representation of Ingres's particular conception of the erotic." Despite a perfunctory discussion of erotic images, Connolly virtually ignores the sexual dimensions of Ingres's harem scenes; instead, he strains to interpret these paintings as elaborate allegories of the senses. The article is disjointed and lacks evidence at every point, the briefly sketched iconographic discussion of *Antiochus and Stratonice* is flimsy, and the essay is generally unconvincing. What is most disappointing is the sense one has of wasted effort. Connolly's fascinating title—"Ingres and the Erotic Intellect"—suggests that at the very least one might expect an exploration of some aspect of Ingres's distinctive way of dealing with erotic content, whether ostensibly veiled as in his portraits, or seemingly open as in his harem scenes. Ingres paints both series with the same erotic sensibility, and indeed here was a fine opportunity to follow

Ingres in these meticulous explorations of the sexual consciousness of upper-class male society in early nineteenth-century France.[7]

Marcia Allentuck's brief study of "Henry Fuseli's 'Nightmare': Eroticism or Pornography?" makes the surprising suggestion that Fuseli's painting is concerned with *"femina erotica"*—that is, with female sexual experience—and indeed that "the *topos* of the picture is *not* a nightmare but a female orgasm, one not in the excitement or peak phases, but in the very beginning of the resolution phase." Allentuck attempts to analyze the moment of orgasm in a clinical language that collides ludicrously with her otherwise slick and allusive style of writing and argument. The article must be challenged for its questionable assumptions, ahistorical conclusions, and lack of visual evidence. For example, Allentuck projects twentieth-century interpretations of female sexuality onto a past that had a quite different set of myths on the subject. She then perceives Fuseli to have depicted this sexuality by means of a pedestrian fidelity of style not in fact characteristic of his painting. Moreover, the entire study is built around the author's uncritical commitment to a Freudian perspective. Freudianism, in the form of badly understood and essentially popularized assumptions, is particularly destructive to attempts to develop a feminist approach; it is this that makes Allentuck's article not merely humorous or mediocre, but to some extent dangerous.[8]

The same bland Freudianism characterizes Gert Schiff's study, "Picasso's *Suite 347,* or Painting as an Act of Love." Schiff combines his Freudian assumptions with a pseudo-hip but actually quite conventional identification of artist, art historian, and reader—all of course presumed to be male. Using this traditional and rather outmoded genre of critical writing, Schiff leads us on a disorderly tour of Picasso's *Suite 347,* a series of prints done in 1968 on the familiar theme of art-as-creative-rape-of-the-model. We—that is, Schiff, Picasso, and the reader—are assured that "the voyeur is a worshipper" for "Picasso's scenes of voyeurism imply nothing of that mixture of hatred, fear and castration-anxiety which together form the clinical syndrome. On the contrary, they represent a fervent homage to life." In Picasso's art, "painting, lovemaking and 'generation' become literally one." The approach is almost a caricature of the modern view that all creative work (Picasso's art, Schiff's interpretation, our appreciation) is essentially equivalent to sex from the standpoint of a man—with the ever-present implication that such endeavors are perhaps not quite so valuable, so virile, as a good fuck.

Schiff fails to see *Suite 347* as it really is. His description, for example, of *Number 314* (one of the variations on Ingres's *Raphael Painting the Fornarina*) ignores the complexity and ambivalence of what Picasso has presented. Over three-quarters of the etching's area is occupied by a variety of strange and surely significant figures and objects. At the left, the Pope—the largest figure in the scene—sits looking across at the entangled artist and model (Raphael having just plunged his over-sized member into the contorted yet somehow spread-eagled relevant parts of the model). The Pope is mournful, uptight, but at the same time clearly malevolent. Under the couple's bed a great flat face peers out, flanked by two big disconnected and useless hands—the jealous husband, apparently, who by staring desperately and directly out at us demands that we deal with his situation as our own. Also facing us is the Raphael painting, now reduced to a tiny oval memento hanging on the wall opposite; part mirror-image, part portrait, part Madonna, part pinup, it has in any case become a quite minor element in the goings-on. Finally, compressed into the upper right corner is the couple. Picasso leaves no doubt as to who controls the pace and character of the sexual action, and indeed the model rather resembles a helpless and somewhat delicate animal impaled by an evil child on a stake. Clearly, Picasso has a sense for the difficulties and confusions of human social relationships as seen from a male point of view, although it may remind one more of Mailer and Hemingway than of Genet or Munch. Schiff, however, utterly misses the point. For him, Picasso has simply shown "the extreme ecstasy of [the painter's] union with the model," and "the final consummation of [the couple's] love."

Picasso's approach to relations between the sexes is particularly interesting in view of his long-standing political involvement. Until recently, socialist and communist movements have accepted much of the alienation imposed by the organization of social relations under capitalism. For example, a "private" or "personal" sphere of experience has traditionally been considered separate from work and political life. Picasso, much like the socialist Courbet a hundred years earlier, fell victim to the pain and distortions that result from such a tearing apart of what might be whole. Consciously or not, Picasso put this experience into his art. Schiff, however, writes as if he were entirely oblivious of and insensitive to the nature of contemporary social and sexual relations. He feels no embarrassment when he literally puts women's experience into parentheses that subordinate it to that of men: "Picasso's painting deals with man's (and woman's) most basic impulses and passions."

Also in the category of relatively disappointing articles is a survey by Robert Rosenblum of the many representations of a woman suckling an adult man, usually her father ("Caritas Romana after 1760: Some Romantic Lactations"). Rosenblum's approach to this "crypto-sexual" theme is to catalog its various manifestations, but given the obviously provocative implications of the motif his text is oddly neutral and limp. The topic has various interesting possibilities for further investigation. For example, eighteenth-century scholarship had discovered that the more substantiated version of the Roman story involved a daughter suckling her mother. Rosenblum declines, however, to explore why artists continued to follow the paternal tradition, merely hinting at "reasons that may demand psychosexual speculation." The story appeared in New World guise around 1800, with Native Americans and European conquerors as protagonists; naturally, wherever a white man appears it is he who is nourished by the milk of the exotic natives. Rosenblum misses the social and political implications in these scenes of "grateful savages" saving the lives of their oppressors.

Rosenblum also attempts to assay the lactation theme as an image of maternity. Here, in what seems to be an unfortunate confusion of subject and object, Rosenblum tends to focus the discussion on women artists (incidentally publishing two out of the grand total of five works by women included among the more than two hundred illustrations to the book). As might be expected, his confusion is rooted in the kind of sexist assumptions that lead him also into serious inaccuracies. For example, he asserts that when the theme of nursing was secularized, "women artists again were drawn to this subject, from Mary Cassatt, who recorded it with a certain primness that countered its potential sentiment and sensuality, to Paula Modersohn-Becker, who venerated the theme in many images of nursing earth-mothers." Rosenblum's own sexist primness has blinded him to the reality of the art of these two painters. Surely it is the unmarried Cassatt herself, not her work, whom he is describing as prim, and the fact of Modersohn-Becker's marriage, rather than her painting, that prompts him to describe her as a venerator of earth-mothers. The work of a Cassatt or a Modersohn-Becker will continue to be seen in these stereotypical terms until the changes created by the women's liberation movement at last permeate the art world, and evidence of what such women artists actually did is adequately developed and forcefully presented.[9]

David Kunzle presents a provocative instance of misogyny in his attempt to tour French and English corset fetishism ("The Corset as Erotic Alchemy: From Rococo Galanterie to Montaut's Physiologies"). This article, which perhaps not too inappropriately takes up almost a third of *Woman as Sex Object,* is yet another example of an important subject treated in a way that renders the article virtually useless, apart from its illustrations. Kunzle's approach is essentially descriptive, and lacks both hypotheses and conclusions. He simply laces, as it were, a great number of topics uncomfortably together, using a hermetic and disorganized writing style that makes the article fairly impossible to follow.

The real subject of Kunzle's article seems to be not corsetry but certain men of the nineteenth century who were fascinated with the notion of a corseted woman as something "about to burst, like some soft-bellied crustacean out of its rigid shell." According to Kunzle these men sought again and again to uncover "the grim reality within the glittering erotic shell . . . the sad truth behind the gaudy artifices of fashionable dress," and above all to reveal "woman as a physiological and social contradiction, as a perversely cultivated, sado-masochistic illusion, fascinating, dangerous, fatal." Kunzle tries hard to reconstruct in himself and his readers the mentality of the male contributors to *La Vie Parisienne* who "could switch from a presentation of female artifice as a kind of super-sensuous and super-seductive reality, to the true, inner reality which it concealed: one which was sordid and repulsive." Kunzle is either unaware or contemptuous of the source and meaning of this schizoid view of women. Moreover, he fails to see corsetry as a vehicle of sexual oppression, dress as an emblem of class position, and dress reform as one of the multitude of nineteenth-century movements responding to real social contradictions. Kunzle's effort in this article to investigate the relationship between high- and low-art images of a social phenomenon and the culture within which they were produced is thus completely distorted by his choice to imprison himself within an upper-class male point of view.

Image versus Reality

A second, more useful group of articles in *Woman as Sex Object* is characterized by its commitment to exploring the dialectic between high and low culture and between image and reality. These essays vary in approach, scope, and quality, but together they begin to lay the necessary groundwork for a feminist interpretation of the image of women in art produced by men.

Beatrice Farwell's very compressed article on "Courbet's 'Baigneuses' [The Bathers] and the Rhetorical Feminine Image" covers a lot of ground and raises a variety of important questions. Farwell defines her task as the unravelling of just what it was that Courbet meant to do in this painting. To answer this question, she finds she must explore a number of issues. In a fascinating but all too brief survey of the motif of the bathing female nude with attendants in an outdoor setting, she emphasizes its evolution from a specific biblical or mythological story to the eighteenth-century scene in which mistress and maid become both anonymous and contemporary. At the same time, the motif of a woman in the intimacy of bath or toilet (with a voyeur either shown or assumed to be the viewer) was moving easily from high art into the realm of popular erotic and pornographic engravings. Farwell documents various changes in these themes at the turn of the nineteenth century and the introduction of lithography, which made erotica more available to a larger audience. For example, the maid begins "deliberately to display her mistress, or even to turn rhetorically to the viewer as though for the approval of a customer, and indeed the image by this time may be seen to have degenerated to a representation of the woman who bestows her charms for a price." New motifs enter the repertory: lesbianism, the dressing and undressing of women, the fetishistic stress on stockings worn by an otherwise naked woman. This material is again fascinating, and deserves extended treatment.

Courbet was of course aware of and interested in popular imagery, as the research of Meyer Schapiro and Linda Nochlin has shown. Farwell investigates the links between popular erotic prints and Courbet's work, for example in *White Stockings* (1861) and *Sleep* (1866). She notes the shift to outdoor settings in erotic lithographs around the middle of the century, possibly in response to the rise of photographic erotica, and connects it to Courbet's *Hammock* of 1844. Finally, Farwell ties together these various explorations into the realms of high art, popular lithography, and erotic photography in order to explain certain puzzling aspects of the 1853 *Bathers*.

Although one might quibble with some of Farwell's conclusions, her approach is extremely intelligent and her observations very valuable. Her main interest is in investigating how traditions of lowbrow erotic imagery were incorporated into high art by the Realist painters, but she is sensitive to a number of other important problems. For example, she notes sardonically how class and race distinctions are articulated in the pictorial structure of the erotic images: in general, maids can be "distinguished from their Olympian mistresses by being either clothed or black (or both)"; in one scene, the "adoring maids include both the Oriental and the black—a third world domestic staff"; in another, the artist carefully "includes the Oriental note frequently encountered in erotica in the age of Turkish invasions and Lady Mary Wortley Montagu, as well as the theme of black maid paying homage to white beauty in an age of colonialism." A more complete and analytical study of the tradition and meaning of this imagery is necessary. As Farwell observes, it is among other things obviously one of the many elements that went into the making of Manet's *Olympia*.

The nineteenth-century preoccupation with scenes of lesbianism is another important topic touched on by Farwell. She also suggests that a complex imagery of sex, class, and race distinctions lies behind the blonde-brunette polarity so frequently found in voyeurist scenes of lesbianism. These subjects deserve a more extensive and thorough investigation.

A third area of great interest briefly mentioned by Farwell is the curious way that fragmentary and incomplete political consciousness expresses itself in art. Farwell suggests that "it is somewhat ironic to reflect that Courbet's seeking out of the popular image was inspired by notions of social reform along egalitarian lines, while the popular image itself—in the case of erotica—represented an aspect of society not only untouched by new ideas, but even retrograde. Women's lib [*sic*] was a long way off." In fact, it is not so much "ironic" as indicative of the limited understanding among most nineteenth-century reformers and socialists of what they were doing. Courbet's painting is an example of the way the image of woman has so often been made a mere vehicle—that is, object—for the transmission of meaning, in this case of ideas concerning social issues and attitudes.

Gerald Needham's examination of "Manet, 'Olympia' and Pornographic Photography" is another of the growing number of studies in which high art is confronted with its counterparts in popular imagery. Needham sets for himself the task of relating Manet's *Olympia* to the contemporary vogue for pornographic photographs. Less ambitious than Farwell's article on Courbet, Needham's essay is straightforward, convincing, and easy to read. He examines the photos, many illustrated, in terms of their subjects, pictorial organization, formal style, and novelty as a medium, concluding that the *Olympia* not only "upset the spectators by her shameless suggestiveness, but she was also directly reminiscent of the pornographic photographs that the male audience at least would have gloated over.'' Needham tries also to go beyond this investigation of the relevant experiences of the contemporary public; like Farwell, he wishes to understand the personal motivations that produced such art. He alludes, for example, to the contradictions in the consciousness of the Realist artists who ''while claiming a virtuous purpose, seem to have at least partially succumbed to the erotic excitement of prostitution and pornography, which combined the allure of the forbidden with a freedom from personal responsibility . . . showing that an advanced attitude in art was no guarantee of freedom from conventional sexual attitudes.''

Needham's evidence and conclusions are useful contributions to our understanding of the portrayal of women and sexuality in high art of the mid-nineteenth century. But Needham does not fully comprehend the implications of what he has found. He sees the *Olympia* simply as a painting ''which exemplified the woman as sex object, albeit temptress.'' He entirely misses the way in which the *Olympia* also presents a stylistically integrated image of autonomy, self-sufficiency, and aggressive independence—truly a visual counterpart to the nineteenth-century social awareness that bourgeois marriage and prostitution were in a hideously hypocritical relationship to one another, and to the feminist charge that marriage was but a legalized, and perhaps even more unsatisfactory, form of prostitution. The social context of the Second Empire did not clearly determine which of the two images projected by the subject and formal structure of Manet's *Olympia*—sex object and self-supporting person—was really dominant. Surely this ability of *Olympia* to be socially and formally autonomous was at least as threatening to the shocked public as her existence as sex object.

Needham also believes Manet to have later developed ''a new concept of femininity,'' one which supposedly shared with the Impressionists an ''openness and directness, a lack of class consciousness, and uncomplicated happiness'' and which was therefore ''fully sexual, but never an exploitation. Contrasting completely with *Olympia,* it points the way to the 'new woman' of the 1890s with her intelligence and independence.'' Needham's analysis of the situation of women in the later nineteenth century and of the real meaning of the imagery of that period is naive and limited, and must be corrected.

Alessandra Comini's discussion of ''Vampires, Virgins, and Voyeurs in Imperial Vienna'' provides an extremely valuable, if short and hard to follow, sketch of the changes in the imagery of women and sexuality around the turn of the century. She begins by briefly tracing how two images of women became increasingly insistent themes: on the one hand, the virgin, and on the other, the female vampire, ''a splendid and scary foil to the virgin-concept, she vied with her innocent sisters for poetic and artistic attention.'' Comini notes that the plague of threatening vampiric creatures, always ready to ''jealously [drain] the life blood of the male's creative ability,'' can only be understood against the background of the rising feminist movement. The same observation could be made of the Viennese Expressionists' attempts to investigate with increasing directness the range of sexual experience, including male and female adolescence, female virginity, voyeurism, hetero- and homosexuality, and masturbation. Comini emphasizes that artists like Schiele and Kubin were also moving toward a self-conscious exploration of their own, specifically male, sexuality. Moreover, ''as artists turned toward themselves, away from women, whether as vampire or virgin, they were appalled to discover the enemy close at hand; to find within themselves those mystifying, foreign, so-called 'feminine' qualities which Weininger and Freud had labelled 'bisexual' . . . a final insight was vouchsafed to the artist; a narcissistic voyeurism in which the antipodes of man's thought about sex, woman and himself battled for resolution.''

Comini is unique among the contributors to *Woman as Sex Object* for her understanding of the dual imagery used to portray women, her sense that the poles of the duality are in a dialectical relationship that reflects social phenomena, her awareness that in late nineteenth-century society and art the strain between the poles was becoming extreme, and her constant and fruitful consciousness that the beholder is throughout presumed to be male. Although Comini's approach is not explicitly feminist, she brings to her subject the kind of sensitivity to issues of sexuality that is necessary.

Two other articles in *Woman as Sex Object* attempt to deal with the image of women in art of the late nineteenth century. Because they are not sufficiently sensitive to the specific tensions of nineteenth-century art and society, these essays do not manage to go beyond a fairly superficial survey of their subjects. Nevertheless, they bring together a certain amount of interesting data, and are therefore useful contributions toward the development of a feminist approach.

Martha Kingsbury discusses ''The Femme Fatale and Her Sisters'' as they existed in high art, popular imagery, and real life. She sees the femme fatale as a particular visual configuration in high art rather than as a social phenomenon, and she takes the configuration as perfectly representative of the social reality. Accordingly, she begins with a tour of the images of Klimt, Munch, and the somewhat easier art of von Lenbach and Sargent. Real-life examples of the femme fatale configuration (actresses) and popular imagery (fashion plates and ads) are then treated simply as versions of the high-art model. The article concludes with a short discussion of the way Carrière and the late Renoir incorporated some of the erotic content of the typology into their scenes of motherhood.

Kingsbury never deals with the femme fatale as a historical phenomenon that takes a specific form in the late nineteenth century. Moreover, her analysis lacks any sense of the relationship between such an imagery and its counterpart, the innocent virgin. Most disturbingly, Kingsbury does not recognize the femme fatale as an artistic and social shaping of experience. Instead, she adopts an essentially Freudian view of women as beings defined totally by their sexuality—that is, as femmes fatales, one way or another. She speaks of women for whom "the possessed are their children, not their lovers; but the pattern is similar, visually and psychologically, and its basis is the same—sexual instinct and the erotic power that is its tool." And the femme fatale has a counterpart in the artist, who "in the exercise of his special creative power also seemed to have something in common with actresses or with women in general, in his absorption by the passion he originated." Kingsbury's subject is a good one, but her treatment of it is seriously distorted by implicit adherence to a psychologistic conception of women and an inadequate understanding of the interrelations between art and society.[10]

Barbara White's article on "Renoir's Sensuous Women" follows the changing portrayal of women in Renoir's work from the 1870s to his last years. The approach is that of a conventional chronological survey of a well-known major motif in an artist's work. What is exciting here is the opportunity to avoid either the gushing platitudes that Renoir's painting of women tend to inspire or their total rejection on modernist formal grounds, and instead to develop a real critique of these works. Although White takes some steps in this direction, her analysis is limited. For example, White sees clearly that "in essence, Renoir created an art about women for men to enjoy," yet she suggests that in Renoir's paintings of the 1870s, "a free sociability enables men and women to relate to one another in a joyful, unpossessive manner. One senses equality between the sexes." This is surely unlikely, and indeed in the next paragraph White quotes approvingly a contemporary comment that these women "would be ideal mistresses—always sweet, gay and smiling . . . the true ideal woman!" A more appropriate approach to the paintings of these years would investigate them as sensitive explorations by Renoir into the ambivalence and difficulty of sex and class relationships; one thinks, for example, of the complexity of form and meaning in the *Bal à Bougival*. Similarly, White's explanation of the change in Renoir's style in the 1880s lacks depth, and deals almost entirely with supposed internal changes in the artist's psychology. She hypothesizes that Renoir "may have felt displaced by having a baby who demanded so much of [his model and wife] Aline's attention . . . Renoir could have been troubled by woman-envy—specifically envy of a woman's ability to give birth to children." White does not really investigate why in the turbulent 1880s Renoir might withdraw and turn socially and artistically conservative, painting idealized nudes that appear to be "all body and no mind or feelings" and writing polemics "against modernity, against industrialization, against the rising tide of feminism."

One feels throughout White's article that despite all good intentions she is held back by the heavy heritage of traditional art-historical approaches. She often veers dangerously close to the laudatory exegeses of conventional Renoir criticism. She relies on superficial and frequently pop-Freudian speculations. And, most disappointingly of all, although White is evidently aware of the issue of sexism, she does not bring a feminist consciousness to her interpretations.

Thomas Hess's article, nattily titled "Pinup and Icon," promises to discuss the convergence around 1950 of popular pinup imagery with the development of Abstract-Expressionism, against the background of the situation of women at that time. In fact, Hess's main focus is on the role of the pinup in the genesis of de Kooning's *Women* series. The violent images in these large paintings of monster-like female figures are I think correctly interpreted as expressions, from a distinctly male point of view, of what society and ideology were forcing women to do in order to survive in post-World War II America. From this perspective, de Kooning's incorporation of the imagery of pinups into these paintings makes perfect sense. What the women's liberation movement has done, however, is to sensitize us to the sexist content of such art. In addition, even more than the Picasso prints discussed by Schiff, de Kooning's *Women* are part of the contemporary world of art and art politics, and for this reason we experience them not only as expressive but as oppressive.

It is in response to this situation that Hess feels he must defend de Kooning from what he fears might be interpreted as male-chauvinist-pig-ism—as if that were the real question. To do this Hess is forced into critical inconsistency. He first argues that the "peculiarly anonymous, ubiquitous pinup" appealed to de Kooning precisely for its "inhuman" and "artificial" qualities. At the same time he asserts that de Kooning's preparatory drawings "affectionately present the pinup as the friendly neighborhood sex-symbol Americans had come to know and love" and that it is only "under the pressure of pictorial necessities" that the large paintings present a more menacing image. In other words, de Kooning's reasons were primarily formal, that is, pure and disinterested, and "the objective substructure of a woman's body freed him to paint as he wanted to, while painters who use abstract shapes . . . are forced to invent them, subjectively." Hess does not bother to tell us why a man's body or an old car body or whatever might not serve just as well.

Oddly enough, Hess is refusing in this essay to admit what as recently as five years ago he freely discussed in his numerous writings on de Kooning: namely, that what de Kooning is really doing is using the pinups and the motif of a woman's body as objects to give not only formal structure but meaning to his paintings. And that meaning involves among other things male ambivalence and confusion about women as ferocious, evil, consuming, iconic, motherly, romantic, vulgar, banal, and so on (all adjectives culled from Hess's earlier writings). Sensing that his new and essentially formalist argument might fail to convince, Hess refers vaguely to the subconscious and to Jungian archetypes. He concludes neatly that "Manet's *Olympia* offers to the spectator the skin of an issue, so to speak; de Kooning's *Woman* reveals the anxieties inside." (Hess is aware enough of modern social criticism to acknowledge that the anxieties are those of the insecure male observer, but he does not quite understand the source of the insecurity.) Finally,

Hess sums up his defense: "Like all great painting [de Kooning's] *Women* are ambiguous and have been interpreted as attacks on women as well as glorifications—and both interpretations have their truth to them." One feels, however, that now that women's liberation has settled in to stay, Hess would like us to believe that de Kooning leans toward the goddess-glorification side, although he is forced to admit that the artist "has never given public support to feminist or Women's Lib [*sic*] causes." In other words, de Kooning (and here I wonder to what extent Hess enters into the tradition of identifying with his subject) is just a well-intentioned fallguy who has been unjustly maligned merely for responding to his presumably purely pictorial needs as an artist.

Hess's essay can be seen as an effort to apply to contemporary art the kind of approach employed by Farwell and Needham for the nineteenth century. The discussions both of popular pinup imagery and of the social history of women are unfortunately quite derivative, as Hess himself acknowledges. What he does not deal with is how his inadequate understanding and simplistic point of view in these areas affect his discussion of Abstract-Expressionism. In addition, a series of other, unspoken, goals further distort Hess's treatment of his material. First, Hess wants to reinforce his conviction that de Kooning is a grand master in the same league as, say, Manet. Second, Hess wishes somehow to demonstrate that de Kooning is a sort of crypto-feminist. And third, Hess would like to establish himself as an understanding sympathizer and interpreter of what he calls "Women's Lib."[11] Hess fails in all three goals, and despite a number of elegantly phrased and quite useful insights, the article is essentially a flashy and inconsistent gloss on an extremely interesting and important topic.

Nochlin and Women's Liberation

Linda Nochlin's brief discussion of "Eroticism and Female Imagery in Nineteenth-Century Art" is the only article in *Woman as Sex Object* that is self-consciously feminist. Curiously, it is by far the shortest piece in the entire collection. Nochlin makes only a few basic points, but these acquire great impact from the sharpness and humor of her presentation.

First, Nochlin observes that art critics and scholars have traditionally ignored (only in print, one might add) erotic implications in works of art. Although it has become permissible to discuss the psychology and the sexuality of the artist, art works themselves have until recently been discussed as if they were somehow chaste. Such an approach, which I would argue is simply another manifestation of the modernist tendency to isolate art from life, is particularly unsuited to the nineteenth century, when "the social basis of sexual myth stands out in clearest relief from the apparently 'personal' erotic imagery of individual artists."

Nochlin points to the obvious convention that the term "erotic" in fact means "erotic-for-men," and asserts that "the imagery of sexual delight or provocation has always been created *about* women for men's enjoyment, by men.'' She poses as an alternative the creation, presumably by women, of an art about men for women's enjoyment, but rejects it as impossible, blocked by ''women's lack of her own erotic territory on the map of nineteenth-century reality. . . . Those who have no country have no language. Women have no imagery available—no accepted public language to hand—with which to express their particular viewpoint.'' As an example of male-oriented imagery Nochlin considers the long tradition in high and low art of the breast-as-apple metaphor, illustrating it with a nineteenth-century magazine photo of an elaborately coiffured woman, nude except for stockings, shiny high boots, and a necklace of pearls, and holding a tray of apples close to her body. The woman's round breasts rest on the tray, alongside and alternating with the fruit. She is presumably available and looks out at us, the male audience, with a glance that invites us to do as the caption below says: ''Achetez des pommes'' [''Buy Some Apples''].

Nochlin suggests that no analogous conventions permit the association of fruit with male sexuality, despite the ''rich underground feminine [*sic*] lore linking food—specifically bananas—with the male organ.'' As a sort of a historical proof for this lack of access to independent imagery, Nochlin constructs what she perceives to be a 1972 women's counterpart to the nineteenth-century photo. Her quite intentionally ludicrous photograph, titled ''Buy Some Bananas,'' captures a heavily bearded and very hairy male model (carefully credited in a footnote as the male model at Vassar College) in a pose much like that of the woman in the earlier photograph. He is entirely nude except for athletic socks and old loafers, holds a tray of bananas at mid-thigh level, and gazes vacuously upwards. Nochlin coyly attributes the erotic failure of her ''Buy Some Bananas'' to our continuing lack of accredited imagery: ''Even today, the food-penis metaphor has no upward mobility, so to speak . . . the linking of the male organ to food is always a figure of meiosis—an image of scorn, belittlement or derision: it lowers and denigrates rather than elevates and universalizes the subject of the metaphor.'' Nochlin's humor in making this comparison should not blind us to the flaws in her argument. First, Nochlin shied away from posing the model to make a true and biting parallel in terms of class, sex, and gender role to the nineteenth-century prototype: the model needs a dogtag around his neck or a tattoo on his shoulder; his tray should be held higher, so that his penis, possibly erect, could lie among the bananas; and he should perhaps be looking aggressively out at us rather than innocently upwards. Moreover, it is not really the lack of appropriate conventions or imagery that makes it impossible for ''Buy Some Bananas'' to be erotic-to-women, even were the improvements suggested to be made. Rather, it is because the politics of contemporary sexual relations are such that a mechanical reversal, in which the man becomes a sex-object available at a price, cannot be made. This is why the athletic socks and the loafers are merely hilarious, for the erotic implications of stockings and shoes are specific to the female sexual role as currently experienced.

Finally, in considering the future Nochlin seems still to be wedded to the idea of an unimaginative reversal of sex roles as the only way out for women. She is very well aware of the issues of sexual politics and the tradition of imagery presenting women as available, submissive, and passive, but the signs of change to which she points positively tend to involve depictions of man as sex-object. She comments approvingly on a painting depicting ''a heavy-lidded male odalisque,'' she misreads Alice Neel's 1933 *Joe Gould* as an early step in a similar direction, and she looks forward to films made by women directors who will employ a reversible sexual imagery. In short, the logical consequence of Nochlin's comments is a simple extension of current sexual conventions, so that men will become more objectified and women will be permitted to participate in sex-ploitation as oppressors. Obviously this solution has attractive aspects, and it is these that Nochlin emphasizes, but essentially it would still keep us all—women and men—imprisoned within a world of alienated and objectified sexual relations. The real alternative would be to create new modes of sexual and indeed human expression.

Behind Nochlin's inability to imagine such a transcendence of current sexual expression is, I think, a relatively superficial understanding of what women's liberation is about and an ultimate allegiance to the status quo. For example, lacking sensitivity to the very real imagery available to women, Nochlin is forced to assume that it does not usefully exist.[12] Nochlin also tends in her work again and again to misunderstand and even ignore the issues of class and race, despite her serious commitment to studying nineteenth-century art as a historical complex of social and artistic relations. She assumes, for instance, a lack of female ''erotic territory'' in both nineteenth- and twentieth-century experience and imagery without any mention of class; implicit in her discussion is a projection of bourgeois class norms onto all women. The evidence of social historians and of sociologists points very clearly, however, to the inaccuracy of such assumptions. The erotic implications of the ''Buy Some Apples'' photo or of Ingres's harem scenes are in each case heightened by the viewer's confident assumption that he is in a superior and controlling class and race as well as sex position. Conversely, Toulouse-Lautrec's brothel scenes frequently lack this kind of erotic power precisely because the artist assumes a sort of human equality with his subjects. And always, Manet's *Olympia* remains the pivotal and perhaps most complex statement of the urgency, difficulty, and even despair felt within nineteenth-century French society as it vainly tried to confront these issues.

Nochlin is also relatively insensitive to the various attempts to build alternatives within the contemporary art world. In another essay, frequently reprinted, she has suggested that there have never been in the past nor are there now any ''great'' women artists.[13] Despite her disclaimers about the meaning of the term ''great,'' one senses that for Nochlin women artists like Cassatt, Morisot, Valadon, Kollwitz, Modersohn-Becker, O'Keeffe, Hepworth, Frankenthaler, Nevelson, and others not only fail to be "great," but by subtle implication they are not even very good, nor worthy of serious research. Nochlin suggests that this situation can and will change (if institutions in the future are forced to reform and readjust), but in the meantime it seems that the focus for Nochlin and her students is on the image of women in the art of "great," and also not-so-great, men. What this means, if done without a feminist consciousness and approach, is simply a new topic to be examined using traditional art-historical methods. In other words, useful but status-quo art history; and by extension, conventional art criticism and mediocre exhibitions.

Linda Nochlin was the first well-known art historian to begin teaching and writing in the area of women and art, and I do not want to belittle her very real and continuing contribution. What disturbs me, however, is that Nochlin's approach to the issues is so far the only one that has been given wide publication and attention. It is surely time that the same broad range of feminist perspectives already developed by scholars in other fields emerge and be made available in the art world. The task is a large one, and I can only outline its contours in the remarks that follow.

Tasks for the Future

A careful and critical reading of *Woman as Sex Object* can do no more than raise issues, suggest fruitful areas of research, and depress the feminist reader by its insistent presentation of the kind of imagery that most objectifies women. The question, then, is what should we do. There are several different groups, somewhat overlapping, of feminists or potential feminists involved with art. There are the feminist artists. There are the critics and historians who write as feminists about art. And there are the teachers who wish to approach their material from a feminist perspective. The immediate needs of each of these types of art workers may be quite different. In the following comments I will consider these different needs, but my own background dictates that I must focus on the situation of the feminist teacher and art historian.

Contemporary Art and Art Criticism

The issue of women, art, and feminism has been most urgently raised by women artists. Several approaches to the problem of making a feminist or a women's art have evolved and are being discussed and developed within the women's art movement. In particular, it has been suggested that some sort of female aesthetic or sensibility exists, involving an imagery and formal style specific to women. Proponents insist that an authentic artistic language is being created, corresponding to the distinct social experience of women, independent of "male-defined" art, and essentially liberating. Others argue that the theory of a female aesthetic really restricts women in that it limits them to suspiciously familiar shapes, colors, forms, and images. In other words, the female aesthetic seems possibly to be no more than a rehabilitated artistic ghetto, gaudily furbished with superficial answers to hard questions. Moreover, some see the rise of a trendy "feminine sensibility" as clearly opportunist. They point, for example, to the odd coincidence that the so-called female aesthetic is strangely reminiscent of the conventions of currently fashionable minimal art, and they predict further shifts in the theory as art-world fashions change.

The theory of a female sensibility seems to be based on two premises, implicit if not explicit. First, it is assumed that an individual's experience is primarily and perhaps completely determined by gender. Women and men are held to inhabit utterly separate worlds, and variations of class or ethnic experience are considered clearly subordinate to gender distinctions. The second assumption is that whatever exists today must be essentially unchangeable: the battle of the sexes is felt to be eternal and ahistorical. It follows, then, that the only way women artists can operate is to accept these terms and develop their own strength, autonomously and in apparent opposition to men.

An alternative approach would argue for a more transcendent view of social experience and of art. Such a point of view corresponds to the sense within some sectors of the women's liberation movement that the meaning of one's personhood and the nature of relationships between the sexes are evolving phenomena which can be grasped and acted upon. Pat Mainardi has outlined one interpretation of what this might mean for women artists: "The only feminine aesthetic worthy of the name is that women artists must be free to explore the entire range of art possibilities. We who have been labeled, stereotyped and gerrymandered out of the very definition of art must be free to *define* art, not to pick up the crumbs from The Man's table. . . . We must begin to define women's art as *what women* [artists] *do,* not try to slip and squeeze ourselves through the loophole of the male art world."

Although the debate around the female aesthetic is absorbing a great deal of energy, the more important questions may be those concerning what is really going on in the art world and who is the audience for art today. Some women artists argue for the development of an explicitly political art outside the reward system of the contemporary art world. Here again Mainardi has clearly articulated one approach to the dilemma:

> Feminist Art is different from feminine sensibility. Feminist Art is political propaganda art which like all political art, should owe its first allegiance to the political movement whose ideology it shares, and not to the museum and gallery artworld system. Since feminism is a political position (the economic, political and social equality of women and men) and feminist art reflects those politics, it could even be made by men, although it is unlikely that at this point men's politics will be up to it. . . . In fact, talking about any form of political art within artworld limitations and audiences is absurd. Doing political art for Rockefeller's MOMA! Good Grief![14]

A serious critique of the art world has not, however, generally been an integral part of discussions of feminism and art. Instead there has been a tendency to somehow separate a "good" from a "feminist" women's art. For example, Cindy Nemser agrees that feminist art is political, but she sees it as quite different from "human art [i.e., true art, which] is what men and women are producing and have always produced."[15] This distinction is basically one between political art and something that is supposed to be better, purer, truer, more elevated, eternal, whatever. It is, I think, an artificial, incorrect and dangerous distinction.

Finally, and perhaps most important, there are women artists all over the country who are creating their art out of an increasingly strong and self-confident sense of themselves as *women* artists. Because they are working within a society that has been forced to recognize the existence of women's liberation as a real social force, they are able to bring their experience as women to their art without the kinds of defensiveness and apology that were necessary before the rise of modern feminism. They may not be aware of the various issues and polemics, no courses on women and art may be offered in their schools, they may not think of themselves as part of a women's liberation movement—yet I believe that the art they are making must be seen as, in the widest sense, feminist. It is these women and their work that must be given support, encouragement, and definition if we are ever to see the kind of forward looking and transcendent feminist art that could really express women's liberation.

Not very much in the way of feminist art criticism of the contemporary scene has appeared so far.[16] In general, what has been published is inadequate, tending variously and contradictorily toward reformism, unrealistic utopianism, and what I would call cultural feminism. For example, Elizabeth Baker and Lucy Lippard have defined the problem for women as essentially a simple question of equal rights within the current art world. Cindy Nemser has gone deeper and attacked the sexist vocabulary available to critics. She calls for the construction of an "androgynous" criticism, but implies that the critic (and artist) can simply *choose* individually to become "androgynous" while still living and operating within a sexist society. This is utopian and idealist. Finally, a trend has emerged recently, particularly in the writings and exhibitions promoting the existence of a so-called feminine sensibility, which is in many ways based on the all-consuming assumption that "female-is-beautiful"; it is this that is best described as cultural feminism. Feminist art criticism of the contemporary art scene will, I think, be forced to remain weak and restricted so long as feminist art, art history, and art teaching continue undeveloped.

Art Courses

Feminist teachers of studio courses and of art history or appreciation courses have the important task of helping to build the necessary context for the creation of a feminist art, criticism, and scholarship. Three general and overlapping areas of interest stand out as obvious running themes for any such course. First, there is the process of learning what women artists have done and what they are doing now. In the case of women artists of the past, we must ask whether and how the specific female experience of a woman artist materialized itself in her work. Moreover, in studying the art of the past, two questions emerge clearly: How did the organization of art in various kinds of societies affect the role of women as artists; and what was the meaning of the distinction between "high" art (usually produced by men) and "low" art (usually produced by women, at least in precapitalist societies)? In the case of contemporary women artists, the issues are somewhat different: What are women artists doing? What are women artists with a self-conscious sense of themselves as women, or perhaps as feminists, doing? Participants in a given class may also decide to ask what each member, as a woman artist, thinks she is doing and what it is she wants to do.

The second area to consider is that of the image of women in art, usually high art by men. We must explore what can be learned when we bring a feminist consciousness and approach to the topics of traditional art history. Here again a distinction must also be made, or at least an awareness kept, of the differences between high and low art and between art by men and by women. How have women been portrayed, and how are they being portrayed now? How has art defined "being female"? What has it seen as woman's role in society? Which women are portrayed and why? What is the relationship of the images to the reality of women's lives? To what extent and why has the image of women in art not reflected social reality? What are the consequences of taking the image of "man" as the human norm?

Finally, there is the general question of whether there in fact exists a specifically female point of view in the response to art, in the creation of art, and in the interpretation or appreciation of art. Do women now, or did they in the past, have such a different experience from men that they bring to art a significantly different perspective? If so, what specifically is it in a given period? When we as women look at art by men, do we from our experience have insights that they don't have? What are they? When we make art, do we do it differently? And should we?

A too-intense focus on any one of these areas—women as artists, images of women, the female point of view—will result in an unsuccessful approach and an inadequate course and teaching experience. Too much concentration on women artists can develop into what I have called cultural feminism—that is, an uncritical overemphasis on women that obscures and denigrates other questions, above all those concerning class and race. Such an approach not only distorts, it is reactionary in that it contains and limits rather than releases energy. An exclusive study of the image of women in art tends to be demoralizing and discouraging, especially if done without a strong feminist perspective. At its worst this approach can become a superficial survey of what seems to be the chauvinism of male artists; the task, however, is not to uncover and catalog the varieties and sins of sexism, but to understand and act on them. An overemphasis on the image of women in the work of male artists can also be relatively reformist and conventional, not to say dull. Finally, focusing exclusively on a female point of view is apt to be abstract and ahistorical. To sum up, a good feminist course on women and art can only be created by combining the three issues within a strong historical framework and a clear and integrated perspective on the issues of race and class. Above all, it must be historical, that is, fully aware of the complexity and specificity of the particular historical moment.

Art History and Feminism: Basics

Perhaps the most pressing and fundamental work to be done by feminist art scholars is that of unearthing, documenting, and interpreting the art produced by women artists. This is an urgent issue because it is an area that has been severely neglected; indeed, it will involve a tremendous effort of basic, almost archaeological research. Moreover, such a project will provide the resources necessary to teach courses dealing with women and art: reproductions, slides, bibliographies, articles, even books. At this point, any work done on women artists is important and useful, if only for the data it provides and the questions it may raise. Eventually, feminist scholars will have to bring the same critical feminist consciousness to the study of work produced by women artists that they are beginning to use in criticizing art made by men. A very few attempts of this sort have been made.[17]

Feminist scholars must also confront the more amorphous problem of modifying and correcting traditional art history. Here the task is emphatically not a one-dimensional search for sexism in art made by men. Rather, we need to learn how to use our consciousness as women and as feminists in order literally to *re-vise*—to look again, to see again, and thus both to reevaluate and to develop new insights. To do this we must first acknowledge several basic methodological necessities and understand the major types of imagery used to depict women.

For women there is always the major question of who is the audience or public for a given work. Although art historians sometimes investigate the upper-class patronage within a particular society quite closely, feminist scholars will of necessity have to be more acutely aware that the patron, buyer, or viewer is virtually always presumed to be *male,* as well as upper-class and white.

Another crucial issue for feminists is the relationship between art and reality. A glance at the depiction of women, family life, or sexuality makes it immediately clear that the tendency within the art world and among many art historians to equate high art with life, and to take the images of art as adequate substitutes for reality, is a bankrupt approach. Far from equating the two, feminist scholars must explore the dialectic between image and reality, as well as develop a thorough critique of the distinction traditionally made between "high" and "low" art. The latter issue has long been a question for those attempting a radical approach to culture, but only feminists have raised it as one involving assumptions concerning sex as well as class.

Feminist art historians and critics will of course have to participate in the increasing skepticism toward traditional Freudian exegeses of art and indeed toward any kind of superficial psychologizing. From a feminist point of view, virtually all psychological theories are particularly distorting in that they simplistically reduce social phenomena to individual sexual ones and at the same time assume the human norm to be male. Moreover, their social biases go so deep that they must be rejected and alternative approaches developed.[18] When one investigates the great recurring theme in the depiction of women—the presentation of a dual image—the limitations of these conventionally based psychological theories become especially clear. The images of duality are taken to be simple projections of "human" (i.e., male) fears and fantasies: virgin versus whore, queen versus slave, Madonna versus Fury, and so on. In fact, this duality is rooted in large-scale social phenomena.

In the case of the art produced over the past several centuries, we must understand the social basis for the duality in the class and accompanying psychic structures of capitalist society. Thus, for example, we will be able to see precisely how Goya was the first to clearly pose the sexual dilemma of the nineteenth-century bourgeoisie, as seen from a specifically male perspective. In his paired depictions of the *Maja Dressed* and the *Maja Undressed,* Goya confronts the viewer with a number of questions: Which of these two women is the real person? Which is the true Maja? Which of the two is the more sexually provocative? Which the more passive object for appropriation by the (male) viewer? Aren't these two women in fact interchangeable? Indeed, aren't all women perhaps whores and belong really to the lower classes? By using a dual structure, Goya suggests his own answers to the questions. Each woman is a fragment, a partial being. Although each is aggressive, strong, and full of a real presence and autonomy, neither one is quite whole. In short, the fears contained in the questions may be real. It took the entire nineteenth century for the prophetic implications of Goya's paintings to mature. The self-confident views espoused by a rising and revolutionary bourgeois culture gave way by the end of the century to the anxious introspection of alienated male artists living isolated amidst turbulent class conflicts. The imagery they developed split women into a proliferation of virginal lady victims on the one hand and vampiric de-classed whores on the other, but the hidden threat that the two types were interchangeable remained. Some aspects of this history of the dual image of women in art are already being investigated by art scholars. What is necessary now is to insist on a feminist interpretation grounded in the social reality that produced the dual imagery.[19]

The other major way the image of woman is used in art is as a "stand-in"—women become the vehicles through which artists express their and society's attitudes and ideas on a variety of issues. A virtual army of these female images could be mustered, representing various virtues, vices, topical issues, crude jokes, didactic slogans, inspirational themes, specific fears, whatever. In these cases, women are not usually stripped of their sexuality; rather they acquire a kind of social as well as sexual objectification. As Farwell and Needham point out in their analyses of the French Realist painters, the progressive aspirations of the social objectification may be seriously contradicted by the reactionary nature of the sexual one. This process is most discouraging, for it is true of virtually all artists who attempt one way or another to build a social critique in their art, that is to make a self-consciously political art. They tend again and again to use images of women as more or less comical stand-ins for the entire range of the sins of the bourgeoisie. In so doing they not only objectify women, they reflect the tragic inadequacy of a political analysis that ignores women while working for social change. Feminist art historians and critics should thoroughly document such imagery for what it means—a confused understanding of who is the enemy. Women today will no longer stand outside the processes of change and revolution, and I would guess that they will less and less appear as objects in art.

Art History and Feminism: Specifics

There are of course a number of special topics that would particularly benefit from a feminist analysis. For example, the study of "erotic art" is generally distorted by ignorance of its basis in a specific gender point of view and of its historical character. The consequences of the "erotic-for-men" perspective have only begun to be explored. Moreover, any investigation of so-called erotic art must take into consideration the historically specific nature of pornography. Recent scholarship suggests that pornography, in contrast to "erotica," is a characteristically capitalist phenomenon. Pornography emerged in the context of the early bourgeois ideology of life, liberty, and the pursuit of happiness for all men (*sic;* compare also the concept of libertinage . . .). As capitalism developed, it proved unable to fulfill its promises of liberty—and pornography was one of many reflections of this failure, in particular of the increasing alienation of relations between the sexes. What better example could there be of the metamorphosis within capitalist society of people into commodity-like things than the fantastic worlds of conventional pornography, both high and low. In these "pornotopias," as Steven Marcus calls them, a mood of emotional anaesthesia hangs over the total sexualization of experience: relations between people become relations between body parts; the human norm tends to be a penis to which is attached, somewhat uncomfortably, a person; and women become natural objects or commodities for consumption. In the 1950s a "new pornography" emerged, and in the 1970s it appears that the social structures supporting the subculture of pornography are beginning, along with capitalist society itself, to crack. All this must be reevaluated and analyzed from a feminist perspective.[20]

Even more interesting than the topic of erotic art is the question of how male sexuality as a point of view is embodied in art. We need to look at much of the work of, say, a Gauguin, a Munch, or a Schiele as the expression of particular types of sexual consciousness. For example, when Gauguin carves a hellish visual catalog of the female life-cycle and titles it *Be in Love, You Will Be Happy,* he does more than merely "[dare to] impose his personal vision on the romantic conventions of the day, to expose the underside of love without coyness."[21] Gauguin is in fact exposing and exploring the nature of his own, specifically *male* illusions about love (as well as about sex, death, etc.). Gauguin, like Picasso in the twentieth century, tends to stress the aggressively macho and superficially unquestioning imagery of male sex roles of his time. Schiele and Munch, by contrast, often suggest the anxieties and fears that inevitably accompany these sex roles. A clear example is any version of Munch's *Jealousy:* the jealousy is, obviously, male jealousy and the work must be interpreted as speaking to the specifics of that emotion as experienced by men. In all these cases, only an approach that refuses to identify uncritically with the artist and his experience can fully explore the great sensitivity and depth with which these artists were giving visual form to the consciousness and reality of the end of the nineteenth century, the very world that was the subject of Freud's early studies. Such an approach to critical interpretation (whether taken by a woman or a man) is not just feminist, it is virtually the only way to *see* the work of these artists as it really is. In other words, the imagery of sexuality, more than any other area, requires that art history and criticism be feminist in order to be adequate.

One aspect of male sexual fantasy is particularly curious and worthy of further investigation: the fascination with scenes of lesbianism. Why scenes of women making love to each other appeal so strongly to the psychic structure of men living in capitalist society is a complex question, and a number of factors must be considered. First, such scenes enable a man to project himself into an intensely erotic world that nevertheless does not require him to expend his own precious sexual energy. At the same time he can enjoy the sensual fantasy of being both subject and object. The scenes may also be attractive in that they suggest entry into the hidden secrets of "woman's sphere," a world apart, unknown, and hence exoticized and eroticized by men, particularly in the nineteenth century. Finally, there is the invitation to a male voyeurism that is seemingly without competitiveness, guilt or fear, because the lovers are both women. The imagery of love between members of the same sex is only one of a number of specific sexual themes that deserve more thorough study. Because it is a subject that may increasingly be found in various forms in the work of women artists, it may also be able to help us understand some of the more concrete ways in which gender experience manifests itself.

What about female sexuality as a point of view in the making of art? For obvious reasons, fewer women than men have articulated their sexual experience in art, at least directly. Still, I would guess that once the basic work of discovering and documenting the art produced by women is underway, we will be surprised at what we find. From Artemisia Gentileschi in the seventeenth century to women artists today, female sexual experience surely expresses itself. In interpreting it, we should remember that the sexual experience of women has varied through history, and we must be sensitive to the complexity and variety of sexual choices available to women at particular moments in history.

The issue of female versus male experience goes far beyond the specifics of sexuality. A feminist approach to art will seek to investigate how the different experience of women and men in most areas of life is expressed in art made by both men and women artists. When it comes to women artists and their approach to the world through a female experience, the assumptions of sex-neutrality of course fail completely. This is true even when a woman artist has undergone a more or less traditional training and appears to participate in the conventions of "high" art. The most obvious example is Cassatt. Her work has always been recognized, yet at the same time it has been devalued and isolated for being either too much concerned with female experience ("all those mother-and-child images") or too limited by it ("her models are confined to the family circle"). A feminist reevaluation of Cassatt's work will see it for what it is: a magnificent exploration of the world inhabited by upper-class women in the last quarter of the nineteenth century. For example, in *Five O'Clock Tea* (1880) the emphasis on the silver tea set, which is given as much space and impact as the two women, is at first surprising and somewhat disquieting; it makes pictorial sense, however, when one enters into the assumptions of Cassatt's sex and class. If the work of even so distinguished and in some ways conventional an artist as Cassatt requires a feminist consciousness in order to be properly understood, what then of the many artists whose work was more obviously affected by the fact that they were women? What about the portrait painters, the genre specialists, the photographers, and (again and again) the women who worked in the forms designated as "low" by the modern art world? Surely here is a task for literally a generation of feminist scholars.

Conclusion: Feminist Criticism and Class Relations

I have focused throughout this paper on the relationship of gender and sexuality to art. At the same time I have noted that once the assumptions of sex-neutrality are attacked, then too the issue of class arises. Similarly, the racism that accompanied the development of capitalism into a worldwide system stands out clearly. In order to underscore these last points, it is useful to review the issues from a perspective that sees them as an integrated expression of the reality of social relations within capitalist society.

In the nineteenth century, for example, culture was intimately involved in the development of imperialism. As the colonial empires of the West expanded, sex, class, and race antagonisms intensified and manifested themselves in all areas of experience, including art. At the start of the century, Ingres's particularly complex treatment of women in his paintings provides an excellent opportunity to tackle the problem of how the issues of sex, class, and race were being joined within French society, and how in turn this tangle functioned in art. Ingres (like Goya, although perhaps less self-consciously) seems to have been acutely and even painfully aware of the splitting and objectification of women into a variety of unreal dual images or projections. More distinctly than any other French artist of his time, he elaborated this duality through two sets of images: a series of portraits of society women, coolly remote yet compelling and in essence sexually charged; and a second series of frozen harem scenes, drawn from a supposedly far-off and erotic orient, but in fact existing more in the imagination than in experience. Ingres's art is thus a kind of catalog of the sexual fantasies and tensions of early nineteenth-century French society, as seen from a bourgeois male point of view.

Delacroix, younger than Ingres by twenty years, experienced European colonial expansion more directly and indeed built his art on it. Ingres had improvised his exotic oriental atmospheres. Delacroix provides a relatively realistic tour of France's recently annexed colonies in North Africa. Ingres produced a stark, idealized, and assertive dual imagery of women. Delacroix, no longer working within a patronage system, could explore the growing male upper-class fascination with a more ambivalent and equivocal conception of women's duality. He focuses mainly on woman-as-slave-and-victim, usually using oriental settings as pretext but sometimes working with Western settings—contemporary, historical, or mythological. Occasionally, one catches Delacroix trying to come to terms with another, more threatening image, that of woman-as-dangerous-avenger.

By the end of the century, the division of the globe among the colonial powers was completed and imperialism clearly defined. The Western cultural expression of the colonial system was the "international" style of Art Nouveau, which drew widely and eclectically on the various cultures of the colonies. A new dual imagery of women, more polarized than ever and clearly responsive to the social conflicts that were simultaneously fueling the feminist and socialist movements, was woven into Art Nouveau and indeed into most late-nineteenth-century art. It is only in this context that Gauguin's complex paintings of Tahiti, for example, with their acutely detailed imagery of sexism and racism, can be fully understood as deeply accurate and sensitive expressions of the personal pain involved when one participates in the class nature of Western society.

Class bias in art seems to be harder to distinguish than sex or racial bias, but it is there nonetheless. In another article I have discussed seventeenth-century Dutch genre painting as a unity of both sex and class assumptions; the fact that the buyer-owner-viewer was to be a more or less prosperous male burgher was quite clearly materialized in the stylistic character of these depictions of domestic life.[22] In the nineteenth century, members of the working class, and especially the myriads of female servants and laundresses who made up more than half the proletariat, were frequently the subject of art. For example, much of the impact of a painting like Toulouse-Lautrec's *Red Haired Woman in a White Caraco*

(1888) derives from its sympathetic class and sex juxtapositions. The woman's dress identifies her as a charwoman or laundress, and Lautrec poses her as if on awkward display for the (male upper-class) viewer. She stares tentatively out from her seat in the foreground of the studio, obviously uncomfortable among the paintings of landscapes, portraits of upper-class women, scenes of couples dancing, and so on. Worse, a satyr with the features of Lautrec seems to lean out from a nearby canvas toward her, as if to leer. In this work, as in many early paintings and prints, Lautrec confronts himself and us directly with the issue of woman-as-victim—and he sees it as an issue in which the questions of class and sex are completely intertwined. Similarly, sex and class are integrated in the many nineteenth-century portrayals of women with children. Often it is not the mother but a servant or nurse who is shown. For example, Cassatt's scenes of women bathing, dressing, or holding children frequently portray the servants whose task was to care for the children, and her art must be interpreted with this in mind.

The class content of art is generally misunderstood or ignored by art scholars, sometimes even by those who are sensitive to specific issues of race or sex. Art works tend to be analyzed as objects without social function, context, or content, probably because they are still perceived as inanimate property, luxury commodities to be isolated in gallery, museum, and private collection. Feminist art historians and critics can make this art live again as it really was and still could be: an integrated response to the realities and relationships of human society. The issue is not just the development of a feminist art history and criticism but indeed the creation of a view of art that will be fully adequate to its reality, meaning, and beauty.

Appendix

The subtitle and epigraph of this article refer to the well-known story of Annie Miller, the "slumgirl" who was W. Holman Hunt's model and mistress. The relationship between Miller and Hunt can be taken as a model of how sex and class tensions are integrated in art and social experience. Although the events took place more than a century ago, they represent a situation that in many ways is still with us today.

Annie Miller was a young woman from the working-class slums of London. Hunt had picked her up in Chelsea, where she was already a part-time model, and probably a part-time prostitute as well. In the milieu of the pre-Raphaelite painters, no real distinction existed between modeling and prostitution. Thus when Miller became both model and mistress to Hunt, she entered a relationship that was typical for mid-nineteenth century England. Hunt was not satisfied with the relationship, however, for he was a man who experienced the strains of Victorian society with great anguish. Like numerous middle-class reformers of all sorts, he could only express his dissatisfaction individualistically. In the case of Annie Miller, he attempted to construct a sort of personal redemption by trying to make her into a living counterpart to the protagonist in his painting *The Awakening Conscience,* a work for which she was in fact the model.

In the painting, a kept young woman starts up from her lover's lap, suddenly repentant and resolved to escape the immoral life she has been living; she is motivated by memories of a more innocent life and love, presumably inspired by a sentimental song the pair have just been singing. In real life, Hunt tried to arrange for Annie Miller to be made into a "lady," and, eventually, his future wife. But Hunt could not control Miller's conscience—or, rather, her consciousness. The brilliantly articulated wealth of detail that he had lovingly woven into the fabric of *The Awakening Conscience* could not be reproduced in Annie Miller's actual experience. Whereas in art a single moment of nostalgia, meticulously described by a heavily loaded iconography of mournful music sheets, allegorically patterned wallpaper, significantly chosen furnishings, and so on, might indicate motivation, in real life the "suitable" education and companionship that Hunt provided for Miller were not sufficient to bring the painting to life in her person. Miller's awareness of contradictions in Victorian society surely matched and indeed probably exceeded Hunt's. Their interests—based on sex and class—clashed, and Miller quite stubbornly and independently refused to subordinate herself to the artist's megalomaniac attempt to play modern Pygmalion. Miller seems to have lived her life as she thought best, surveying her alternatives and opting for the best choices available as she saw them. After the stormy affair with Hunt, she was for years the mistress of the seventh Viscount Ranelagh, and eventually married his cousin—apparently an excellent match.

While Hunt's depiction of *The Awakening Conscience* embodied his perception of his relationship to Annie Miller, Miller's point of view can only be read between the lines. She was in fact caught in an almost impossible situation. As a woman, her "pure whiteness" and "conscience" were in theory presumed to be eternally capable of being "awakened," no matter how far she might have fallen. But as a member of the nineteenth-century British proletariat, she was virtually by definition an "outcast" whose "pure whiteness" was already "soiled with dust and rain." Thus when Miller became involved with Hunt, these contradictions were simply intensified.

Annie Miller's resistance and independence should be seen as an individual response to a quite general situation. Elsewhere, the same kinds of conditions were giving rise to collective responses in the form of the emergence of feminism, the heightening of class struggle, and the development of a variety of socialist movements. In the course of the nineteenth century, the comfortable and well-tailored correspondence of image to reality—always a somewhat problematic and vulnerable relationship even in the best of circumstances—came under severe strain and began to crack. Ideological norms no longer seemed adequate to lived consciousness, bourgeois culture tended to float free from most human experience, art and life appeared to be irreconcilable. Cultural and ideological dislocation naturally expressed the intensification of social conflict accompanying the development of capitalism. And the same contradictions gave rise to pain and dislocation in the daily experience of individuals. This then is the background to Annie Miller's predicament, to her struggle, and to *The Awakening Conscience*.[23]

The story of a man's attempt literally to remold a living human being according to an image of his own design is familiar. The means Hunt used were caricatural and somewhat pathetic, but the scenario provides a virtual paradigm of sex and class contradictions within capitalist society. Moreover, Hunt's behavior follows the essentially romantic or bourgeois typology of the artist, which contains an analogous set of contradictions. The artist is seemingly an all-powerful Pygmalion, a creator whose generative aesthetic act has steamy overtones of an aggressive sexuality verging on rape. At the same time, the artist is a pitiful and impotent figure, a man thrust out of the truly powerful and productive workings of society, arrogantly isolated yet in the end lonely, ineffective, and dependent.

Hunt's effort to transcend the widening gulf between what he saw as art and life failed. He tried to make whole a social matrix that was being twisted and torn by forces he did not understand. His attempt was doomed, but it was not isolated. Almost as soon as the rise of capitalism threatened the traditional relationship between art, artists, art education, patrons, and audience, a search began to find new relationships reflecting the more positive aspects of their situation: liberation of the individual, validation of the importance of private feelings, increasing democratization of art and of the role of the artist, expansion of the art audience, possibility for immediate and mass distribution of art, and so on. Artists began to tackle the problem of making a modern art for a modern audience. Indeed, the development of art over the last two hundred years can be understood in terms of how these categories or concepts—"modern," "art," and "audience"—were variously interpreted and acted upon. The desire to transcend and make whole our shattered experience endures, and is in fact one of the strongest factors motivating contemporary movements for change—including the women's liberation movement.

Notes

For the story behind the subtitle and epigraph, see the Appendix. I would like to thank Pat Mainardi, Carol Duncan, and Lillian Robinson for their discussion and criticism of this article. I must also mention the students in my classes on women, art, and feminism at the Massachusetts College of Art; the intelligence and excitement with which they participated in our discussions of these issues have been invaluable.

1. For an earlier discussion of sex, class, and race as part of the reality of artist, critic, audience, and art, see Lillian S. Robinson and Lise Vogel, "Modernism and History," *New Literary History* 3 (1971): 177–99, reprinted as No. 88 in the series *M.I.T. Publications in the Humanities* (and revised in *Sex, Class, and Culture*, by Lillian S. Robinson [New York: Methuen, 1986]). Robinson's most recent work on these issues was included in a talk entitled, "Criticism—Self-Criticism," delivered at the 32nd session of the English Institute, September 1973; this paper

will be published in *College English*. The present article incorporates my own extensions and revisions of the earlier essay.

2. My observations on the relative absence of critiques of the art world refer to the situation over the last twenty-five years or so. The social consciousness of the pre-Cold War period was as brutally suppressed within the art world as elsewhere, despite the supposed isolation of art from political realities. In the last several years. a strong analysis of the art world has been frequently and excellently expressed in the course of various polemics, but to my knowledge the only easily available critiques are: Kurt W. Forster, "Critical History of Art, or Transfiguration of Values?," *New Literary History* 3 (1972): 459–70, and Carol Duncan, "Teaching the Rich," *New Ideas in Art Education: A Critical Anthology,* ed. Gregory Battcock (New York: Dutton, 1973), pp. 128–39. See also Robinson and Vogel, pp. 196–99. Specialized articles and studies that incorporate a more or less critical view have appeared in the last year or so, and there is also a renewed interest in developing an adequate Marxist approach to the visual arts.

3. Only one art course—Linda Nochlin's seminar at Vassar College on the image of women in art—is included in the most comprehensive compilation of syllabi and bibliographies available: *Female Studies II* and *III* (December 1970 and December 1971; available from KNOW, Inc., Pittsburgh, Pa.). A modest one-and-one-half page proposal outlining aspects of an approach to the issue of art and feminism appears in *Female Studies V* (1972). Although it is clear that courses on women and art are being offered (see the listings in the annual *Guide to Current Female Studies,* also KNOW, Inc.), the course published in *Female Studies II* remains the only relatively accessible model for a "women and art" course. Contrast the multitude and variety of syllabi and bibliographies that have appeared both before and since in the fields of literature, sociology, history, economics, and so on. See also the author's syllabus, selected bibliography, and essay, "Women, Art, and Feminism," in *Female Studies VII. Going Strong. New Courses/New Programs,* ed. Deborah Rosenfelt (Old Westbury, NY: The Feminist Press, 1973), pp. 42–53.

4. Thomas B. Hess and Linda Nochlin, eds., *Woman as Sex Object: Studies in Erotic Art, 1730–1970* (New York: Newsweek, Inc., 1972).

5. For the record, the following changes were made: "Antiochus and Stratonice: Passion and Protocol in the Reign of Louis Philippe" became "Ingres and the Erotic Intellect." "Eroticism and Female Imagery in Renoir's Paintings and Drawings of 1884–1887" became "Renoir's Sensuous Women." And "Fashion, Art, and Women: The Sexual Transformation of the Female Body in the Illustrations of Henri de Montaut for 'La Vie Parisienne' ca. 1870–1885" became "The Corset as Erotic Alchemy: From Rococo Galanterie to Montaut's Physiologies."

6. Corinne Robins called it "a truly dirty book" in her review for *The New York Times Book Review,* 25 March 1973: 18. She observed also that "in this book art and the women's movement serve as a publishing gimmick," given that "sex sells and pseudo-movement literature is money in the till." Incidentally, nowhere in the book is there any mention or acknowledgment of the CAA symposium. In mid-1973 a second book appeared, *Art and Sexual Politics* (New York: Collier Books, 1973), pretentiously subtitled *Women's Liberation, Women Artists, and Art History,* and bearing on its cover the demoralizing query, "Why Have There Been No Great Women Artists?" This book is an unfortunately abridged and rewritten version of an interesting but hardly stunning issue of *Art News* (69.9 [January 1971]). Both these books appear to be under the editorial guidance of Thomas B. Hess, who seems to be trying to corner a market he does not understand.

7. For discussions of the tensions in Ingres's portraits and harem scenes see, for example, Robert Rosenblum, *Ingres* (New York: Abrams, 1967), pp. 64, 104–7, 142–45, 164, 170–72. Rosenblum

senses the interconnection of the formal, sexual, racial, and even class tensions, but shies away from an explicit investigation.

8. Allentuck does not cite the source for her detailed descriptions of the body changes accompanying female orgasm (for example, "Along the female's somewhat swollen face is the suggestion of a measles-like rash characteristic of the last stages of orgasm among many women"). It is obvious, however, that she relies on the work of Masters and Johnson, the researchers whose work also proved conclusively that the clitoral orgasm is physiologically indistinguishable from the mystical and elusive vaginal orgasm so prized by Freudians. One wonders whether Allentuck's commitment to Freudianism has perhaps made her loathe to cite Masters and Johnson.

9. A good deal of basic work has already been done on Cassatt, notably by Adelyn D. Breeskin. An interesting and feminist discussion of Cassatt's treatment of the mother-and-child theme criticizes it for its tendency toward saccharin sentimentality and accompanying pictorial disorder, and compares these to Cassatt's generally more architectonic ("prim"?) approach to other subjects; see Ann Gabhart and Elizabeth Broun, "Old Mistresses: Women Artists of the Past," *Walters Art Gallery Bulletin* 24.7 (April 1972), also excerpted in *Women: A Journal of Liberation* 3.2 (1973): 64–67. No book on Modersohn-Becker has yet been published in English. Alfred Werner has recently (one wonders why!) pointed to the relative lack of interest in her work in his "Paula Modersohn-Becker: A Short Creative Life," *American Artist* 37 (1973): 16–23 +. Preliminary attempts to reevaluate Cassatt and other women artists appear in issues of *Women and Art, Feminist Art Journal,* and *Womanspace Journal.*

10. For some of the points considered here, see: Dora Jane Janson, "From Slave to Siren," *Art News* 70.3 (May 1971): 49–53 +, and especially Jan Thompson, "The Role of Woman in the Iconography of Art Nouveau," *Art Journal* 31 (1971–72): 158–67.

11. See note 6 above for more on what Hess is doing in this sphere; among other reasons, surely one is sheer opportunism in an area where women have as yet been unable to get commercial book contracts.

12. For example, Nochlin reads Sylvia Plath's comparison of the male sex organs to turkey giblets in *The Bell Jar* without a trace of what has come to be known as "women's consciousness," and thus mistakes it as an indication of simple disappointment. In the novel, the boyfriend has been displaying himself and the narrator records her response: "Then he just stood there in front of me and I kept staring at him. The only thing I could think of was turkey neck and turkey gizzards and I felt very depressed." Coming at the end of Plath's brilliant portrayal of the confused and benumbed emotional interactions between these two adolescents, the observation in context is marvelously to the point—the honest responses of a young girl speaking out of the social experience, conventions, and imagery shared by many who grew up female in America in the early fifties.

13. Linda Nochlin, "Why Are There No Great Women Artists?" *Woman in Sexist Society,* eds. Vivian Gornick and Barbara K. Moran (New York: Signet, 1971), pp. 480–510. Reprinted under the title "Why Have There Been No Great Women Artists?" in *Art News* 69.9 (January 1971): 23–39 + (slightly altered), and in *Art and Sexual Politics,* pp. 1–39 (abridged).

14. Pat Mainardi, "A Feminine Sensibility?" *Feminist Art Journal* 1.1 (April 1972): 4 + (a statement originally made in mid-February of 1972), and "Women Artists Speak Out," photocopy, January 1973. I have cited Mainardi above all because she has written most clearly and extensively on the relationship between women, art, and feminism. Cf. also Marjorie Kramer, "Some Thoughts on Feminist Art," *Women and Art* (Winter 1971): 3.

15. Cindy Nemser, "Art Criticism and Gender Prejudice," *Arts Magazine* 46.5 (March 1972): 44–46.

16. Elizabeth C. Baker, "Sexual Art-Politics," *Art News* 69.9 (January 1971): 47–48+, revised in Hess and Baker, *Art and Sexual Politics,* pp. 108–19. Lucy R. Lippard, "Sexual Politics Art Style," *Art in America* 59.5 (September–October 1971): 19–20. Cindy Nemser, "Art Criticism"; see also "Stereotypes and Women Artists," *Feminist Art Journal* 1.1 (April 1972): 1+. In this discussion I have on the whole cited only easily accessible art world establishment periodicals; a similar spectrum of critical positions can be found in *Women and Art, Feminist Art Journal,* and *Womanspace Journal.*

17. See, for example, the discussion of Artemisia Gentileschi, Adélaïde Labille-Guiard, Lily Martin Spencer, and Mary Cassatt, in Gabhart and Broun, "Old Mistresses" (the version in *Women: A Journal of Liberation* is severely cut throughout, lacking footnotes and entirely omitting the discussion of the American "amateur" painter Spencer). Another particularly useful discussion is Patricia Mainardi, "Quilts: The Great American Art," *Feminist Art Journal* 2.1 (Winter 1973): 1+, reprinted in *Radical America* 7.1 (January–February 1973): 36–68. See also Vogel, "Women, Art, and Feminism."

It is especially necessary to stress the importance of studying women artists in view of Nochlin's persistent devaluation of all women artists, even those like Cassatt and Köllwitz who are generally recognized (although usually kept within a special ranking—e.g., one would think Cassatt is more significant than, say, Pissarro or Sisley, but usually she is isolated in her own, "great"-but-special category). For Nochlin's treatment of women artists, see "Why Are There No Great Women Artists?"; note also the omissions in her recent study of *Realism* (Baltimore: Penguin, 1971).

In this and the following sections my emphasis will be on the art of the last several hundred years, for it is here that I believe a feminist approach will be most productive of new insights and material as well as most relevant to contemporary problems.

18. When the artist is a woman the necessity of rejecting a conventional psychological perspective should be obvious, but the lack of an adequate theory of psychology affects all cultural interpretation. Even when an artist may seem to fit the sex and class preconceptions of most psychological theory, or when an artist's consciousness and work may themselves have been shaped by a belief in such a psychological framework, we must still approach the artist and his/her work with a critique of the inadequacy of the preconceptions and framework.

19. Janson's "From Slave to Siren" is a good if brief application to nineteenth-century visual imagery of Mario Praz's largely literary survey, *The Romantic Agony* (London: Oxford University Press, 1933). Much the same ground is covered from a more feminist and socially based perspective in Thompson, "The Role of Women." Other relevant studies are the pieces by Comini, Farwell, and Needham in *Woman as Sex Object,* and Vogel, "Women, Art, and Feminism."

20. This discussion of pornography is based in part on David Foxon, *Libertine Literature in England 1660–1745* (New York: University Books, 1965) and Steven Marcus, *The Other Victorians: A Study of Sexuality and Pornography in Mid-Nineteenth Century England* (New York: Bantam, 1966). See Susan Sontag, "The Pornographic Imagination" (1967), in *Styles of Radical Will* (New York: Delta, 1969), pp. 35–73, for a consideration of the "new pornography" of the 1950s, and the work of Phyllis and Eberhard Kronhausen for the recent changes in the climate for erotica.

21. Wayne Andersen, *Gauguin's Paradise Lost* (New York: Viking, 1971), p. 116. This book is notable for its extraordinarily uncritical commitment to Freudian analysis and for its author's relentless identification with the artist; it will nevertheless, I think, prove very useful in the hands of a feminist interpreter.

22. Robinson and Vogel, "Modernism and History," pp. 192–95.

23. Some useful recent discussions of Hunt's *The Awakening Conscience* are included in: Helene E. Roberts, "Marriage, Redundancy or Sin: The Painter's View of Women in the First Twenty-Five Years of Victoria's Reign," *Suffer and Be Still: Women in the Victorian Age,* ed. Martha Vicinus (Bloomington: Indiana University Press, 1972), pp. 45–76; Janson, "From Slave to Siren"; Nochlin, *Realism,* pp. 201, 268–69. The relationship between Miller and Hunt is extensively discussed in: Diana Holman-Hunt, *My Grandfather, His Wives and Loves* (London: Hamilton, 1969), and G. H. Fleming, *That Ne'er Shall Meet Again: Rossetti, Millais, Hunt* (London: Joseph, 1971). Hunt's Pygmalion-like treatment of Miller was not at all unique; see Holman-Hunt, p. 96 and Fleming, p. 127. The illustrations in Graham Ovenden, *Pre-Raphaelite Photography* (London: St. Martin's Press, 1972) provide a good visual sense for the character of the relationships between the painters and their models; one is reminded of Nell Kimball's remark that to her mind, art presented "men's ideas . . . , the average john's idea of people they didn't know a goddamn thing about; except the dreams we were supposed to make real for them" (*Nell Kimball: Her Life as an American Madam, by Herself,* ed. Stephen Longstreet [New York: Berkeley, 1970], p. 21).

The Aesthetics of Power in Modern Erotic Art

Carol Duncan

In this essay, I am using the term erotic not as a self-evident, universal category, but as a culturally defined concept that is ideological in nature. More specifically, I am arguing that the modern art that we have learned to recognize and respond to as erotic is frequently about the power and supremacy of men over women. Indeed, once one begins to subject erotic art to critical analysis, to examine the male-female relationships it implies, one is struck with the repetitiousness with which the issue of power is treated. The erotic imaginations of modern male artists—the famous and the forgotten, the formal innovators and the followers—reenact in hundreds of particular variations a remarkably limited set of fantasies. Time and again, the male confronts the female nude as an adversary whose independent existence as a physical or spiritual being must be assimilated to male needs, converted to abstractions, enfeebled, or destroyed. So often do such works invite fantasies of male conquest (or fantasies that justify male domination) that the subjugation of the female will appear to be one of the primary motives of modern erotic art.

In Delacroix's *Woman in White Stockings* (1832), for example, an artist's model (i.e., a sexually available woman) reclines invitingly on a silken mattress. The deep red drapery behind her forms a shadowy and suggestive opening. The image evokes a basic male fantasy of sexual confrontation, but the model does not appear to anticipate pleasure. On the contrary, she appears to be in pain, and the signs of her distress are depicted as carefully as her alluring flesh. Her face, partly averted, appears disturbed, her torso is uncomfortably twisted, and the position of her arms suggests surrender and powerlessness. But this distress does not contradict the promise of male gratification. Rather, it is offered as an explicit *condition* of male pleasure—the artist's and the viewer's.

This article originally appeared in *Heresies*, January 1977. It is an excerpt from the forthcoming book *The New Eros*, ed. Joan Semmel (Hacker Art Books).

The equation of female sexual experience with surrender and victimization is so familiar in what our culture designates as erotic art and so sanctioned by both popular and high cultural traditions, that one hardly stops to think it odd. The Victorian myth that women experience sex as a violation of body or spirit or both, and that those who actively seek gratification are perverse (and hence deserving of degradation), is but one of many ideological justifications of the sexual victimization of women devised by the modern era. In the twentieth century, the theory and practice of psychology has given new rationalizations to the same underlying thesis.

The visual arts are crowded with images of suffering, exposed heroines—slaves, murder victims, women in terror, under attack, betrayed, in chains, abandoned or abducted. Delacroix's *Death of Sardanapalus* (1867), inspired by a poem by Byron, is a *tour de force* of erotic cruelty. Ingres's *Roger and Angelica* (1867) also depicts woman as victim. Here, an endangered and helpless heroine—naked, hairless and swooning—is chained to a large, phallic-shaped rock, immediately below which appear the snakelike forms of a dragon. This fantastic but deadly serious statement documents a common case of male castration anxiety. But the artist-hero (he is Ingres-Roger) masters the situation: he conquers the dangerous female genitals. First he desexualizes Angelica—reduces her to an unconscious mass of closed and boneless flesh; then he thrusts his lance into the toothy opening of the serpent—Angelica's vagina transposed. Given the fears such an image reveals, it is no wonder that Ingres idealized helpless, passive women. The point here, however, is that neither Ingres's fears nor his ideal woman were unique to him.

Americans, too, thrilled to images of female victims. Hiram Powers's *The Greek Slave* (1843) was probably the most famous and celebrated American sculpture in the mid-nineteenth century. Overtly, the viewer could admire the virtuous modesty with which Powers endowed the young slave girl, as did critics in the nineteenth century; but covertly, Powers invites the viewer to imagine himself as the potential oriental buyer of a beautiful, naked, humiliated girl who is literally for sale (he specified that she is on the auction block). The narrative content of this sculpture supports the same underlying thesis we saw in the Delacroix: for women, the sexual encounter must entail pain and subjugation, and that subjugation is a condition of male gratification. But even in paintings where nudes are not literally victims, female allure is treated in terms related to victimization. For Ingres, Courbet, Renoir, Matisse, and scores of other modern artists, weakness, mindlessness and indolence are attributes of female sexiness. Germaine Greer's description of the female ideal that informs modern advertising could as well have been drawn from modern nudes: "Her essential quality is castratedness. She absolutely must be young, her body hairless, her flesh buoyant, and *she must not have a sexual organ*."[1] That is, in the modern era, woman's desirability increases as her humanity and health (relative to male norms) are diminished.

Hiram Powers, *The Greek Slave*, 1843
Marble.
(*The Corcoran Gallery of Art, Washington,
D.C., Gift of William Wilson Corcoran*)

The need to see women as weak, vapid, unhealthy objects—while not unique to the modern era—is evidently felt with unusual intensity and frequency in bourgeois civilization, whose technical advances so favor the idea of sexual equality. Indeed, as women's claims to full humanity grew, the more relentlessly would art rationalize their inferior status. For while literature and the theatre could give expression to feminist voices, the art world acknowledged only male views of human sexual experience. In that arena, men alone were free to grapple with their sexual aspirations, fantasies, and fears. Increasingly in the modern era, artists and their audiences agreed that serious and profound art is likely to be about what men think of women. In fact, the defense of male supremacy must be recognized as a central theme in modern art. Gauguin, Munch, Rodin, Matisse, Picasso, and scores of other artists, consciously or unconsciously, identified some aspect of the sexist cause with all or part of their own artistic missions. Art celebrating sexist experience was accorded the greatest prestige, given the most pretentious aesthetic rationales, and identified with the highest and deepest of human aspirations.

Nudes and whores—women with no identity beyond their existence as sex objects—were made to embody transcendent, "universally" significant statements. In literature as in art, the image of the whore even came to stand for woman in her purest, most concentrated form, just as the brothel became the ultimate classroom, the temple in which men only might glimpse life's deepest mysteries: "A Henry Miller, going to bed with a prostitute [in *Tropic of Cancer*], feels that he sounds the very depths of life, death and the cosmos."[2] Picasso's famous brothel scene, the *Demoiselles d'Avignon* (1907), where the viewer is cast as the male customer, makes similar claims—claims that art historians advocate as "humanistic" and universal.[3] Art-making itself is analogous to the sexual domination of whores. The metaphor of the penis-as-paintbrush is a revered truth for many twentieth-century artists and art historians. It also insists that to create is to possess, to dominate, and to be quintessentially male.

> I try to paint with my heart and my loins, not bothering with style. (Vlaminck)[4]

> Thus I learned to battle the canvas, to come to know it as a being resisting my wish (dream), and to bend it forcibly to this wish. At first it stands there like a pure chaste virgin . . . and then comes the willful brush which first here, then there, gradually conquers it with all the energy peculiar to it, like a European colonist. . . . (Kandinsky)[5]

The kind of nudes that prevail in the modern era do not merely reflect a collective male psyche. They actively promote the relationships they portray, not only expressing but also shaping sexual consciousness. For the nude, in her passivity and impotence, is addressed to women as much as to men. Far from being merely an entertainment for males, the nude, as a genre, is one of many cultural phenomena that teaches women to see themselves through male eyes and in terms of dominating male interest. While it sanctions and reinforces in men the identification of virility with domination, it holds up to women self-images in which even sexual self-expression is prohibited. As ideology, the nude shapes our awareness of our deepest human instincts in terms of domination and submission so that the supremacy of the male "I" prevails on that most fundamental level of experience.

Twentieth-century art has equally urged the victimization and spiritual diminution of women, shedding, however, the narrative trappings and much of the illusionism of the nineteenth-century. The abandoned Ariadnes, endangered captives and cloistered harem women of nineteenth-century art become simply naked models and mistresses in the studio or whores in the brothel. In nudes by Matisse, Vlaminck, Kirchner, Van Dongen, and others, the demonstration of male control and the suppression of female subjectivity is more emphatic and more frequently asserted than in nineteenth-century ones. Their faces are more frequently concealed, blank or masklike (that is, when they are not put to sleep), and the artist manipulates their passive bodies with more liberty and "artistic" bravado than ever.

The image of the femme fatale, especially popular at the turn of the century, would seem to contradict the image of woman as victim. Typically, she looms over the male viewer, fixing him with a mysterious gaze and rendering him willless. Yet she is born of the same set of underlying fears as her powerless, victimized sisters, as the depictions often reveal. Munch's *Madonna* (1893–94), a femme fatale *par excellence,* visually hints at the imagery of victimization. The familiar gestures of surrender (the arm behind the head) and captivity (the arm behind the back, as if bound) are clearly if softly stated. These gestures have a long history in Western art. The dying *Daughter of Niobe,* a well-known Greek sculpture of the fifth-century B.C., exhibits exactly this pose. The raised arm is also seen in numerous fifth-century statues of dying Amazons and sleeping Ariadnes, where it conveys death, sleep or an overwhelming of the will. It may also convey the idea of lost struggle, as in the Amazon statues or in Michelangelo's *Dying Captive* (The Louvre), themselves masterpieces of victim imagery with strong sexual overtones. But in the modern era, the raised arm (or arms) is emptied of its classical connotation of defeat with dignity and becomes almost exclusively a female gesture—a signal of sexual surrender and physical availability. Munch used it in his *Madonna* to mitigate his assertion of female power; the gesture of defeat subtly checks the dark, overpowering force of Woman. The same ambivalence can also be seen in the spatial relationship between the figure and the viewer: the woman can be read as rising upright before him or as lying beneath him.

However lethal to the male, the late-nineteenth-century femme fatale of Munch, Klimt, and Moreau ensnares by her physical beauty and sexual allure. In the twentieth century, she becomes bestial, carnivorous, and visibly grotesque. In images of monstrous females by Picasso, Rouault, the Surrealists, and de Kooning, the dread of woman and male feelings of inferiority are projected,

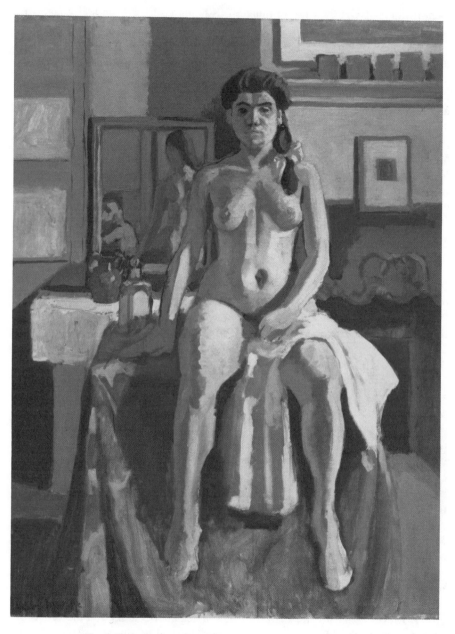

Henri Matisse, *Carmelina*, 1903
Oil on canvas, 32″ × 32¼″.
(Courtesy Museum of Fine Arts, Boston; Tompkins Collection)

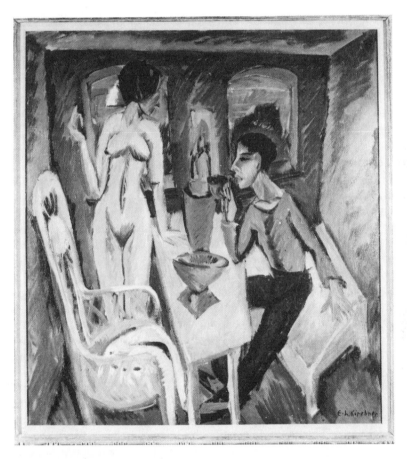

Ernst Ludwig Kirchner, *Tower Room, Self-Portrait with Erna*, 1913
Oil on canvas, 91 cm. × 81 cm.
(*Private collection, U.S.A.*)

objectified and universalized. Yet here too the devouring woman implies her opposite, combining features of both the powerless and the threatening. The women in Picasso's *Demoiselles d'Avignon,* although physically mutilated and naked (vulnerable), aggressively stare down the viewer, are impenetrably masked, and display sharp-edged, dangerous-looking bodies. Picasso ambivalently presents them with sham and real reverence in the form of a desecrated, burlesque icon, already slashed to bits. De Kooning, in his continuing *Woman* series, ritually invokes, objectifies and obliterates the same species of goddess-whore. Here too a similar ambivalence finds its voice in shifting, unstable forms whose emergence and destruction are accepted in the critical literature as the conscious "aesthetic"'pretext for his work. The pose his figures usually take—a frontal crouch with thighs open to expose the vulva—also appears in the *Demoiselles d'Avignon* (in the lower right figure), which, in turn, derives from primitive art. Like Picasso's figures, de Kooning's women are simultaneously inviting and repelling, above and below the viewer, obscene modern whores and terrifying primitive deities.

The pronounced teeth in de Kooning's *Woman and Bicycle* (1950)—the figure actually has a second set around her throat—also speak of primitive and modern neurotic fears of the female genitals. The *vagina dentata,* an ancient fantasy into which males project their terror of castration—of being swallowed up or devoured in their partner's sexual organs—is commonly represented as a toothed mouth. The image, which appears frequently in modern art, is a striking feature of Miró's *Woman's Head* (1938). The savage creature in this painting has open alligator jaws protruding from a large, black head. The red eye, bristling hairs and exaggerated palpable nipples, in combination with the thin weak arms, help give it the same mixture of comic improbability and terribleness that characterize Picasso's *Demoiselles* and de Kooning's *Women.* But in addition—and true to Miró's love of metamorphosing forms—the image can be read literally as the lower part of a woman's body, seen partly as if through an X-ray. Inverted, the arms become open legs, the dark, massive head a uterus, and the long, dangerous jaws a toothed vaginal canal. The predatory creature in Picasso's *Seated Bather* (1929) not only has saw-toothed jaws, but several features of the praying mantis.

The praying mantis, who supposedly devours her mate, was a favorite theme in Surrealist art and literature. In paintings by Masson, Labisse, Ernst, and others, the cannibalistic sexual rites of this insect become a metaphor for the human sexual relationship, and the female of the species becomes the Surrealistic version of the femme fatale. More subhuman and brutal than her nineteenth-century predecessors, she testifies to the higher level of sexual anxiety and hostility experienced by the twentieth-century male. For as women increasingly demanded a share of the world, the defense of male authority became more desperate. "Now become a fellow being, woman seems as formidable as when she faced man as a part of alien Nature. In place of the myth of the laborious honeybee or the mother hen is substituted the myth of the devouring female insect: the praying mantis, the spider. No longer is the female she who nurses the little ones, but rather she who eats the male."[6]

Pictures of nudes in nature also affirm the supremacy of the male consciousness even while they ostensibly venerate or pay tribute to women as freer or more in harmony with nature than men. From the *Bathers* of Delacroix to those of Renoir and Picasso, nude-in-nature pictures almost always ascribe to women a mode of existence that is categorically different from man's. Woman is seen as more *of nature* than man, less in opposition to it both physically and mentally. Implicitly, the male is seen as more closely identified with culture, "the means by which humanity transcends the givens of natural existence, bends them to its purposes, controls them in its interests."[7]

This woman/nature–man/culture dichotomy is one of the most ancient and universal ideas ever devised by man and is hardly new to modern Western culture. However, in Western bourgeois culture, the real and important role of women in domestic, economic and social life becomes ever more recognized: increasingly, the bourgeoisie educates its daughters, depends upon their social and economic cooperation and values their human companionship. Above all, the idea that women belong to the same order of being as men is more articulated than ever before. In this context, to cling to ancient notions of women as a race apart from men—as creatures of nature rather than of culture—is to defend blatantly an ideology that is everywhere contested and contradicted by experience. Nevertheless, the majority of nude-in-nature pictures state just this thesis.

In countless nineteenth- and twentieth-century paintings—Romantic, Symbolist, or Expressionist—female nudes in outdoor settings are treated as natural inhabitants of the landscape. Although modern artists have characterized it differently, they agree that this woman-nature realm is an inviting but alien mode of experience. It both attracts and repels the male. It beckons him to step out of rationalized, bourgeois society and to enter a world where men might live through their senses, instinct, or imaginations. But the condition of entry—shedding the social identity of the bourgeois male—also entails loss of autonomy and of the power to shape and control one's world. The male artist longs to join those naked beings in that other imagined realm, but he cannot because he fails to imagine their full humanity—or his own. While he values his own instincts, or that part of himself that responds to nature, he regards this portion of his nature as "feminine," antagonistic to his socialized masculine ego, and belonging to that other, "natural" order. Nor can he acknowledge in women a "masculine principle"—an autonomous self that knows itself as separate from and opposed to the natural, biological world. Like Munch before his *Madonna*, he hovers before his dream in ambivalent desire.

Rarely do modern artists imagine naked men in that other realm. When they do, as in works by Cézanne or Kirchner, the male figures tend to look uncomfortable or self-conscious. More often, the male in nature is clothed—both in the literal sense or metaphorically—with a social identity and a social or cultural project. He is a shepherd, a hunter, an artist. Matisse's *Boy with Butterfly Net* (1907) is a magnificent image of a male in nature (or rather a male acting against nature), highly individualized and properly equipped for a specific purpose. In beach scenes by the Fauves and the Kirchner circle, males—when they are present—are not "bathers," i.e., placid creatures of the water, but modern men going swimming in bathing suits or in the raw. They are active, engaged in a culturally defined recreation, located in historical time and space. The female bather, who has no counterpart in modern art, is a naked existence, outside of culture. Michelet, the nineteenth-century historian, poetically expressed the ideas implicit in the genre: man, he wrote, creates history, while woman "follows the noble and serene epic that Nature chants in her harmonious cycles, repeating herself with a touching grace of constancy and fidelity. . . . Nature is a woman. History, which we very foolishly put in the feminine gender, is a rude, savage male, a sun-burnt, dusty traveller. . . . "[8] Even in Matisse's *Joy of Living* (1906), where men and women share an Arcadian life, cultural activities (music-making, animal husbandry) are male endeavors while women exist merely as sensual beings or abandon themselves to emotionally expressive but artless and spontaneous dance.

How we relate to these works becomes a compelling issue once their sexual-political content is apparent. The issue, however, is difficult to grasp without first coming to terms with the ideological character of our received notions of art. For in our society, art—along with all high culture—has replaced religion (that is, among the educated) as the repository of what we are taught to regard as our highest, most enduring values. As sanctified a category as any our society offers, art silently but ritually validates and invests with mystifying authority the ideals that sustain existing social relations. In art, those ideals are given to us as general, universal values, collective cultural experience, "our" heritage, or as some other abstraction removed from concrete experience. Physically and ideologically, art is isolated from the rest of life, surrounded with solemnity, protected from moral judgment. Our very encounters with it in museums, galleries, and art books are structured to create the illusion that the significance of art has little or nothing to do with the conflicts and problems that touch common experience. Established art ideologies reinforce this illusion. According to both popular and scholarly literature, true artistic imaginations transcend the ordinary fantasies, the class and sex prejudices and the bad faith that beset other human minds. Indeed, most of us believe that art, by definition, is always good—because it is of purely aesthetic significance (and the purely aesthetic is thought to be good), or because it confirms the existence of the imagination and of individualism, or because it reveals other "timeless" values or truths. Most of us have been schooled to believe that art, *qua* art, if it is "good" art, is never bad *for* anyone, never has anything to do with the oppression of the powerless, and never imposes on us values that are not universally beneficial.

The modern masterpeices of erotic art that I have been discussing enjoy this ideological protection even while they affirm the ideals of male domination and female subjugation. Once admitted to that high category of Art, they acquire an invisible authority that silently acts upon the consciousness, confirming from on high what social customs and law enforce from below. In their invisible and hence unquestioned authority, they proclaim—without acknowledging it—what men and women can be to themselves and to each other. But once that authority is made visible, we can see what is before us: art and artists are made on earth, in history, in organized society. And in the modern era as in the past, what has been sanctified as high art and called True, Good, and Beautiful is born of the aspirations of those who are empowered to shape culture.

Notes

My gratitude to Flavia Alaya and Joan Kelly-Gadol, whose own work and conversation have enriched and clarified my thinking.

1. Germaine Greer, *The Female Eunuch* (New York: Farrar, Straus & Giroux, 1972), p. 57.

2. Simone de Beauvoir, *The Second Sex* (New York: Alfred A. Knopf, 1961), p. 181.

3. See, for example, Gert Schiff, "Picasso's Suite 347, or Painting as an Act of Love," in *Woman as Sex Object,* ed. Thomas B. Hess and Linda Nochlin (New York: Newsweek, Inc., 1972), pp. 238–53; and Leo Steinberg, "The Philosophical Brothel, Part I," *Art News* (September 1972): 20–29.

4. In Herschel B. Chipp, *Theories of Modern Art* (Berkeley: University of California Press, 1970), p. 144.

5. In Max Kozloff, "The Authoritarian Personality in Modern Art," *Artforum* (May 1974): 46. Schiff actually advocates the penis-as-paintbrush metaphor.

6. de Beauvoir, *Second Sex,* p. 179.

7. Sherry Ortner, "Is Female to Male as Nature Is to Culture?" *Feminist Studies* 1.2 (Fall 1974): 10.

8. Jules Michelet, *Woman [La femme]*, trans. by J. W. Palmer (New York, 1960), pp. 104–5.

The Reemergence of the Archetype of the Great Goddess in Art by Contemporary Women

Gloria Feman Orenstein
In memory of Ana Mendieta

As the archetype of the Great Goddess reemerges into consciousness today, women artists, through transpersonal visionary experiences, are bringing to light energic psychic forces, symbols, images, artifacts, and rituals whose configurations constitute the basic paradigm of a new feminist myth for our time. "When a psychological need arises it seems inevitably the deeper layers of the collective unconscious are activated and sooner or later the memory of a myth of an event or an earlier psychic state emerges into consciousness."[1]

Evoking the memory of an earlier psychic state, one in which divinity was seen to reside in matter and the energies of the earth were revered as sacred, the Goddess has become that symbol of transformation which activates those forces within woman identified with holiness and with creative power. If the artist is the avatar of the new age, the alchemist whose great Art is the transformation of consciousness and being, then contemporary women artists such as Mary Beth Edelson, Carolee Schneemann, Mimi Lobell, Buffie Johnson, Judy Chicago, Donna Byars, Donna Henes, Miriam Sharon, Ana Mendieta, Betsy Damon, Betye Saar, Monica Sjoo, and Hannah Kay, by summoning up the powers associated with the Goddess archetype, are energizing a new form of Goddess consciousness, which in its most recent manifestation is exorcising the patriarchal creation myth through a repossession of the female visionary faculties.

This new Goddess consciousness might be described most effectively as a holistic mind-body totality. As we move away from the cultural dominance of the masculine archetype, characterized by a mind-body duality, we find that the model of the sorcerer's vision serves as a corrective alternative for a consciousness

This article originally appeared in *Heresies,* Spring 1978.

expansion in which intuitive body-knowledge is reaffirmed as a faculty of intelligence. Transcending the false dualities and dichotomies established by patriarchal systems of thought which split mind from body, spirit from matter and sacred from profane, the Great Goddess as a psychic symbol suggests the rebirth of woman to a holistic psychophysical perception of the sacred, as a new form of her feminist evolution.

Artists who are in touch with the archetype of the Goddess are now using the female form in both image and ritual as an instrument of spirit-knowledge. They are training the body so that it functions as a conscious perceptor and transformer of the powerful energies that reside in matter, both animal and vegetable. Through the psychophysical participation in Edelson's magical ceremonies of evocation, through the transformation of the body into a living totem in Damon's rituals, through the stimulation of the body via meditation upon the power points in the body icons of Kurz's self-portrait as the Durga, or Mailman's mirror image as God, through the fusion of the body with the earth itself in Mendieta's alchemical burials, through the sacrilization of the body in Lobell's Goddess Temple, and through a merging with the spirit of the Goddess in Suzanne Benton's masked ritual theater, women are gradually repossessing the powers long associated with the various manifestations of the archetype of the Goddess.

This new art (in which the archetype of the Goddess plays a catalytic role) is not based upon an original creation myth connected with the fertility and birth mysteries. In its modern transformed meaning, it is about the mysteries of woman's rebirth from the womb of historical darkness, in which her powers were so long enshrouded, into a new era where a culture of her own making will come about as a result of a new Earth Alchemy.

If the alchemy performed by the male magician sought essentially to purify brute matter by transforming it into spirit, taking gold or the philosopher's stone as the symbol of spiritual enlightenment, the supreme goal of alchemy for women artists today is to restore the spirit already inherent in the natural world; to consider matter itself as a storehouse of the potent energies most available for transformations in their natural organic state. Women are attempting nothing less than the magical dealchemizing of the philosopher's stone, the reconstitution of the Earth Goddess's original herborium on the planet and the energizing of the self through the internalization of its sacred spirits. It is no mere coincidence that the alchemical symbols of "witchcraft," the magic of the wise women who worshipped the Goddess, are herbs, grains, plants, and seeds. The desire to alter both mental and physical functioning translates an impulse to integrate the Earth Goddess's chemical secrets into the body and to carry the Goddess within the self. In so doing, women now activate a Goddess consciousness within matter by means of which all contemporary culture will be awakened.

Jung said: "To carry a god around in yourself is a guarantee of happiness, of power, and even of omnipotence in so far as these are attributes of divinity."[2]

Contemporary woman's need to carry a "god" around within the self, her desire to transform herself into the image of the Goddess, arises from a deep historical imperative. Research into the history of Goddess worship gives ample evidence of the desecration of Goddess temples, shrines, altars, and sanctuaries, and of the systematic erasure of all traces of Goddess worship from the face of the earth. Through the persecution of witches, sacred knowledge of the Old Religion had to be transmitted through visual and oral lore from generation to generation. Where once the Goddess was worshipped at sacred natural sites with the Earth identified as the body of the Great Mother, today women are transforming their own bodies into those sacred repositories of Goddess knowledge and energy.

The repossession by woman of the attributes of the Great Goddess is necessary in order to provide fundamental changes in vision and reality. Under the hegemony of patriarchal religions, notably Christianity, which has conditioned Western consciousness over many centuries through image-making and ritual, a profound mystification has been perpetrated on so large a scale that one of the first functions of this new art is to exorcise the sexist impact and interpretation of all sacred imagery. Christian art, for example, by establishing the paradoxical image of the Virgin Mother, has encouraged women to hallucinate an impossibility as if it were a natural image of reality. In order to reestablish the validity of the natural image of Mother and Child as incorporated in the archetype of the Fertility Goddess, contemporary artists are celebrating sexuality by invoking ancient images of the Great Mother that exalt procreation and superimposing them over the former image of the Virgin and Child.

Another integral part of the process of Goddess-culture art are the expeditions to caves, mounds, sanctuaries, shrines, or megalithic sites in search of the energy evoked and the artifacts or symbols of veneration left by ancient cults which worshipped the Goddess. In this kind of search artists are making the heretofore invisible, manifest again. This visionary technique of rendering the invisible and the real visible once more and ultimately abolishing the separation between the spiritual and the material plane reestablishes the human and the natural as the legitimate realm of the divine. The energy formerly required to accept Christian illusion is now released for the accomplishment of the true work of alchemical transformation—that of preparing and retraining the mind-body perceptor so that women may now perform their highest functions.

This exaltation of natural energies releases enormous potential so that women may begin to transform themselves into living repositories of sacred knowledge, storing their total history within their bodies, their psychic memory and their art as a natural form of protection against future persecution or annihilation. As bearers of sacred tradition, contemporary feminist artists use ritual to resacrilize the female body, creating a new sacred space for the enactment of those magical rebirth ceremonies that are first coming into our culture through art.

In *Beyond God the Father,* Mary Daly, redefining God as a verb, as a participation in being, rather than anthropomorphically as a being, suggests that women's participation in history, her new sisterhood, is a means of saying "us vs. nonbeing": "What we are about is the human becoming of that half of the human race that has been excluded from humanity by sexual definition . . . . What is at stake is a real leap in human evolution, initiated by women."[3] The Goddess, then, is that archetype which mediates between image, energy, and history, evolving and unfolding destiny through the redirection of energy into a revolutionary manifestation of being. When imaged and celebrated in contemporary art, the Goddess signifies Being as a verb, as a creative energy, as a transformative energy, as sacred earth-energy and as psychic energy. Contemporary women artists are using the documentation that is being gathered on the various manifestations of the Goddess from the Upper Paleolithic and Neolithic communities to the present both as visual and as informational data, as elements of the new art works or events they are creating in accordance with the elaboration of a new myth synonymous with the exigencies of female culture in the 1970s.

Architect Mimi Lobell and two other women, one a Jungian, have designed a Goddess temple which expresses the theme of initiation and rebirth into a Goddess-centered culture. They consider the temple to be the externalization of an archetypal structure that exists within the psyche. The temple, whose eventual site will be a mountainous region near Aspen, Colorado, is conceived as analogous to the body of the Goddess through which the initiate will pass in a ceremony of transformation. Its form and materials function as a catalyst for this process. According to Lobell, "To go through the temple will be to experience an initiation into the mysteries of the feminine and activate a prelogical consciousness."[4]

As planned, the temple is approached via an uphill walk along a "sacred way" lined with figures of animals. The entrance is at the lower level, which appears to be buried in rock. Deep in this rock the veiled entry leads to a nine-ring labyrinth. Reversing the process of birth one enters through the vaginal orifice and journeys toward the third eye of enlightenment. The walls of the labyrinth are covered with exotic fabrics and tapestries, weavings, batiks, silks, and lace from various ethnic sources. In the center of the labyrinth lies the sunken grail pool, inscribed with a serpentine spiral. A helical ladder, 15 feet high, rises out of the pool and ascends to the upper temple, which at eye level becomes a 360-degree open-windowed panorama of the mountains and valleys. Over the windows are 29 perforations in the shape of the moon, one for each of its monthly day cycle. The altar is a part of the Great Eye of Vision of the Eye Goddess.

We are one with that all receptive 360 degree panoramic perception in the Oculus of the Eye Goddess, warmed by the fires of Vesta, the libidinous energy that keeps us integrated with our bodies and with all of our sensuous lenses onto the mysteries of the universe. The water of the hydolunar force has been transmuted into the fire that ignites the feminine wisdom of Sophia and the Muses and the Oracles and Sybils.[5]

Becoming conscious of the presence of Goddess imagery in one's work is a long arduous process of visual reeducation. Carolee Schneemann, who in childhood saw the radiant face of the Great Mother in the moon and believed that the world was permeated by invisible energies, unconsciously made her first Goddess image in 1963 when she was working on her theater piece *Chromolodeon*. In her desire for a companion figure for the piece, she made the head of a horned bull and mounted it on a clothed dressmaker's dummy. Seven years later she was to discover that the bull was the sacred beast of the Great Goddess. In the 1960s Schneemann did not yet understand the real significance of the bull iconography in her work. In her series of body pieces, such as *Meat Joy* of 1964, she began to put the materials from the static works onto herself, and in *Eye Body* (1963) she used two snakes on her body in a set of transformative actions. Later, reviewing her artistic evolution through the 1970s, Schneemann came to understand that the serpents in her earlier works were related to the Minoan Snake Goddess through a series of iconographical similarities and personal connections.

The figure of the Minoan Snake Goddess, arms upright, is currently featured in much Goddess-culture art. This merging of the self with that of the Goddess functions as a mirror reflection in which women see themselves as the Goddess and the Goddess in themselves.

The process of the evolution of Goddess consciousness itself became the theme of *Homerunmuse* (performed at the Brooklyn Museum during the "Women Artists 1550–1950" show, Fall 1977). In a meditation upon the female and the muse, whose presence is indicated in the word "museum," but whose usual absence from the institution was made obvious by the fact of the women artists' show, Schneemann rejects "the abstracted token Muse as fragmentation." Through a collage of texts Schneemann reiterates the theme of woman remaking herself into the image of the Goddess.

Israeli artist Miriam Sharon performs desert rituals that are rites of exorcism overthrowing the patriarchal model that constructed alienating cityscapes of concrete over the ancient earth shrines and sacred sites. Her pilgrimage to the desert put her in contact with the Bedouins, "the last survivors of the Earth Living Culture." Her own *Space Project-Earth People* which grew out of her stay in the desert is a ritual act of identification with the Earth Culture. Through meditation rituals in the wilderness, Sharon expresses the wish to recreate an ancient lost myth of the Earth. Sharon's reclamation of the barren earth as the natural holy shrine and her use of the desert as a temple for meditation exemplify the return to primal matter as holy matter. Her participation with the Bedouins in the life of the desert as Goddess-space parallels the initiatory experience of Lobell's Goddess Temple. However, Sharon defines "holy" as without shrines or temples, holy in its being only.

> The Bedouins (whom I adopted some years ago as part of my work) are part of this "meditative" existence of the desert. They meditate daily in front of the wide seas or wide wilderness

of the desert. They kiss the earth for their existence. They never thanked their "god" by building huge temples, but just kissed the sands. When they will disappear they will never leave behind any traces for their existence, except the stones of their burial places. I try through my art, not to build static sculptures or monuments in the spaces but only put human energy through my art (a ritual art) into something that is disappearing.[6]

Sharon's recent *Sand Tent Project* involved the participation of a Bedouin tribe and a Kibbutz settlement (Kerem Shalom). The Bedouin Mother who taught her how to create such a tent is the last survivor of the tent life in that area. Sharon's apprenticeship to the wise women who know the secrets of the earth is an affirmation of woman as Goddess-incarnation. The desert, for Sharon, symbolizes patriarchal spiritual values (the barren emptiness) which must be exorcised and is, at the same time, that pure clear space of the new frontier, representing the new female space of herstory upon which our lost traces will be reinscribed and our new destiny will be written.

Ana Mendieta, who came to the U.S. from Cuba in 1961, thinks of the Earth as the Goddess. She recalls a mountain in Cuba, La Mazapan de Matanza, that is in the shape of a reclining woman. Her transformational rituals explore the boundaries between spirit and matter. In a piece she did in a labyrinth, *Silueta de Laberinto* (1974), she worked with the metamorphosis of the self that occurs in sorcery and trance. In this piece someone traced her silhouette on the ground. When Mendieta left the labyrinth, her image was imprinted upon the earth, suggesting that through a merging with the Goddess spirits are evoked that infuse the body and cause such occurrences as out-of-body journeys or astral travel. In Earth Sorcery, of which all her works are examples, the Earth Goddess is the shaman and the spell is invoked through a magical rite in which unification with the Earth Mother transpires. Mendieta is concerned with rebirth and her grave and burial mound pieces suggest that material death does not imply spiritual death.

In some of her works, Mendieta wraps herself in black cloth, imposing her mummified form upon the ground which is then dug out around her. A series of these imprints are eventually lit with gun powder, leaving silhouetted afterimages embedded in the earth as a testimony to the magical site of transformation, the dwelling of the Goddess, where the human and the divine had come to mingle as preparation for a new destiny. Her art concretizes that process of Earth Alchemy, using prime matter itself as the alchemistic vessel through which spirit will be made to reenter matter and transform woman into the vital incarnation of the Earth Goddess once more.

Buffie Johnson's paintings celebrate the natural symbols of the universe which were recognized as sacred in the worship of the Great Goddess. The plant and animal manifestations of the Goddess are energizers of transformation which function like the star and cross in the Judeo-Christian tradition. They are reminders of the numinous state in which all of nature was held to be sacred. Erich Neumann writes: "Because originally human life was so strongly affected by its

Ana Mendieta, *Untitled* (*"Mujer de piedra"* [Stonewoman] Series), 1983
Marble chips attached to frame, executed in Miami, Florida, 60" × 46".
(*Photo courtesy of the New Museum of Contemporary Art, New York*)

Ana Mendieta, *Untitled* (*"Arbol de la Vida"* [Tree of Life] Series), 1977
Earth-body work with tree and mud, executed at Old Man's Creek in Iowa City,
Iowa, 20″ × 13¼″.
(*Photo courtesy of the New Museum of Contemporary Art, New York*)

Ana Mendieta, *Guanbancex* (*Goddess of the Wind/Diosa del viento*), from the *Esculturas Rupestres* (Rupestrian Sculptures), 1981
Carved cave wall executed at the Cueva del Aguila, Escaleras de Jaruco, Havana, Cuba, 40¾" × 53¼".
(Photo courtesy of the New Museum of Contemporary Art, New York)

Ana Mendieta, *El laberinto de la vida* (The Labyrinth of Life) ("*Laberinto de Venus*" [Labyrinth of Venus] Series), 1982
Clay and earth sculpture, executed in Iowa, 41" × 61".
(*Photo courtesy of the New Museum of Contemporary Art, New York*)

participation mystique with the outside world that stone, plant, and man [*sic*], animal and star were bound together in a single stream, one could always transform itself into another.''[7] These symbols reinforce in us an awareness that we are all manifestations of the one "single stream," the spirit of the Mother Goddess.

The general "theme" of Johnson's work since the late 1940s is drawn from the Jungian concept of the collective unconscious and from her scholarly research on the Great Goddess. The paintings which evolved with specific reference to the Goddess show her aspects as *Mistress of the Beasts* and *Lady of the Plants*. Around the latter, she has created single-image plants in varying aspects of cyclical transformation, which stimulate the unconscious and evoke mythic memories. The paintings serve as sacred icons to resurrect the layers of consciousness in which our most primordial images, those of the Great Goddess and of our true origin, lie buried. In *Ariadne* ("Barley Mother," 1971), the Goddess of Vegetation is evoked by the image of the long-grain barley flowing gently down in a skirt of rain. A pomegranate bursting from within (*Pomegranate*, 1972) recalls the myth of Persephone and Demeter and their connection with the lifegiving powers of the Feminine. The monolithic opium seed-pod *Lapis* (1970) is a cosmic starglobe exploding with life, a metaphor for the Goddess from whose womb all is born. In *Pasiphae* (1976) the image of the iris, the sacred lily of Crete, merges with that of a bovine head, so that both animal and plant symbols of the Goddess coalesce in a new charged sign. References to the myth of the Minotaur and the labyrinth are suggested, the labyrinth of the Goddess being the place where one loses and finds oneself again—the unconscious. The collective symbols are here employed as forces of awakening, the artist reaching deep into the buried past when the Goddess and all of nature were revealed as One.

Donna Byars's work shows the creative processes at work in the deciphering of the oracle of the Goddess as She speaks to the artist through the labyrinth of dream and visionary experience. *Oracle Stone Grove,* for example, evolved from a dream.

> A stone woman who sat in a grove of trees spoke to me in vapors, not words. She was very poetic and mystical and spoke only in truths. All of a sudden, like in a faint, she slid from her chair into a hole in the underground. I grabbed her before she went underground and when she came up she was no longer able to speak. I woke up with a terrible feeling of sadness.[8]

In the piece itself, "All the components . . . sit on the floor and do not occupy any wall space, two stones are arranged perpendicular to each other sitting on an old paint scratched rocker in a grove of four weeping fig trees. For Byars, the Grove becomes a shrine."

In works such as *Vested Relic* where stone and silver wings are enclosed within a blindfolded cage, creating a secret altar and a reliquary, Byars preserves the magical objects that reveal to her the presence of the Goddess as a guardian spirit in her world. The blindfolding of the cage symbolizes that these sacred objects can only be perceived with the inner eye. Byar's glass collages make visible the apparitions of the Mother Goddess in images of a winged being and a shaman, who appears to us during altered states of consciousness.

For Byars, the world is vibrant and alive with signs and guideposts. Many of her pieces are themselves omens, assembled from objects and materials which spoke to her in oracular modes. One such object is *Swathe,* which combines feathers and a wing on a swathed ironing board that has lilies of the valley wrapped in chamois placed upon it. These totems and talismans conjure up archaic imagery from the distant past. Animal horns, wings, feathers, shells, trees, serpents, brought together in these mythopoetic assemblages, activate intimate relationships between natural materials, objects and living things that illuminate essences which were formerly only visible to seers and shamans. The presence of the Goddess is thus revealed and brought into contemporary consciousness.

Mary Beth Edelson's work has long been intimately involved in the explorations of the Goddess. In 1961 her painting of Madonna and Child entitled *Godhead* introduced concentric circles as sources of energy from the Madonna's head. In these early paintings[9] her women were frequently depicted with their arms uplifted, reminiscent of the posture of many early Goddess figures. The primal image of the outstretched arms of the ancient Goddess, whose power must be reclaimed by women for themselves today, is seen by Edelson not only as a spiritual signifier, but as a contemporary symbol of our political activism.

In 1969 she began to evolve a more defined and specific area of archetypal imagery, out of which emerged the exhibition *Woman Rising,* revolutionary in the way it brought to consciousness psychic material about the Great Goddess. Her most innovative images she has created through performing private body rituals where the body itself is the house of wisdom. In these, the artist calls upon Goddess energy, using her own body as a stand-in for the Goddess and as a symbol for Everywoman, whose expanded states of body-consciousness and multiple transformations are evoked through contact with powerful natural energies.

On March 1, 1977, Edelson performed a mourning ritual ceremony for her exhibition, "Your 5,000 Years Are Up," entitled *Mourning Our Lost Herstory,* at the Mandeville Gallery, University of California at La Jolla. Ten women sat in a circle in the center of a fire ring, the only source of light, chanting and wailing while seven silent eight-foot high black-draped figures, which had previously seemed to be an uninhabited formal sculptural installation on the back wall, came alive and began to move around the cavernous gallery. More recently, she performed a mourning-reclamation ritual at A.I.R. Gallery, New York City, entitled *Proposals For: Memorials to the 9,000,000 Women Burned as Witches in the Christian Era.* This ritual, based on research about witch burning in relation to women who were Goddess worshippers evoked the spirits of individual women who were tortured during the Inquisition. Edelson is not content, however, to exorcise the past; her art is about mythic recreation of holy spaces for women's culture today.

Donna Henes's *Spider Woman,* a series of process environmental sculptures, makes reference to the Mother Goddess of the Navaho Emergence Myth about whom Sheila Moon has written, "She is the protective feminine objectivity. Spider Woman is the unobtrusive but powerful archetype of fate—not in the sense of determinism, but in the sense of the magical law of one's own 'gravity' which leads always beyond itself towards wholeness."[10] In a state of trance and meditation, Henes spins her web of various kinds of fibers in natural settings and in public places, where they can be altered by the specific environmental conditions of each location. Her manifesto[11] defines the web as a map of the subconscious and as a form of primal meditation.

Henes performs a yearly winter solstice celebration *Reverence to Her: A Chant to Invoke the Female Forces of the Universe Present in All People.* The winter solstice is the time when "the Great Mother gives birth to the sun, who is Her son, and stands at the center of the matriarchal mysteries. At the winter solstice, the moon occupies the highest point in its cycle, the sun is at its nadir, and the constellation Virgo rises in the east."[12] Henes's participatory chant invokes the Great Goddess, the archetypal female principle of communal creation and continuity, and gives reverence to the female power "who exists in all beings in the form of consciousness, reason, sleep, hunger, shadow, energy, thirst, forgiveness, species, bashfulness, peace, faith, loveliness, fortune, vocation, memory, compassion, mother, fulfillment and illusion."

If the webs are a materialization of a female spirit-presence in the environment, a kind of feminine structure within matter itself, her work makes us visualize this presence, evokes it, and brings it forth out of the void, making manifest the interconnectedness of all space and time through the weaving of the great web of life, which is the work of the Mother Goddess. This is the actualization of a creation myth which posits the female life-force as an energy that is at work in the universe in invisible ways.

Betye Saar's work, through its mystical, visionary imagery, probes the collective unconscious for those images of female power specific to black women. By delving deeply into the religious practices of Africa and Haiti, Saar resurrects images of the Black Goddess, the Voodoo Priestess and the Queen of the Witches, collecting the amulets and artifacts of these cultures and placing them in her boxes in order to create potent talismanic collections of magically charged objects and icons. For Saar, contemporary black women are all incarnations of the Black Goddess, and in reclaiming black power, women are instinctively venerating an ancient female force still worshipped in other cultures today. *Voo Doo Lady W/3 Dice* (1977) is a mixed-media collage on fabric that identifies black woman in her image of oppression with the mystical Black Goddess, implying through its iconography that women should worship the deity within themselves, and that a familiarity with occult and mythological traditions will reveal the true face of the Goddess to all women.

In her piece *7,000 Year Old Woman,*[13] performed publicly May 21, 1977, Betsy Damon covered herself with small bags of colored flour which she punctured in a ritual ceremony. As each small bag of flour emptied, like a miniature sandtimer, it was as if the artist and her assistant, through intense concentration and meditation, had incorporated a bit of lost time into the aura of their consciousnesses. This piece demonstrates how contemporary Goddess-culture art seeks to transform the body and the consciousness of modern woman by infusing it with a sense of herstory, reclaimed and reintegrated into the present sense of the self.

Damon has been performing rituals in nature for several years, working collectively with women, creating rites of anger, rebirth and transformation, such as the *Birth Ritual,* in which each woman gives birth to another, chanting, "I am a woman. I can give birth to you." In the *Naming Ritual,* performed in Ithaca, women chanted, "I am a woman. I give you my hand. We are women. Our circle is powerful." After the chanting they intoned the names of all the women in the ritual. It was during her performance of *Changes,* in Ithaca, that she dreamed of the *Maypole Ritual.* This fertility rite was held in that same city and participants brought corn, food, poetry, and other offerings to the celebration. They painted their bodies, danced, and wove maypoles out of colorfully dyed gauze.

Hannah Kay, an Israeli artist living in New York, paints the ultimate breakthrough of Earth Goddess energy that parallels the advent of female autonomy in the new era of feminist consciousness. She writes that in her art woman

> became a landscape and then the whole universe. A woman's body is, in itself, the whole universe: birth, life, death, and communication. The human body manifests all the laws of the universe; and for me the woman's body is the sensuality of the universe. The sensuality of mountains, and oceans, and planets in their orbits about the stars.[14]

Enclosed invites us to hallucinate the female form as the basic force behind the intertwined branches of the worldscape. In this visionary art we come to see the spirit that resides in matter: our perception is altered so that the invisible being of the Goddess becomes manifest, and we are transformed into seers whose eyes may behold the divine revelation of the existence of a female principle at work in the universe.

Judy Chicago has made a major contribution to this tradition by conceptualizing and creating a traveling multimedia exhibition, *The Dinner Party Project,* an environmental recasting of the history of Western civilization in feminist terms.[15] Accompanying the Dinner Party Project's exhibition is a book in the form of an illuminated manuscript of five sections, some of which include a rewriting of Genesis as an alternate creation myth in which the Goddess is the supreme Creatrix. It also contains a section of myths, legends and tales of the women, a vision of the Apocalypse which is a vision of the world made whole by the infusion of feminist values, and the Calling of the Disciplines, a list of the women represented in the table relating who they were and what they did.

Chicago's work has long been making links between female iconography and a feminist reinterpretation of the Creation Myth. In her series of porcelain plates entitled *The Butterfly Goddesses: Other Specimens* (1974), which includes *The Butterfly Vagina as the Venus of Willendorf, The Butterfly Vagina as the Great Round,* etc., sexuality is expressly connected to spiritual transformation. For Chicago, the butterfly symbolizes both liberty and metamorphosis. The new specimens in *The Butterfly Goddess* series represent a new breed of women: these are women yet to be born to a world in which the Goddess is recognized as the original deity; women whose sexual energy is accepted as a legitimate form of creative power.

Her *Womantree* series suggests the principle of a female Tree of Life out of which these "Ancient New Beings" will emerge, possessing all the secrets of the matriarchal past transmitted over time through the sacred matrilineage women now reclaim. Chicago's flower forms, seed shapes, and pod forms relate to the principles of feminist alchemy and suggest the final transmutation into "The Ancient New Being" of which the butterfly is her prime symbol.

Chicago's dream has always been to bring art out of the world and back into the culture so that it will affect the people as it once did in the Middle Ages.

Monica Sjoo's synthesizing of artistic, political, and mythological material has served as a catalyst of Goddess-consciousness in England. Her underground pamphlet, *The Ancient Religion of the Great Cosmic Mother of All,* which will be published by *Womanspirit* in the coming year, is a poetic attempt to cull all information that can be obtained through a feminist occult reading of history, symbolism, myth, art, and literature, and bring it into a powerful reevaluation of many of the philosophical underpinnings of contemporary thought. Her art works create Goddess emblems which narrate the story of the real crucifixion, that of women who have been sacrificed upon the cross of patriarchal culture. They speak of female rebirth into a new ethos through the revolutionary force of women as workers and visionaries.

Contemporary Goddess-culture art, with its many varied manifestations, is creating a whole new constellation of charged signs, aspirational images, icons for contemplation, talismanic artifacts, and symbolic rites of passage that constitute the source of a new reality for women.

Artists of the Surrealist tradition like Leonora Carrington, Leonor Fini, Meret Oppenheim, Frida Kahlo, and Remedios Varo, artists participating in the Sister Chapel exhibition (*Womanart,* Winter 1977) such as Diana Kurz and Cynthia Mailman, Canadian artists Jovette Marchessault (totemic sculptural figures) and Suzanne Guité (stone sculpture), Thérèse Guité (batik) and other contemporary American artists such as Faith Wilding, Suzanne Benton (welded sculpture and mask ritual theater), Julia Barkley, etc., are creating a new feminist myth in which woman becomes the vital connecting link between all forms of life in the cosmos; the great catalyser and transformer of life energies. By the repossession of Goddess power and by a full participation in Her Being, women are bringing into existence a vastly expanded state of ecstatic consciousness.

Through the many ceremonies of rebirth and reclamation, the rituals of mourning and self-transformation, the energizing of new psyco-physical centers of being, the activation of a new Earth-Alchemy, the rewriting of sacred texts, myth, and history, and a new scanning of the universal system of hieroglyphics, using trance, meditation, and dream, women artists are bringing about a planetary goddess-consciousness revolution, a cycle of female rebirth, and a new feminist ethos in our time.

Notes

1. June Singer, *Androgyny: Towards a New Theory of Sexuality* (New York: Anchor, 1976), p. 71.

2. Jolande Jacobi, *Complex, Archetype, Symbol in the Psychology of C. G. Jung* (Princeton: Princeton University Press, 1959), p. 101.

3. Mary Daly, *Beyond God the Father: Toward a Philosophy of Women's Liberation* (Boston: Beacon Press, 1973), p. 34.

4. Mimi Lobell, "The Goddess Temple," *Humanist Ideas in Architecture* 19, no. 1: 20.

5. Lobell, "Goddess Temple," p. 21.

6. Miriam Sharon, personal communication, Dec. 10, 1977.

7. Erich Neumann, *The Great Mother* (Princeton: Princeton University Press, 1955), p. 262.

8. Quote by artist from dream narrative.

9. "Mary Beth Edelson's Great Goddess," *Arts Magazine* (Nov. 1975).

10. Sheila Moon, *A Magic Dwells* (Middletown: Wesleyan University Press, 1970), p. 152.

11. Donna Henes, "Spider Woman Manifesto," Lady-Unique-Inclination-of the-Night (Cycle III 1978).

12. Neumann, *Great Mother.*

13. Betsy Damon, "The 7,000 Year Old Woman," *Heresies* (Fall 1977): 9–13.

14. Quote from unpublished statement by the author.

15. Arlene Raven & Susan Rennie, "Interview with Judy Chicago," *Chrysalis* 4: 89–101.

Textual Strategies: The Politics of Art-Making

Judith Barry and Sandy Flitterman-Lewis

To say that there is a crisis in contemporary criticism might seem like overstating the case for a situation in which critical definitions and methods merely lack precision and rigor. Yet it cannot be disputed that in terms of the feminist issue of the representation of women and the figuration of female sexuality in art, a crisis does exist. In order to develop a truly effective feminist artistic practice, one that works toward productive social change, it is necessary to understand the question of representation as a political question, to have an analysis of women's subordination within patriarchal forms of representation. This article emerges from the need for a feminist reexamination of the notions of art, politics, and the relations between them, an evaluation which must take into account how "femininity" itself is a social construct with a particular form of representation under patriarchy. We have come together, a feminist film theorist and a feminist artist, to discuss these issues, and more specifically to determine to what extent current definitions of art as a political activity are limited. It is indeed a crisis of definitions and methods where women are concerned.

Traditional notions of art have emphasized personal expression, from the subjective lyricism of the Romantics to the individual virtuosity of the avant-gardists. Initially in the women's movement feminists emphasized the importance of giving voice to personal experiences; the expression and documentation of both women's oppression as well as aspirations, provided women's art with a liberating force. However, a radical reconceptualization of the personal to include more broadly social and even unconscious forces has necessitated a more analytic approach to these personal experiences. The experiential must be taken beyond the consciously felt and articulated needs of women if a real transformation of the *structures* of women's oppression is to occur.

This article was published in *Screen*, Summer 1980, in an edited and unauthorized version. The version printed here is the original form which was printed in *LIP: Feminist Arts Journal*, 1981/82.

While we recognize the value of certain forms of radical political art, whose aim it is to highlight feminist issues that are generally submerged by dominant cultural discourse, it seems that this kind of work, if untheorized, can only have limited results. These more militant forms of feminist art such as agit-prop, body-art, and ritualized violence, can produce immediate results by allowing the expression of rage, for example, or by focussing on a particular event or aspect of women's oppression. But these results may be short-lived, as in the case of heightened activism resulting from an issue-oriented art work. A more theoretically informed art can prove capable of producing enduring changes by addressing itself to the structural and deep-seated causes of women's oppression rather than to its effects. A radical feminist art would include an understanding of how women are constituted through social practices in culture; once it is understood how women are consumed in this society it would be possible to create an aesthetics designed to subvert the consumption of women, thus avoiding the pitfalls of a politically progressive art work which depicts women in the same forms as the dominant culture. Consequently, we see a need for theory that goes beyond the personal into the questions of ideology, culture, and the production of meaning.

To better understand the point at which theory and art intersect it might be useful to consider women's cultural production in four categories.[1] Our attempt here is to describe a typology rather than criticize these positions for their shortcomings. In evaluating these types of women's art, our constant reference point will be the recognition of the need for a theory of cultural production as an armature for any politically progressive art form. When we talk about culturally constructed meaning, we are referring to a system of heterogeneous codes that interact. The meaning we derive from any interaction is dependent on our knowledge of a set of conventions ensnaring every aspect of our lives, from the food we eat to the art we like. Every act (eating an orange, building a table, reading a book) is a social act; the fundamentally human is social. Theory enables us to recognize this and permits us to go beyond individual, personally liberating solutions to a "socially" liberated situation. Any society will impose a certain selection or priority of meaning upon the multiplicity of meanings inherent in a given situation. Culture as a mechanism that imposes an assumed unity on this diversity of codes, has a naturalising function in that it makes this constructed unity appear as given and enduring. Theory, as a systematic organization of the range of cultural phenomena, can produce the tools for examining the political effectiveness of feminist art work.

Each of the four categories in our typology of women's art-making implies a specific relation between strategy and action. By examining each of the categories and applying the definition of theory that we have suggested, we can ascertain the assumptions that characterize these relations. From doing this it should be clear that sets of assumptions do not constitute a theory, although they may be sufficient to establish a particular type of artistic practice. When we speak of the political in discussing art work we must ask the question, "Action, by whom, and for what purpose?" Each of the four categories will propose different answers to these questions, because they each have different goals and strategies.

One type of women's art can be seen as the glorification of an essential female art power. This power is viewed as an inherent feminine artistic essence which could find expression if allowed to be explored freely. This is an essentialist position because it is based on the belief in a female essence residing somewhere in the body of woman. It is an orientation that can be found in the emphasis on "vaginal" forms in painting and sculpture; it can also be associated with mysticism, ritual, and the postulation of a female mythology. It is possible to see this type of art which valorizes the body as reversing the traditional dichotomy of mind over matter. If we accept the premise that Western metaphysical thought hierarchizes binary opposition so that one term always predominates, this form of art can be seen as an aesthetics of simple inversion. Within the context of a logic that reduces the multiplicity of difference to the opposition of two positivities, feminist essentialism in art simply reverses the terms of dominance and subordination. Instead of the male supremacy of patriarchal culture, the female (the essential feminine) is elevated to primary status.

Much of the art work in this category has its aim the encouragement of self-esteem through valorization of female experiences and bodily processes. This art seeks to reinforce satisfaction in being a woman in a culture that does the opposite. The strategy is that by glorifying the bodies of women in art work an indentificatory process is set up such that the receivers of the art work (the women for whom the work is intended) will validate their own femaleness. This type of art work can also be seen to redefine motherhood as the seat of female creativity from which spring female deities, witchcraft, and matriarchal cultural heritage. Operating on the assumption that our society isolates women and inspires competition, this kind of art seeks to encourage the mutual glorification and bonding of women. One of the main ways some of the art works achieve this is through emotional appeal, ritual form, and synesthetic effects in performance, with the aim of enveloping spectators in feminine solidarity.

One example of women's art that would fall into this category is the work of Gina Pane, the French body-artist whose performances for the last ten years have involved self-mutilation and the ritualized drawing of her own blood. She defines the incision of her face with a razor blade in one performance as a "transgression of the taboo of the sore through which the body is opened, and of the canons of feminine beauty," and at least one critic has appropriated current terminology in his praise of her work because it "privileges the signifier on the side of pain." Complications arise, however, when the assumptions underlying this type of art are examined. When an aesthetics of pain is counterposed against the assumed pleasurable discourse of dominant artistic practice, a rigid pleasure/pain dichotomy is already accepted as given. By confronting one half of the dichotomy with its opposite, Pane's work is seen to offer an act of artistic contestation. However, this confrontation seems rather to continue the dualistic tradition of Western metaphysics.

The very definition of opposition thus comes into question. By elevating pain to the status of an oppositional artistic force, it would seem that Pane is simply reinforcing a traditional cliché about women. If women are assumed to be outside the patriarchal discourse, would the first rumble of self-expression take the form of very traditional pain or self-mutilation? Pane's comments about her work seem to indicate that she feels in wounding herself she is wounding society. However, because her wounds exist in an art context, they are already ritualised and easily absorbed into an artworld notion of beautiful pain, distanced suffering, and a whole legacy of exquisite female martyrdom. The solidarity in suffering that this work seems to want to promote is actually a form of solidarity that has been imposed on women for centuries. It is bondage rather than bonding.

Hannah Wilke adopts a related strategy of body-art by creating an art work that has as its aim "that women allow their feelings and fantasies to emerge . . . (so that) this could lead to a new type of art." In her *S.O.S. Starification Object Series* (1975) she says, "I am my art. My art becomes me." She sets up an equivalency between her body's poses and its alteration after vaginally shaped pieces of chewing gum are attached to the exposed areas, and language where the meaning of a word or series of words is transformed by a slight change or modification in the letter(s)—scarification becomes starification. Wilke explains that "my art is seduction." Often her poses take on the characteristics of a centrefold, her eyes directed to the assumed male spectator of nude paintings and *Playboy* magazine. In *Ways of Seeing,* John Berger points out "Men look at women. Women watch themselves being looked at. The surveyor of the woman in herself is male; the surveyed female. Thus, she turns herself into an object."[2] In objectifying herself as she does, in assuming the conventions associated with a stripper (as someone who will reveal all), Wilke seems to be teasing us as to her motives. She is the stripper and the stripped bare. She does not make her own position clear; is her art work enticing critique or titillating enticement? It seems her work ends up by reinforcing what it intends to subvert. In using her own body as the content of her art, in calling her art "seduction," she complicates the issues and fails to challenge conventional notions of female sexuality. The consequences are such that they permit statements like the following to issue forth from male critics: "By manipulating the image of a sex kitten (female sex object), Wilke manages to avoid being trapped by it without having to deny her own beauty to achieve liberation."

Wilke and Pane are only two, very divergent, types of women's art that fall into our first category. Yet they both enable us to draw certain conclusions about this type of art-making. Because this kind of art has no theory of the representation of women underlying it, it presents images of women as unproblematic. It does not take into account the social contradictions involved in "femininity." In much of this art, women are reinstalled in society as the bearers of culture, albeit an alternative culture. In this way what is assumed to be a progressive position is actually retrograde. Although the content of this art is different (nineteenth-century women instructed their children in art appreciation and manners, here they embody and illustrate the virtues of womanhood), the function remains unchanged; in both cases they are the custodians of what is deemed true, good and beautiful. Being-a-woman is the essential presupposition underlying this art work: what this notion entails is assumed to be generally accepted, uncontradictory, and immutable. Whether the art focusses on pain (immolation) or pleasure (eroticism), it does not challenge a fixed and rigid category of "femininity."

The second strategy or type of feminist artistic practice views women's art as a form of subcultural resistance. It postulates a kind of artisanal work, often overlooked in dominant systems of representation, as the "unsung province" of women's art activity.

An example of this type of work is the valorization of crafts, such as patchwork quilts, and the activities of women in the home. It posits the development of a feminist counter-tradition in the arts, by the valorization or reconstruction of a hidden history of female productivity. The strategy here is one of encouragement and nurturance and has the positive effect of stimulating women's creativity in the discovery of new areas of female expression. By redefining art to include crafts and skills heretofore neglected, it obviates the ideological distinction between "high" and "low" cultural forms. In so doing, it emphasises that this distinction is a tool of patriarchy that has served to downplay or negate creative avenues for women.

However, this can also be seen as an essentialist position since it views women as having an inherent creativity that simply goes unrecognised by mainstream culture. It therefore cannot be seen as a broadly effective political practice because it emphasises the personal at the expense of the social, and thus is ineffectual in transforming the structural *conditions* that oppress women. This is not to say that this kind of art-making is unimportant, but simply to point out the limitations of an untheorized strategy.

Although Jackie Winsor is not usually considered a feminist artist, she does fit into our second category of women's art, and in fact at least one critic considered her a feminist artist when she first came to national attention in 1970–71. Her constructions of wood, hemp, and other "natural" materials convey a postminimal fascination with geometric forms and the imposition of order and regularity. While she lists her concerns as repetition, weightiness, and density, there is in her work-process itself careful attention to craftlike details, particularly in the spinninglike monotony of some of the hemp and wood pieces and even of the actual carpentry itself. In *From the Center,* Lucy Lippard characterizes her work in the following way:

> Repetition in Winsor's work refers not to form, but to process, that is, to the repetition of single-unit materials which finally make up a unified, single form after being subjected to the process of repeatedly unraveling, then to the process of repeatedly binding or to the process of repeatedly nailing into wood or to the process of repeatedly sticking bricks in cement or to the process of repeatedly gouging out tracks in plywood.[3]

Jackie Winsor's work is considered much "tougher" than the work of other women who might be placed in this category, for example the "pattern painters" such as Harmony Hammond. Her work has been seen as speaking a rugged female masochism encompassing the outdoors, and including skills usually reserved for men. Yet, in discussing her work Winsor often ties the origin of a particular sculpture to an early emotional childhood experience, as in *Nail Piece*. When she was a child, her father planned a house which her mother built while he was away at work. At one point, says Winsor, "My father gave me an enormous bag of nails and left, saying to nail them down to keep the wood in place. I did . . . and used the whole bag of nails to do it. The part he told me to nail down needed about a pound of nails. I think I put in about twelve pounds. My father had a fit because I'd used up all his nails. They made such a fuss about it that it left quite an impression on me." And like much traditional women's work, Winsor's pieces conceal the actual labor involved in their construction.

A parallel might be drawn at this point between this aspect of Winsor's work and a related phenomenon with regard to women's craft work as in quilts or baskets. The mechanisms of repression have functioned traditionally in patriarchal culture to negate the complexity or degree of work involved in women's traditional handiwork. By foregrounding this "other" of conventional high art, the art work that falls into our second category emphasises that there *is* another art, which has a history, and which has been repressed due to specific historical needs of the dominant culture. The "alternative tradition" approach emphasizes the social and functional aspects of things such as weaving or pottery-making in communities. We agree that this type of contribution to feminist art-making is an important one; however it is equally important to point out the limitations of a form of self-contained subcultural resistance, one which does not work in a dialectical relation with the dominant male culture. A possible consequence is the "ghettoization" of women's art in an alternative tradition, thereby limiting its effectiveness for broad social change.

Our third category of women's art derives as well from this aspect of isolationism. This category of women's art views the dominant cultural order as a monolithic construction in which women's cultural activity is either submerged or entirely outside its limits. This position is an antidote to feminist essentialism in that it recognizes that what has traditionally been known as the "form" and the "content" of culture both carry meaning.

However, ironically, it is also the basis of *both* "separatist" (artists who do not identify with the artworld) and nonfeminist (women artists who maintain that they are people who happen to be women) argumentation. Thus this category includes two groups of women at opposite ideological poles. One group wants to establish a separate social order unaffiliated with the patriarchal culture. The other group, women who disavow their sex, attempts to ignore the issue of "women in crisis," seeking total identification with the patriarchy.

The strategy of the first group is that by establishing their own society, women will be able to combat the patriarchy. However, by failing to theorize how many women are produced as a category within the social complex, or how femininity is a social construction amidst a whole range of intersecting determinations, these artists lose sight of a solution that is workable in practice. As with many utopian visions, lack of integration within the wider social sphere presents obstacles. It is particularly difficult in the case of feminist separatism in that the postulation of an alternative separate culture can often be founded on simplistic notions.

The example of Terry Wolverton presents both the benefits and the limitations of the separatist strategy. As codirector of the Lesbian Art Project (which provides a program of Sapphic Education) and producer-codirector of a feminist science fiction theatre exploration, Wolverton informs her art work with the desire to shape an alternative female culture. This takes the form of validating craft projects such as bread-dough sculptures and costumed happenings because they are produced by lesbians in the community. One positive consequence is that this type of art allows women to explore their feelings and attitudes, enabling them to develop self-esteem and pride in the discovery of their love and trust for one another. The productive result is an attack on the destructive dissatisfaction with being a woman that patriarchal culture fosters. However, the separatist position seems to be an example of this self-validation gone awry: the very notion of positive (lesbian) images of women relies on the already constituted meaning of "woman." Again, this unproblematic notion of "femaleness" does not take into account that meaning is a dialectical process which involves an interaction between images and viewers. By failing to theorize how this meaning is produced within the social complex, this art considers the notion of femininity as unproblematic and positions women's culture as separate and different from mainstream culture. This can produce very disturbing results, as in the case of some of the art work validated by Wolverton, in which the prominence given to the exposed breasts of the subjects of the art work is strikingly similar to that in the photography of Les Krims, an artist noted for his particularly virulent expressions of misogyny.

The second group of women within our third category of artistic practice cannot be said to have a strategy because they do not view themselves as artists engaged in the feminist struggle. It is at this stage that women who have been favored through more strident forms of careerism make the assertion that women's art has outgrown its need for feminism. For these women, feminism is no longer useful, primarily because it was seen as a means to an end. But this form of separatism—women who deny their sex—does not necessarily have to exploit feminism. Artists falling into this category, such as Rosalyn Drexler ("I don't object to being called a woman artist as long as the word 'woman' isn't used to define the kind of art I create") and Elaine de Kooning ("We're artists who happen to be women or men among other things we happen to be—tall, short, blonde, dark, mesmorph, ectomorph, black, Spanish, German, Irish, hot-tempered, easy-going— that are in no way relevant to our being artists") simply deny that their work is embedded in a social context, or that art-making, like being a woman, is a form of social practice. Yet in the dialog in which these two artists made the above statements, when each describes how she began her career in art, both mention being "taken" to an exhibit by a man (husband or teacher) and being thereby "introduced" to certain aspects of the art world.[4]

The final type of artistic practice situates women at a crucial place within patriarchy which enables them to play on the contradictions that inform patriarchy itself. This position sees artistic activity as a textual practice which exploits the existing social contradiction toward productive ends. Accordingly, this position takes culture as a discourse in which art as a discursive structure and other social practices intersect. This dialectic foregrounds many of the issues involved in the representation of women. In these works the image of women is not accepted as an already produced given, but is constructed in and through the work itself. This has the result of emphasizing that meanings are socially constructed and demonstrates the importance and functioning of discourse in the shaping of social reality.

In discussing our fourth category of feminist art-making, we can clarify the issue of theory by underlining the difference between women making art in a male-dominated society and feminist art working against patriarchy. Activism alone in women's art has limited effects because it does not examine the representation of women in culture or the production of women as a social category. We are suggesting that a feminist art evolves from a theoretical reflection on representation: how the representation of women is produced, the way it is understood, and the social conditions in which it is situated. In addition to specific artistic practices that fall into this category we should point out that important critical work is being done in theoretical journals such as *m/f, Camera Obscura,* and *Discourse,* all of which contain articles analysing cultural production from a feminist perspective.

In *Post-Partum Document* Mary Kelly deconstructs the assumed unity of the mother/child dyad in order to articulate the mother's fantasies of possession and loss. By mapping the exploration of psychic processes, she indicates the ways in which motherhood is constructed rather than biologically given. One section, displayed as a series of transparent boxes, is a record of "conversations" between mother and son just as the child is leaving the family to enter school. Each box contains a drawing done by the child, remarks by the child, the mother's reaction, and the mother's diary. This information is supplemented by a Lacanian psychoanalytic text describing the constitution of the mother's subjectivity under "motherhood" (patriarchy). This method allows the spectator to construct several positions simultaneously.

In a September 1976 press release Mary Kelly described her work in the following way:

> I am using the "art object" explicitly as a fetish object in order to suggest the operations of the unconscious that underly it. The stains, markings, and word imprints have a minimum sign value in themselves, but a maximum affective value in relation to my lived experience. In psychoanalytic terms, they are visual representations of cathected memory traces. These traces, in combination with the diaries, time-tables, and feeding charts, constitute what I would call a discourse which "represents" my lived experience as a mother, but they are consciously set up in an antogonistic relationship with the diagrams, algorithms, and footnotes, thereby constituting another discourse which "represents" my analysis, as a feminist, of this lived experience.

Martha Rosler's videotapes address the ideology of bourgeois culture. In *Semiotics of the Kitchen* an antipodean Julia Child demonstrates the use of gourmet cooking utensils within a lexicon of "rage and frustration," alluding to a less civilized time when preparing the meal had no more to do with survival than commodity fetishism. In *Losing—A Conversation with the Parents* an at-home TV interview style is adopted as two middle-class parents describe the death of their daughter by anorexia nervosa, the self-starvation disease that afflicts (mostly) teenage women from middle-class families. In the attempt of the parents to present a "coherent narrative" of their misfortune, many of the social contradictions contained in their position(s) are indexed, most specifically, "starvation in the midst of plenty."

Rosler's bound volume of three postcard novels is entitled *Service: A Trilogy on Colonization.* Each novel, *A Budding Gourmet* (about a middle-class housewife who takes a gourmet cooking class because she feels "it will enhance 'her' as a human being"), *McTowers Maid* (about a woman employee who organizes the workers in a fast-food chain), and *Tijuana Maid* (about a Mexican woman who comes to San Diego to work as a maid in a middle-class household—the novel is in Spanish with the translation appended in the trilogy), deals with women and food in relation to issues of class, sex, and race. Originally Rosler sent these food novels through the mail as postcard series, one card about every five to seven days. As she makes clear in an introductory note to the trilogy, the spectator or reader of an art work is an integral part of the piece itself.

> Mail both is and isn't a personal communication. But whether welcome or unwelcome it thrusts itself upon you, so to speak, and must be dealt with in the context of your own life. Its immediacy may allow its message to penetrate the usual bounds of your attention. A serial communication can hook you, engaging your long-term interest (intermittently, at least). There was a lot of time—and mental space—around each installment of these novels, time in which the communication could unfold and reverberate. So they are long novels, and slow ones.

When various representations are placed in a crisis in a work of art, the work has a fissuring effect, exposing the elements that embody its construction. This is important to Judith Barry (our third example of art work in this category) "in considering how women are represented by art, particularly in performance art where diverse conventions/disciplines intersect making possible a natural dialogue within these cultural conventions." In *Past Future Tense* woman's position as icon is juxtaposed to a disparate psychological and social narrative detailing the question of woman as subject. The format of this piece calls into question the taken for granted assumption of a unified "ego" of the woman, making apparent her real heterogeneity in its place. *See How to Be an Amercian Woman* situates feminist social theory clichés informing seven horror stories of women's existence via a prerecorded multitrack tape (rape, childbirth, abortion, marriage, divorce, old age, etc.) against the naked, immobilized body of a woman in an Italian arcade and museum. Several dualities are telescoped: American feminism's unproblematic relationship to the body of the woman/European body art (including another duality: nudity/pornography), woman as individual subject/popular history, performer/spectator, and the art world/larger social world. These dualities are readily identifiable, yet because they are not resolvable they remain in a contradictory stasis.

Kaleidoscope, a series of eight five-minute scenes employing conventions from TV, cinema, and theater, explores the relationship of middle-class feminism as it shapes the private and public lives of a heterosexual couple. The contradictory positions exhibited by the two protagonists (both played by women) as they attempt to live their beliefs, underscores the unresolvable contradictions contained in even the most progressive views of social organization. Barry says of this piece:

> It is in trying to come to terms with the world as perceived (a perception which is ideological) that psychoanalysis intervenes. As dreams, jokes, and neuroses indicate, the unconscious does not describe a one-to-one relationship with the world. Jacques Lacan has shown that this unconscious is produced in language, hence the identity of the individual as speaking subject is fictional. Consequently, ideology's arbitrary nature within the domain of this fictional subject becomes apparent and yet simultaneously must remain unknown on some levels.

From our descriptions of the work of these three artists it should be clear that an important aim of the art in this category is the critical awareness (both on the part of the spectator, and informing the work) of the social construction of femininity. For it is only through a critical understanding of "representation" that a representation of "women" can occur. We do not want to simply posit a definition of "good women's art," for at this historical moment such a definition would foreclose the dialectical play of meaning that we are calling for; our intention is to be suggestive rather than prescriptive. One strategy of this fourth type of art transforms the spectator from a passive consumer into an active producer of meaning by engaging the spectator in a process of discovery rather than offering a rigidly formulated truth. Moreover, the art work strives to produce a critical perspective that questions absolute or reified categories and definitions of women. Both the social constructions of femininity and the psychoanalytic construction of sexual difference can be foregrounded if the art work attempts to rupture traditionally held and naturalized ideas about women. Finally, a theoretical approach implies a break with the dominant notion of art as personal expression, resituating it along the continuum connecting the social with the political and placing the artist as producer in a new situation of responsibility for her images.

Notes

1. An initial formulation of these categories has been made by Laura Mulvey in an interview in *Wedge* 2 (1978).

2. John Berger, *Ways of Seeing* (Harmondsworth: Penguin, 1972), p. 47.

3. Lucy Lippard, *From the Center: Feminist Essays on Women's Art* (New York: Dutton, 1976), p. 203.

4. Rosalyn Drexler and Elaine de Kooning, "Dialogue," In *Art and Sexual Politics: Why Have There Been No Great Women Artists?*, ed. Thomas B. Hess and Elizabeth C. Baker (New York: Collier, 1973), p. 57.

Visions and Re-Visions:
Rosa Luxemburg and the Artist's Mother

Moira Roth
In memory of Beverly Bolton

The rejection of the dualism, of the positive-negative polarities be-tween which most of our intellectual training has taken place, has been an undercurrent of feminist thought. And rejecting them, we reaffirm the existence of all those who have through the centuries been negatively defined: not only women, but the "untouchable," the "unmanly," the "nonwhite," the "illiterate": the "invisible" which forces us to confront the problem of the essential dichoto-my: power/powerlessness.

Adrienne Rich, *Of Woman Born,* 1976

At the beginning of the feminist movement, the artist, art, issues and audiences were fresh. Women artists plunged into previously taboo subjects and materials—autobiography, politics, rape, silk, and blood—and exhibited these in the new feminist alternative spaces and all-women shows to be seen by the new audience of other women. (At the same time, these taboo subjects and materials assailed the bewildered, frequently hostile audiences of the established and sexist art world.) Everything was grist for the feminist art mill. Simply taking on such subjects and materials produced, with astonishingly high frequency, effective feminist art. In 1980 this is no longer the case. What constitutes effective feminist art *now?*

In 1980 we can and should celebrate the spectacular achievements of a de-cade of women's art. Yet, it is high time that we take critical stock of the present state and future direction of both feminist art and feminist art criticism. As the criteria for feminist art (let alone for effective feminist art) have changed radically

This article originally appeared in *Artforum,* November 1980. © Artforum, November 1980, "Vi-sions and Revisions," Moira Roth.

in the last couple of years, so have those for feminist art criticism. The urgent central question confronting feminist critics in 1980, parallel to that for artists, is: What constitutes effective feminist art *criticism* now?

At the beginning of the '70s courageous feminist critics and historians—Lucy Lippard and Linda Nochlin among others—took on, with passion and intelligence, three tasks:

1. The discovery and presentation of art by women, past and present.
2. The development of a new language for writing about this art—often polemic and poetic, always antiformalist.
3. The creation of a history of and theories about the forms and meanings of this rapidly growing, astonishing quantity of art by women.

Today these tasks continue to legitimately occupy much of feminist critical writing, and passion and intelligence are still the order of the day. But there is a new task which must be taken on—which many feminists, including myself, have been hesitant to address—or feminist art criticism will at best flounder and at worst fail to be effective any longer. To the list of earlier tasks must be added another:

4. The undertaking of a far more critical mode of writing about this art than was possible or necessary in the last decade.[1]

Surrounding this new task is the highly volatile issue of support. Should feminist critics protest against ineffective feminist art and against the use of the word "feminist" when it is not an appropriate description? *Yes.* And will such feminist critics risk incurring the often paralyzing accusation that they are being unsupportive to women artists and to the feminist art movement in particular? *Yes.*

As I see the state of feminist art in 1980, there are several critical issues that need tackling. For me, two are paramount:

1. Should we redefine what we mean by "feminist art"?
2. Is it possible to be a feminist artist without making overtly feminist art?

Around 1970, after a decade of heated politics but for the most part of super cool art, women artists led the way in exploring autobiography, unorthodox "feminine" materials, ritual, and politics. These explorations provided the exciting, fresh, and appropriate staple fare of early feminist art. Highly successful then, these subjects and media are now in trouble.

As critics and artists, we are faced by the dangers of boredom and cooptation. Currently, in feminist art, there is the problem of quantity: the sheer surfeit of such material. There is also the problem of quality: the frequency of overworked and exhausted statements and forms. There is the problem of feminist art that has become neutralized: so much genuinely good feminist art, originally effective in a feminist context, has been appropriated by an art world fascinated a priori with autobiography, narration, Marxism, and decoration. And there is the final problem, misrepresentation: on occasion, both artist and critic claim certain works as feminist when others believe that they are not. So what is "feminist art"?

Suzanne Lacy, the feminist performance artist and theorist, talked recently of the need to qualify the definition of feminist art: "At first we defined feminist art as all art which reflects a woman's consciousness, but as our politics evolved some of us chose stronger definitions. For me, now, feminist art must show a consciousness of women's social and economic position in the world. I also believe it demonstrates forms and perceptions that are drawn from a sense of spiritual kinship between women."[2] Lacy's statement articulates one of the more thorny issues in contemporary discussions among feminists, including feminist artists: the relationship and balance between the overtly political and spiritual strains of current feminist theory and practice. Within these two major territories are a multitude of further divisions.

The spectrum of political feminism ranges from the liberal aspirations (associated with the National Organization for Women), which are concerned with the ratification of ERA, with the protection of women's abortion rights, etc., to the more radical goals of socialist feminists, who are working according to theoretical structures which attempt to encompass Marxism and women's issues. The spectrum of spiritual feminism ranges from an all-out, literal adoration of the Great Goddess to a more abstract belief in intense, emotional and mystical bonds among women, which create a women's spiritual community. How should feminist art respond to such different directions in feminist energy? As I am writing this essay in the summer of 1980, ERA and abortion rights are in an increasingly beleaguered position (the Republican Party platform has come out against both), and at the same time the summer solstice rites for the Great Goddess have just been celebrated in various parts of the country. What should feminist art *do* in 1980?

At the moment, the word "feminist" is too often a blanket term used by the artists themselves and by both friendly and hostile critics to describe all art by women that concerns itself with the enormous subject of women's experiences and consciousness. I believe that a commitment both to political ideologies and to a spiritual kinship between women, whatever the particular form, must provide the underpinnings to virtually all feminist art in 1980. However, such commitments also characterize feminist artists who may or may not make overtly "feminist art." This brings us to a question that I raised earlier. Is it possible to be a feminist artist without making overtly feminist art? *Yes.*

I would define a feminist artist as a woman who believes in and practices feminism outside her studio and thus comes to her work with a developed feminist sensibility; *however,* that does not mean inevitably that her work should be called "feminist." It has customarily received that description because until now no real theoretical distinctions have been drawn between the "feminist artist" and "feminist art." Indeed, earlier on it was not possible to make such distinctions. Now, it is not only possible but necessary: "feminist art" is on the verge of becoming a morass of vague, sometimes contradictory, images and messages.

I would suggest that we use the term "feminist art" more sparingly and more exactly, and that we continue to speak of the feminist artist in the spirit that I have just described. Otherwise, the feminist artist is left with no choice but to insist on her claims to making "feminist art" in order that her very loyalty to feminism not be put in question. If we agree to this separation of concepts, then we can begin to consider an affirmative answer to the first question. Should we redefine what we mean by "feminist art"? *Yes.*

I think we need to address this question by recognizing that the tasks of feminist art today differ profoundly in their priorities from those in the early seventies, even though they are continuous with them. In 1970, there were two principal tasks: to describe and to demand. One main undertaking for the emerging feminist artist was to make art about women from the woman's point of view. Feminist art took on this task of description in tones that ranged from despair to extreme anger. A second major objective was to teach others about the conditions of women in a way that would lead to changing those conditions. In 1980, the objectives of feminist art must be redefined to encompass the collective, interactive character of women's political and spiritual strengths. This means that the main tasks for current feminist art include:

1. The creation of visual symbols of women's unity and power.
2. The making of connections and bonds among women previously separated by race, class, age, geography, and history.
3. The portrayal of past, present and future obstacles to women's power and unity, and the analysis and criticism of such impediments in the light of feminist theories.
4. The invention of a visual language to help forge the political and spiritual components of feminism.
5. The development of effective strategies for protecting feminist art from cooptation and misrepresentation.
6. The creation of feminist visions of and for the future.

Among the women working in these areas of feminist art are Helene Aylon, Judith Barry, Judy Chicago, Mary Beth Edelson, Feminist Art Workers, Leslie Labowitz, Suzanne Lacy, Faith Ringgold, Martha Rosler, Carolee Schneemann, Miriam Schapiro, May Stevens, and Faith Wilding. I have decided to focus here on Lacy and Stevens—partly because they represent strikingly different theoretical backgrounds and different arenas of geography and mediums, but primarily because these two artists are working out some of the most effective strategies in contemporary feminist art for combining and balancing the strains of politics and spirituality, a dualism that I view as absolutely central to the making of effective feminist art today.

Both Lacy and Stevens are deeply involved in the intense and lively feminist art communities of Los Angeles and New York respectively. In these areas (and in many others outside of the two major coastal centers for feminist art), women are spending an enormous amount of time, energy, and passion in developing networks and communities for women artists—locally, nationally, and, increasingly, internationally.[3] (They are also struggling with the question: How do you extend this network outside the art world? How do you reach other women and other women's communities?)

Communities and networks among women also constitute a pivotal theme in the art of Lacy and Stevens, as they do in that of many others in the movement. Such artists are working on the creation of powerful visual forms for, and images and symbols of these past, present, future, imagined and real networks and communities. And, through their art, the artists are further intensifying and broadening these connections—both inside of and beyond the art world.

In the future, as the networks multiply, surely more and more feminist artists will respond to this theme. As it is, over the last decade an impressive body of feminist art has already been developed to represent such networks and communities: Faith Ringgold in *For the Women's House,* 1971, responded to the needs and visions of the inmates of a women's prison; Miriam Schapiro in *Connections,* 1976, and Sheila Levrant de Bretteville in *Pink,* 1974, have explored the grid format to symbolize the connection of information and objects, gathered from many women; Judy Chicago with *The Dinner Party,* 1979, formed a women's community through which to shape a work of art; and Faith Wilding with *Seed Piece,* 1980, created rites based on sowing and harvesting to connect a worldwide community of women.

Two of the most powerful visions of women's spiritual and political communities to emerge in feminist art of the seventies are *Mysteries and Politics,* a painting by Stevens, and *In Mourning and In Rage,* a collaboration between Lacy and Leslie Labowitz. One can see the symbolic connection between the two works: the ten giant female mourning figures of *In Mourning and In Rage,* their stance and garb simultaneously expressing grief and enraged strength, could well act as the mythic guardians of the tranquil community of women in *Mysteries and Politics.*

These two works were created in the latter half of the seventies, a time of theoretical appraisal and commotion in feminist art circles.[4] Martha Rosler presents a vivid picture of this time in the opening paragraph of her pivotal and controversial article, "The Private and The Public: Feminist Art in California," when she writes of the earlier confusion between the terms "women's art," "feminist art," "woman artist," and "feminist" and of the lack of differentiation between political and art world feminism. Rosler then comments: "In the early 70s . . . the unity and high energy of the women's movement seemed to obviate the need for

Suzanne Lacy and Leslie Labowitz, *In Mourning and In Rage*, Los Angeles City
Hall, December 13, 1977
Performance.
(*Photo by Susan Mogul*)

May Stevens, *Mysteries and Politics*, 1978
Acrylic, 78" × 142".
(Photo by eeva-inkeri)

May Stevens, *Two Women*, 1976
Mixed media, 6′ × 12′.
(Photo by Bevan Davies)

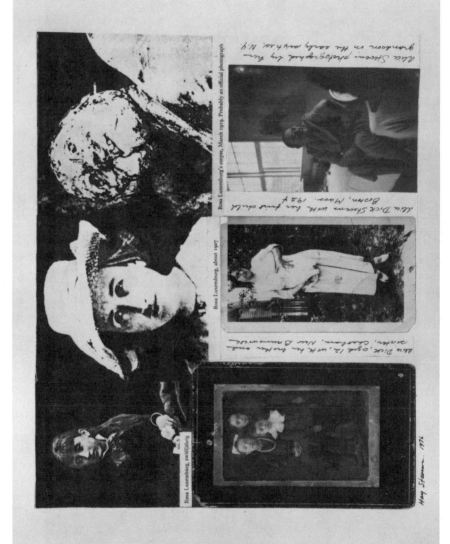

ORDINARY. EXTRAORDINARY. A COLLAGE OF WORDS AND IMAGES OF ROSA LUXEMBURG, POLISH/GERMAN REVOLUTIONARY LEADER AND THEORETICIAN, MURDER VICTIM (1871-1919) JUXTAPOSED WITH IMAGES AND WORDS OF ALICE STEVENS (BORN 1895—) HOUSEWIFE, MOTHER, WASHER AND IRONER, INMATE OF HOSPITALS AND NURSING HOMES. A FILMIC SEQUENCE OF DARKS AND LIGHTS MOVING THROUGH CLOSE-UP TO LONG-VIEW AND BACK.

OBLIQUE. DIRECT. FRAGMENTS OF ROSA'S THOUGHT FROM INTIMATE NOTES SENT FROM PRISON TO HER COMRADE AND LOVER, LEO JOGICHES, AND TO HER FRIENDS; FROM AGIT-PROP PUBLISHED IN DIE ROTE FAHNE; AND FROM HER SERIOUS SCIENTIFIC WRITINGS, IMAGES FROM HER GIRLHOOD, HER MIDDLE LIFE, AND THE FINAL PHOTOGRAPH OF HER MURDERED HEAD. ALICE'S WORDS FROM THE MEMORY OF AND LETTERS TO HER DAUGHTER. EXAMINING AND DOCUMENTING THE MARK OF A POLITICAL WOMAN AND MARKING THE LIFE OF A WOMAN WHOSE LIFE WOULD OTHERWISE BE UNMARKED. ORDINARY. EXTRAORDINARY.

May Stevens, Handwritten Explanatory Note from *Ordinary/Extraordinary*, 1980 fine distinctions. That moment has passed, and renewed theoretical activity has begun."⁵

A year before the 1977 Rosler article, in this atmosphere of "renewed theoretical activity," May Stevens began to work for the first time on the subject of Alice Stevens (her mother) and Rosa Luxemburg (the radical and political martyr); in 1978 these two women appear among others in the painting, *Mysteries and Politics*. Why Rosa Luxemburg and the artist's mother? How did Stevens arrive at this combination of women? *Slowly. Obsessively.*

Stevens's earlier commitments had been more exclusively to socialism. In the sixties as a young painter, she had turned first to the figures of civil rights leaders and martyrs for subjects of her art. Then at the end of the decade, she became obsessed for a number of years with the image of *Big Daddy*, a figure based on her own father. In *Big Daddy* (to quote a statement in *Heresies*, the journal published by the New York feminist collective of which Stevens is a member), "The personal and the political are fused in autobiographical images which are also symbols of authority and patriarchy."⁶

In the middle seventies, guided by both political and psychological motives, Stevens turned to the joint subject of her mother and Luxemburg. A series of large photocollages quickly followed her first exploration of this subject, the 1976 collage *Two Women;* finally, this year, Stevens published an artists' book, whose content and title, *Ordinary/Extraordinary,* she explains in a handwritten note in the book.

Stevens's book combines, both formally and emotionally, the characters, lives and destinies of these two women, who, through Stevens the daughter and the socialist, poignantly reach out to each other through time and space—to where an ordinary and an extraordinary woman meet.

In 1978 Stevens painted *Mysteries and Politics,* in which feminist politics and feminist mysteries meet. In this large painting a group of thirteen women are arranged in a semicircle according to their primary commitment and concern for either politics or mysteries. Stevens appears in it twice: once as a child in her mother's arms on the "mysteries" side, and once as a mature artist, standing near the large disembodied head of Luxemburg on the "politics" side. Revealingly, the adult Stevens is turned toward the center of the group in which the literal and symbolic meeting of mysteries and politics takes place. I feel that this potent combination in Stevens's art was made possible by the politically and psychologically motivated juxtaposition of her mother and Rosa Luxemburg.

Stevens credits three sources of inspiration for her painting *Mysteries and Politics:* first, her reading of *Of Woman Born* by Adrienne Rich (a key work in the literature of "spiritual" feminism);⁷ second, her "desire to reproduce consciousness as we experience it, on many levels"; and third, her experience of working within the *Heresies* collective. Recent feminist "spiritual" literature, a greater sensitivity to the multifaceted nature of feminist perceptions, and the experience of working in a theoretically oriented feminist collective—the three "inspirations" of Stevens's painting—are important wellsprings for exploring the highly complex relationship of politics and mysteries in feminist art.

In 1980, women need to unite the ordinary and extraordinary woman, to unite the past and the present, the public and the private, politics and mysteries, and to act on these necessities. Feminist art can be a powerful force for symbolizing these unities and for inspiring action among women.

Notes

1. Two questions are germane to this task of writing more critically, when necessary, on feminist art: First, who should take on this criticism? (Women only? Also men?) Second, where should this criticism be aired? (In the studio only? Among the feminist art community only? Is it politically permissible to air criticism in a nonfeminist public context, and does this affect the form and tone of that criticism?)

2. From a conversation with Suzanne Lacy in the spring of 1979, which I quoted in my article "Autobiography, Theater, Mysticism, and Politics: Women's Performance Art in Southern California," published in *Performance Anthology: Square Book for a Decade of California Performance Art,* Carl E. Loeffler, ed., Darlene Tong, associate ed. (San Francisco: Contemporary Arts Press, 1980). This anthology also includes an interesting article by Judith Barry on "Women, Representation and Performance Art: Northern California."

3. Two current projects are typical of the increasingly international flavor of these exchanges: the San Francisco-Berlin show of woman's art facilitated in the States through the newly formed Women's Building in San Francisco and the coming together of Californian and English women performance artists in Franklin Furnace, New York. Both are scheduled for the spring of next year.

4. The second half of the 1970s was the period of crystallization of the scholarly accounts of women's art history, of the initial theoretical studies on feminist art, and of the feminist "spiritual" literature. Any brief chronology of the feminist movement and feminist art movement between 1975 and 1978 must include:

   1975: Susan Brownmiller, *Against Our Will: Men, Women and Rape* (New York: Bantam Books, 1975); Judy Chicago, *Through the Flower: My Struggle as a Woman Artist* (Garden City, N.Y.: Doubleday, 1975).

   1976: Ann Sutherland Harris and Linda Nochlin's exhibition and catalog, *Woman Artists: 1550–1950* (New York: Alfred A. Knopf, 1976); Lucy Lippard, *From the Center: Feminist Essays in Women's Art* (New York: E. P. Dutton, 1976); Adrienne Rich, *Of Woman Born* (New York: Bantam Books, 1976); Merlin Stone, *When God Was a Woman* (New York: Harcourt Brace Jovanovich, 1976).

   1977: Faith Wilding, *By Our Own Hands* (Santa Monica: Double X, 1977); and *Heresies* and *Chrysalis,* which began publication this year.

   1978: Mary Daly, *Gyn/Ecology* (New York: Harper & Row, 1978); Susan Griffin, *Woman and Nature* (New York: Harper & Row, 1978).

   (This chronology is drawn from the collaborative work by Janet Burdick, Alice Dubiel, and myself on "Toward a Chronology of Performance Art by Woman (History and Women's History)" to be published shortly as part of a catalog/book on *Women and Performance Art,* a response to the exhibition (curated by Mary Jane Jacobs) on that subject in New Orleans in 1980.)

5. Martha Rosler, "The Private and the Public: Feminist Art in California," *Artforum,* September 1977, p. 66.

6. *Heresies: A Feminist Publication on Art and Politics,* January 1977, p. 28. In an essay, "My Work and My Working-Class Father" (published in *Working It Out, 23 Women Writers, Artists,*

Scientists and Scholars Talk about Their Lives and Work, Sara Ruddick and Pamela Daniels, eds., New York: Pantheon Books, 1977) May Stevens describes the shift in her art to an autobiographical framework for her politics:

> I began to paint my own family background. I painted out of love for those lower-middle class Americans I came from and out of a great anger for what had happened to them and what they were letting happen, making happen, in the South and in Vietnam . . . I had two recent photographs—one of my father, one of my mother. They were snapshots, terrible to see, revealing of what life had done to these people I loved, and what they had done to each other. The photograph of my mother was too terrible for me to deal with. I started to paint my father.
>
> My mother, when I was growing up, did not sew, did not cook well, and did not keep a beautiful house. . . . When my brother died at sixteen and I left home, the long disorientation consumed her and she was committed to a state mental hospital.
>
> Sexism and classism, male authority and poverty-and-ignorance were the forces that crippled my mother, the agent in most direct contact with her was, of course, my father. (p. 112)

7. Adrienne Rich's *Of Woman Born,* 1976. Mary Daly's *Gyn/Ecology* and Susan Griffin's *Woman and Nature,* both 1978, are some of the most notable explorations of the mystical side of feminism. Most of this literature argues for a separatist reading of history and nature, emphasizes the intimate, unique relationship of women with nature, and invokes the Great Goddess as the literal or symbolic statement of women's ancient powers and future destiny. This is a highly complex and controversial issue, and so is the question interlocked with it: Are there, in fact, unique forms which characterize women's thinking, writing and art-making?

Against the Grain:
A Working Gynergenic Art Criticism

Cassandra L. Langer

Introduction

Since 1969 ''aware'' feminists have attempted a systematic inquiry into the literature of art history as it is presently taught through patriarchal texts in our institutions of learning. Although I would like to say that the shocking revelations of the sixties concerning sexism are a thing of the past (or at least common knowledge) recent statistics compiled for the College Art Association of America's ''newsletter'' and women's experiences reveal that this is far from true.[1] Some blame rests squarely on the shoulders of these so-called aware women who nonetheless have not been gynergenically centered critics. Although reflection on these problems in the intervening years has led some contemporary art historians and critics to undertake a partial revision of the discipline, many have maintained that the status quo is fine just as it is and several others have actively and successfully thwarted any attempt at a balanced presentation of facts. As a result of such activity we have yet to see a fully balanced survey of art history.

Not surprisingly the majority of revisionist scholars are active feminists, if not gynergenic activists. The essential difference between these individuals is their comprehension of the issues. The feminist revisionist is conscious of women's oppression due to gender. She understands that women exist for the patriarchy: to propagate, to carry on the male name, and to assure a legitimate passage of the father's property and wealth to a designated heir. She also knows that she provides a cheap source of labor in a male-dominated market place. Comprehending this, however, is only a necessary first step in reaching a mature political consciousness, something I believe most feminist art historians and critics have failed to achieve. The gynergenic activist, on the other hand, makes it her

This article originally appeared in the *International Journal of Women's Studies* 5.3 (1982).

business to advance her cause; she actively attacks the ideology that supports women's oppression through male institutions: family, work, school, and media. She recognizes these as the components that not only allow but serve to foster the growth of discrimination against women, regardless of class, due to their sex. The gynergenic critic recognizes that an active commitment to the frustratingly slow process of shaping and enunciating women's own cultural history is primary. To formulate effective alternatives to the robotic identities created for women by males, i.e., daughters, wives, mothers, and mistresses (objects that speak only to a collective persona "woman"), is crucial. Engaged criticism requires actively seeking our own women-centered terms, expressions, and roots; it recognizes the essential difference between being merely "feminist" and "aware" and being actively involved in revolt against a sexist society.[2]

My purpose in this paper is to undertake a multilevel analysis of a number of issues that have arisen in this context. The first part of the essay will examine the "woman question" within the confines of a sexist art history created primarily for a white male audience. This requires an understanding that traditional art history is one in which women's contributions and those of others outside the mainstream are devalued or classified as inferior to those of white males. Here I will also conduct a reexamination of the pertinent literature concerning women in art. Using representative examples through a survey of these contributions, I will attempt to summarize these showing similarities and differences among nineteenth and twentieth century art historians, critics, and writers.[3]

The problem of how to carry our observations beyond these immediate issues is the crucial one for theorists, critics, and those making art. Required here is a methodology for the implementation of not merely a revisionist history of art and its criticism but instead a gynergenic practice. In an attempt to formulate some criteria relative to what I saw as an emerging feminist practice in the field of art history, I once posed some fundamental questions which a self-consciously aware feminist revisionist might ask: What implicit assumptions underlie my definition of a specific art historical problem? How do these influence my choice of method? Can the method I choose affect my conclusions? How does my language affect how my conclusions are read by others?[4]

Essentially, the issue is how can I practice art history and its criticism in such a way as to minimize its service to the continuation of sexist domination? Having roughed out a framework, the logical question now becomes "Can one practice more than a feminist criticism and, if so, what might such a practice reveal in relation to both traditional and feminist practices of art history and criticism?" In the second section of this article, I will attempt to carry this notion several steps further, that is, into the realm of an active gynergenic criticism. I will examine two well-known visual themes, eroticism and maternity. My object in doing so is not only to show how female and male artists differ in their interpretations but how language might function in "gynergenic" criticism.[5] It is hoped that by taking a gynergenic perspective, which I understand to place emphasis on women's perceptions, language and experiences in our society, and by comparing and contrasting it with male consciousness of these same events, some new insights may be gained. My interpretations are not intended as absolute gynergenic reading of these conceptions: none currently exists (nor would I wish it to be otherwise). Finally, the third section will address the difficulties, possibilities, and implications of such gynergenic criticism. Here, as in the preceding section, my intent is not to offer a closed system of interpretation, but a new beginning.

In the last paragraphs of Kate Chopin's *The Awakening,* the heroine Edna imagines the concert pianist Mademoiselle Reisz laughing and commenting, "And you call yourself an artist! What pretentions, Madame! The artist must possess the courageous soul that dares and defies!"[6] This is exactly what has been required of women artists, revisionist art historians, and feminist critics of our own generation.

Freedom fighters on the art front can look back on twelve years of unsuccessful struggle to free themselves from patriarchal art historians, curators, gallery directors, and art professionals. *Patriarchal* and *patriarchy* in this context refer to the social system based on father-right that universalizes male experiences, institutionalizes the values of that experience in all facets of social life, and presents these social norms based upon power relationships as objective truths. Thus reified, these values are expressed through a system of sanctions that reward upholders and punish transgressors of establishment conventions. In effect, the power of originating, of naming, is thus appropriated as a masculine prerogative, and with it the power of defining what is good, right, proper and significant.

Evelyn Reed suggests that "the essence of male sexual dominance in our society is the husband's exclusive possession of his wife who by law must restrict her sexual activities to him alone."[7] An analogous situation exists in modern intellectual life. Rooted in the medieval university, for centuries shaped by male definitions of what constitutes legitimate intellectual inquiry, it is not surprising that the modern academy continues to reflect masculine bias.[8] While the intellectual capacity of contemporary women is generally acknowledged, the legitimate exercise of that capacity has been defined and limited to those areas certified by male practitioners of the past as valid. Sanctions are enforced through administrative rules that grant or withhold status on the basis of "scholarly" criteria.[9] "Scholarly" in this sense, however, carries both a descriptive and a commendatory meaning. Applied to a process of methodological investigation as rigorous inquiry and rational ordering of information, it described fact; but used to direct the proper focus of such activities or to judge the significance of their finds it conveys approval or disapproval of the subject itself as a legitimate object of investigation.[10] Thus, would-be feminist critics are discouraged from pursuing this avenue of inquiry. Adrienne Rich sums it up best in "Diving into the Wreck":

> We are, I am, you are
> by cowardice or courage
> the ones who find our way
> back to the scene
> carrying a knife, a camera
> a book of myths
> in which
> our names do not appear.[11]

The attempt to rid ourselves of sexist language, images, values, and aspirations has been, and continues to be, a daily battle requiring constant application of feminist theory to daily professional practice, whether that practice be art criticism, art education, art history, or the creation of art itself. With the recent publication of six explicitly feminist-inspired histories of women's art, it would seem that art historians and interested others have been particularly successful in pressing the cause of feminism in the visual arts, but this is deceptive in view of the conservative backlash we are presently experiencing. In this context, my purpose here is to explore this apparent praxis through a critical examination of this literature.[12]

In her essay "Why Have There Been No Great Women Artists?" Linda Nochlin predicted contemporary feminists would take one of two lines of argument in responding to the question. The first would be the defensive assertion that, indeed, there had been great women artists but that they had been somehow excluded from art history by sexist male art historians. Having "swallowed the bait," as Nochlin puts it, these outraged defenders are then stuck with ferreting out the great women artists of the past using the traditional patriarchal standards of value to justify their selections, thus perpetuating the form of the initial oppression they wish to combat. The second possibility lay in the suggestion of a different standard of measure to evaluate the work of women artists of the past, a position premised upon the existence of a discernable "feminine sensibility." Many women artists and a number of art historians and critics have explored this corridor of discovery; thus we have seen a proliferation of essays and art dealing with the search for female rootedness.[13]

While the accuracy of this prediction is amply borne out by contemporary literature on the subject, I cannot help but be struck by a certain sense of déjà vu when I find variations on the same themes pursued by Mrs. Ellet, Clara Erskine Clement, and Walter Shaw Sparrow.[14] It will no doubt be suggested that there is an inherent flaw in any attempt to compare apples and oranges, but in the context of this essay a few brief notes concerning the historical conditions and class of these writers might prove helpful.

In an effort to comprehend the "feminism" of our three earliest contributors, Ellet, Clement, and Sparrow, it is necessary to understand the term "feminist intellectual," which Susan Conrad defines as one who "makes contributions to feminist thought without necessarily adopting an activist stance."[15] In this sense all three historians may be seen as forerunners of a feminist art history. All are essentially products of nineteenth-century romantic thinking and middle- to upper-class schooling. They themselves may be characterized as "professional" writers who charted the shifting cultural values of their era. Much the same may be said of their latter-day inheritors.

The works discussed in my previous articles and summarized here are written on different levels by white women (with the exception of Sparrow, a white male) who are products of middle- and upper-class educational systems.[16] Although these books seem aimed at different publics they all essentially address the dominant culture. While they vary greatly as to both the scope and depth of their enterprise, in a very real sense they ultimately share the same subject matter and class biases. All of our authors are shaped by middle- to upper-class educational systems and their scale of values when it comes to writing about and evaluating art. This in some part may account for their lack of revolutionary spirit and unwillingness to make real waves when it comes to the discipline itself. Doubtless, the consequences of challenging the dominant system of values is such that eventually melding into its mainstream, even as a stepchild, seems the lesser evil. Be this as it may, it has been my contention in this paper and others that through examination of the premises underlying the pursuit of this common subject and the methods adopted in their application we might better comprehend the relationship between feminism, women's studies in the arts, and the more general context of the discipline of art history as a whole.

To the extent that there is an emerging pattern evident in these publications, it is the revelation of a shared consciousness of the fact that, as presently constituted, the discipline has either relegated women artists to inferior status or excluded their contributions altogether. In a sense, a pattern exists in that this common assumption underlies the fact that each author undertakes to fill in the void. Thus, they are all revisionist to a degree, but they differ in the extent to which this consciousness enables them to be critical of the field itself. These works, then, cannot be viewed in terms of linear development, but rather must be seen in terms of their relationship to two polarities of disciplinary self-criticism. The more conservative formulation differs from traditional art history primarily in the focus of its attention. It upholds, if only tacitly, the same long-established categories of "high art," "great artists," individual genius and the purity of formal aesthetic criteria. Its object is to prove that there have been great women artists worthy of scholarly consideration by the same standards applied to their male contemporaries. All these works are expressive, albeit in varying degrees, of this formulation by virtue of their unwillingness to challenge the status quo and rock the methodological boat in its totality. This is not surprising in view of the upper-class educations of most of these women, e.g., Harris, Nochlin, and Tufts (see *Who's Who in American Art*). Mrs. Ellet, Clement, and Tufts are closest to the pole in terms of the established notions of "fine arts" and "creative genius" as the proper object of art historical investigation. Petersen and Wilson, Fine, and Munro deviate from this traditional wisdom by suggesting that social conditions influence the creative process and by introducing the status and role of women in a given period as a necessary augmentation of the study of their art.

A more aggressive and accusatory stance is taken by Harris and Nochlin and Greer. Fine and Greer, however, remain true to the concept of painting and sculpture as the highest expressions of artistic energy. In Greer's case one is obliged to say that *The Obstacle Race,* which the author styles a sociology of art and "feminist art history," is a far cry from the rigorous model provided by Harris and Nochlin. In fact, Ms. Greer's attempt is a case in point of how *not* to create gynergenic art history. As one astute reviewer put it, "The book isn't history. It isn't even passionate criticism. It is a facile potboiler, the latest and glossiest reminder that women can still capitalize on each other as a cause célèbre."[17] Remarkable indeed is Greer's insensitivity to the requirements of a feminist critique. Particularly painful from a gynergenic point of view is her use of patriarchal vocabulary and its implications in her text. More striking, however, is her blatant exploitation of women artists through her use of penny-dreadful sensationalism when it comes to their lives and art. Most astonishing of all is to see those who claim to "live in the tradition of the Furies" sidestep the requirements of feminist ethics in reviewing this book.[18] Women-centered thinking does not mean lack of integrity when it comes to "critique." Gynocentric criticism is risky and in this sense Eleanor Munro's *Originals* is anything but risk-taking. The author takes a sociobiographic and psychological approach to the lives of select women artists. In tracing the careers and aspirations of American women artists from Mary Cassatt to contemporary women artists of the seventies Munro follows patriarchal form. She provides subjective information using the language of the ruling class and attempts no critique. It should be noted that her book is the outgrowth (much like Petersen and Wilson's) of a media event, in this case a television series produced by WNET. As such it has all of the virtues and drawbacks of that inspiration.

Clearly, Petersen and Wilson, Munro, and most markedly Harris and Nochlin (who after all must be credited with setting the standard for this sort of analysis) differ from these other writers in recognizing that social conditions have resulted in the concentration of women's creative expressions primarily in the "minor arts," including the decorative and applied arts. In practice, however, all of these writers should be viewed as gradualists rather than as active revolutionaries, reformers rather than as radicals.

The radical formulation, by contrast, is not content just to add women artists to the existing honor roll of art historical judgments.[19] In examining the social and institutional causes for women's "success" or "failure" in the arts, it proposes to look at art and its language with new eyes and with the purpose of describing it in women-centered terms.[20] By bringing a sociological perspective to bear upon the study of art, it dismisses the idea of objective criteria for "artistic quality" and emphasizes instead the importance of such concepts as class, sex, and culture in the determination of what constitutes "good" art and for whom in a given period.[21]

For the purposes of this commentary and in the most general sense a distinction should be made between "female art history" and "gynergenic criticism," understanding that these are not necessarily mutually exclusive categories. Filling in the gaps and setting the record right would seem to me to be practicing female art history. This is something which devotes itself to the examination of women artists and their visual contributions to culture. By contrast, I would define "gynergenic critique" as a self-consciously aware and aggressively women-identified attack on the male-identified status quo from a women-centered perspective, in this particular case the history of art as it is presently known, taught, and practiced in male institutions. Moreover, it is actively concerned with creating alternatives to patriarchal art, art history, and criticism shaped and defined by men. While this is a far from conclusive definition, it is a necessary first step. Thus, on the one hand, "female art history" may be viewed as the conservative formulation since it differs from standard art historical practice only in the object of its gaze. Gynergenic criticism, on the other hand, is the radical practice in that it demands active commitment and participation in social change.

To summarize, in the creative arts, as in all patriarchally dominated endeavors, it is assumed that men originate ideas and women follow them. Moreover, while it is a simple fact of sociopolitical and economic history that the rights of men generally do not care to recognize the rights of women, for the obvious reason that it is not to men's advantage to do so, the problem is further complicated by a number of factors.[22] Even in Socialist and Marxist circles, where it is fashionable to address the women question, women are objectified. It is evident that, like Socialism, Marxism, anarchism, and other "isms," "feminism" may be practiced by both sexes provided they share the conviction that females have been oppressed by a sexist society. It would seem that many males participate in supporting women's concerns because it appeals to their bourgeois sense of liberalism. Their interest is an ego trip at the expense of real social radicalism, which requires them to abdicate male privilege (which they have no intention of doing). Indeed, if this latter-day "liberal" man is to be credited with anything, as compared with nineteenth-century socialist thinkers, then rape is his best answer to today's revolutionary heroine.[23] One cannot ignore, as Jane Rule points out in her essay on "Sexuality in Literature," that: "The vocabulary of sexual love is male ammunition for the ancient war. Even the medical terms which are used for parts of the female body . . . are descriptive only of male uses for them." "By way of contrast she cites a work by Phyllis Webb, "Naked Poem":

> And
> here
> and here and
> here
> and over and
> over your mouth[24]

The gynergenic critic seeks woman's total identity, not man's infantile, exploitive cannibalism which compartmentalizes woman by how she functions for him, i.e., sexually. Doubtless, as Adrienne Rich notes, choosing real alternatives has its consequences: two women sleeping together have more than their sleep to defend.[25] Given the considerations I have outlined above, it is logical for gynergenic critics to investigate the implicit tensions inherent in the relationship between the two sexes in order to shape their language and expression according to woman-centered perceptions. In this sense, the obvious areas for a gynergenic critic to focus on are eroticism and maternity. It is to an exploration of these themes that we now turn.

One of the major issues to emerge during the last twelve years of art critical activity is the role that visual images of women play in shaping perceptions of women in the lived-in world. Certainly, the objectification of women in a sexist culture is such that it need not be substantiated by visual illustrations: they are all around us everywhere we look. Psychologist Naomi Weisstein summed it up nicely: "When feminists say that women are treated as sex objects, we are compressing into a single perhaps rhetorical phrase an enormous area of discomfort, pain, harassment, and humiliation."[26]

Turning to any standard history of art will provide ample support for her thesis. It is clear to any aware professional woman that her ideas of herself are influenced by these pictures. In a sexist society, woman is a creature defined by her biological function and erotic possibilities, a thing that at once generalizes and condenses both male fears and fantasies. Any woman who refuses her proper place in the patriarchal scheme of things is immediately in danger of being labeled a radical-feminist-man-hating dyke. Thus is the lesbian evoked as a spectre of things to come. The lesbian is unavailable to men and therefore no longer participates in a patriarchal assumption that all females are available to male needs. As a consequence, patriarchally trained women, who are all of us, run the risk of implicit penalties when we choose otherwise. In this case, the rejection of our "femininity" results in our being made outcasts. The moral code, however, is strictly enforced only when it is to the advantage of the ruling class to make an issue of it. As Mary Daly points out: "Fear of the label 'lesbian' has driven many into matrimony, mental hospitals, and—worst of all—numbing, dumbing normality. In her own light the Self sees/says her own light/insight. She sees through the lurid male masturbatory fantasies about made-up 'lesbians' who make out in *Playboy* for men's amusement.''[27] The point that needs to be made here is simply that she be free to emphasize the female experience as subject rather than as object without consequences. The result of such choice might be that for the first time it may be possible to see what eroticism would be for liberated women.

In 1975, at Douglas College, feminist critic Carol Duncan discussed the problem of love and beauty in terms of art's image of woman and noted the relationship between erotic art and the aesthetics of power.[28] Her point, that erotic art is culturally defined, was not a new one. It is obvious that women and men in our society are taught to respond and identify with the social interactions depicted in pictures. Duncan and a number of other feminists asserted that male artists, particularly those of the nineteenth and twentieth centuries, approach the female nude in a number of masculine-centered ways, none of which are realistic or reassuring from a female-centered perspective. A nude woman, they argue, is for the majority of male artists a threat, an adversary to be conquered, or just plain property to be used in any way they choose.

The drama of portrayal which ensues from this is one of ritual subjugation of the female via various means which titillate both the male artist and male viewer to whom these creations are undoubtedly addressed. Since identification with such themes as Delacroix's *Death of Sardanapalus,* or more recent examples from popular culture, i.e., *Lipstick* or *Dressed to Kill,* do nothing for female audiences, who naturally have to identify with the female victim, it is obvious that these are male media events. Short of absolute masochism there is nothing erotic here for women. If death, brutality, violation, and sadism are erotic for the patriarchy when it comes to female bodies, what, one wonders, does this say about misogynist culture in general? Clearly, violence and force are used by the male artist to show this ritual surrender which reinforces images of male superiority and power, no matter how sick or distorted from a gynocentric perspective. In looking at the majority of examples available to us in the history of the visual arts, it is clear that much high art, craft art, and popular media deal with exploring only male desires and fears concerning women. Female viewers, thinking of their highest aspirations, would hardly seek to consciously imitate art in their lives by partaking of relationships similar to those depicted in these works of art. What this leaves the gynergenic critic asking is, ''What is there for us?''

This question was posed by Linda Nochlin at the 1969 meeting of the College Art Association when she made her point with a witty juxtaposition of a French dirty picture postcard and her own contemporary version of this same theme, manufactured for her presentation, showing a reversal.[29] Her nude, hirsute young man with his black garters, high-heeled loafers, and penis resting on a tray of bananas bore the caption ''Buy some bananas?'' The message was clear. While the audience of usually staid art historians roared with laughter, Nochlin made the point that there were simply no real equivalents for "Achetez des pommes?" for the female sex. The reactions of those same art historians were not nearly so cordial nearly a decade later when Alessandra Comini addressed them on sexism in art history at the New Orleans meeting.[30] Using Larry Rivers's phallic measures, which asserted that *America's Number One Problem* was size, Comini pointed out that 49 percent of the population had made it the other 51 percent's problem too.

While male artists can be trusted to deal with the penis, the same cannot be said of female artists. The censorship afforded the works of Eunice Golden, Joan Semmel, Judith Bernstein, and Sylvia Sleigh serves to underline the double standard when it comes to patriarchal morals and the sexual revolution. In his book *Eroticism in Western Art,* Edward Lucie-Smith opines in relation to the female *Odalisque:* "Totally submissive, she awaits the man who will possess her, and every line of the pose tells us that she will not resist him, whoever he is. Her body is not her own. And when we look at her face we see that it is anonymous, a beautiful blank."[31]

Turning to Sylvia Sleigh's nudes of Philip Golub and Paul Rosano, we see no "beautiful blanks." Instead, she paints individual portraits of what she considers young and beautiful male subjects. Unlike contemporary male artists such as Mel Remos, John Kacere, and Allen Jones, to mention only a few, Sleigh's emphasis is not only on the alert, self-possessed and sexy male, but on a concept of the beautiful as viable in art as well. She is respectful of her subjects' individuality and does not objectify them as mere things. What we have here is not a simple reversal of this art historical cliché but instead, perhaps for the first time, a contemporary female expression of erotic appreciation. Not surprisingly, given the newness of it all, these visions have been met by male and patriarchally conditioned female audiences with titters of self-conscious derision. The irate male audience is particularly sensitive to the change in position from vertical to horizontal, from superior to object. Ironically, this same moral male hierarchy sees the objectification of wombs, vaginas, and breasts by men as perfectly acceptable in works of art and worthy of inclusion in its national presses and prestigious institutions. It is indeed a paradox that these same art lovers are capable of censoring the work of women artists who have the unmitigated audacity to use male anatomy in a similar fashion.

Even more provocative from the standpoint of this new woman-centered perspective is the debate raging around Judy Chicago's *Dinner Party*.[32] Of all gynergenic art theory, that of Chicago's central imagery remains the most controversial. It is a concept which patriarchal thinkers insist on reading as merely genital, which may tell us something interesting about Freudian conditioning in a sexist society. Understanding, however, that the *Dinner Party* is an explicitly "hagiological" piece facilitates a more in-depth interpretation of it.[33] Obviously, its iconography is a radical vision which attempts to restore revolutionary women to their rightful place in our shared inheritance. One instance of this is

Sylvia Sleigh, *Philip Golub Reclining,* 1971
Oil on canvas, 42″ × 60″.
(Photo by Geoffrey Clements)

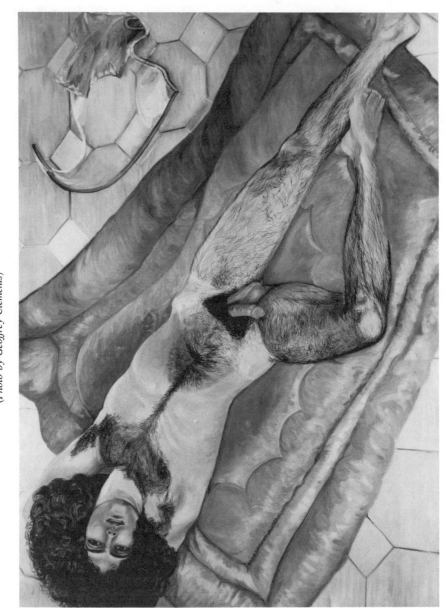

Sylvia Sleigh, *Paul Rosano Reclining*, 1974
Oil on canvas, 54″ × 78″.
(*Photo by Geoffrey Clements*)

Chicago's choice of Georgia O'Keeffe as a gynocentric being, as woman who says no to men and yes to herself, and as the living artist most responsible for giving birth to a language that provides a foundation for a female-centered art. It is unfortunate that Chicago's own concept of "femaleness" is so intellectually limited.[34] She sees the original female being as genital. To Chicago this being is one from whom all life emerged: "the primal vagina — her center dark and molten; all of her energy emanates from her bloody core. She is the sacred vessel, the gateway to existence and the doorway to the Abyss."[35] Once we accept her new gynocentric iconography, which many misogynist critics insist on ignoring or ridiculing, it is clear that Chicago's content and theme are explicitly and implicitly critical. In spite of the vulgarity of her concepts, comprehending this intention facilitates a fairer reading of her work. As a consequence, it is no longer shocking that Chicago's symbolic portrayal of O'Keeffe emphasizes her undeniable "femaleness." It is not simply a matter of vaginal imagery but instead may be read as a sign of femaleness, a metaphor for female experience and aspiration.[36] Tokenism is, in the guise of bourgeois liberalism, alive and flourishing in the land of the fathers. As a consequence, the *Dinner Party* is shown and written about. Chicago's is the most threatening sort of feminist vision, in spite of accusations against it of sexism and racism, because of its ability to project itself into society at large; the repercussions in male-dominated museums and presses have been predictable. Most significant from a political perspective is the fact that such an image cannot be transferred into a male metaphor or coopted by a sexist society. It is part of an emerging affirmation of a new gynergenic hagocracy.

A similar argument can be made in relation to maternity. Among the variety of ways this theme has been portrayed by artists, that of the "happy mother" is perhaps one of the most enduring images in traditional art history.[37] What such an image suggests to young women is that it is both natural and desirable for them to be mothers. When one examines this premise and its visual manifestation from a gynergenic critic's perspective, however, it takes on a somewhat different meaning.

Mary Cassatt has been soundly condemned by the male art establishment for her paintings of women and children. This has often been pointed out as a justification for evaluating her art as inferior to that of her male contemporaries. In point of fact, as Breeskin's painstaking research has revealed, Cassatt, much like her male contemporaries, painted her environment.[38] Given her social class, upbringing, and the expectations of her upper-class American parents, she provides yet another example of a woman artist who rebelled against the social codes and role assigned to her. Granted, Cassatt's economic status may have provided the independent wealth which facilitated her rebellion, but it was Mary herself who chose to become a painter against her father's wishes, to study and live abroad, and to exhibit with the independent Impressionists. Her work depicts upper-class mothers and children with extraordinary empathy. In these pictures she displays an individuality and a unique lack of the sappy sentimentality with which so many of her male counterparts have treated this same subject (i.e., Monet or Renoir). Astonishingly, until Breeskin insisted on the visual fact of Cassatt's point of departure, her work was either trivialized or forgotten altogether. Traditional art history insisted upon presenting her as a pupil of Degas, which she was not, and as a female artist limited by her unambitious subject matter. Her childlessness was pointed to by patriarchal explicators as the reason for her choice of theme. Implicit in this interpretation was the notion that she was compensating for not having fulfilled her "natural destiny" as wife and mother by painting a wished-for reality. This sort of implication, like the spectre of the lesbian, is meant to warn more "natural" women of following such examples. From a gynergenic point of view and in Mary Daly's language, she becomes a "Spins-ter" who serves as a role model for other young women artists.[39]

The German Expressionist Paula Modersohn-Becker is another case in point of a middle-class woman rebelling against the expectations of her parents and loved ones. Certainly an artist as talented, innovative and courageous as Modersohn-Becker deserves a place in any art history text; lamentably, she does not yet appear. Her visual statements about women's experiences, and particularly her sympathy for the toiling farm women in Worpswede (where she worked and lived), constitute a moving testimony not only to her stylistic innovations but to her social consciousness as well.[40] She presented one of the most striking portrayals of motherhood ever created in her *Reclining Mother and Child* of 1906. She seems to try and capture the impressions she jotted down in her diary of 1898: "And the woman was giving her life and her youth and strength to the child in all simplicity, without realizing that she was a heroic figure."[41] With a magisterial sense of monumental presence, this woman is at one with nature. The artist has given this age-old subject a new freshness and power. Unattractive and threatening as this symbol may have been to the polite bourgeoisie of the early twentieth century, it was nonetheless acceptable because it reinforced their conviction and Becker's that woman's natural role in the scheme of things is to procreate and nurture. It is only with the rise of the Nazi Socialists that her work became seen, along with many expressionistic and socially conscious artists, as decadent.

One of the most radicalized views of women and motherhood is presented by another German Expressionist, Käthe Kollwitz. The product of a socially and politically sophisticated middle-class family, she early turned to images of the working class. Going against her father's wishes, she decided to marry and move to Berlin where her husband Karl was to be employed as a Kassenartz (Health Insurance Doctor).[42] Her overriding concern during this decisive period was whether she could be married and still be the artist she wanted to be. In the last decades of the nineteenth century, Ludwig Pietsch, an establishment critic, included in his review Goethe's misogynistic phrase "when the road leads to an evil place, woman has a head start in the race."[43] In spite of such insulting criticism, the last years of the nineteenth century found her emphasis solidly on the urban working-class poor, especially the women. It should be noted that she found these people more beautiful and true than her own supposedly "better" class. A reflection of this conviction is noted in her journal: "Much later on, when I became acquainted with the difficulties and tragedies underlying proletarian life, when I met the women who came to my husband for help and so, incidentally, came to me, I was gripped by the full force of the proletarian's fate."[44] In her art she attempted to capture the "full force of the proletarian's fate" in industrial society, and nowhere with more impact than in her heroic mothers. In such stunningly powerful and moving works as *Das Opfer, Mütter, Sauglin an irh Gesicht drückend* (ca. 1925) and *and Die Mütter* (ca. 1919), Kollwitz pours out her outraged protective maternal instincts. Kollwitz's working-class mothers are not content to merely accept passively the rewards or lack of them that a patriarchal industrial society sees fit to give. Her toiling women cry out in desperation and rage, they rebel, are dangerous and strike back with surprising ferocity when their children are threatened. Need we "save our children" from Kollwitz's vision, asks the self-consciously aware gynocentric critic.

A different and less political response to motherhood is that of middle-class English sculptress Barbara Hepworth. Her sculpture is clearly a product of the revolutionary abstract art consciousness of the 1930s. The influences of the school of Paris are evident in her forceful geometrics, i.e., *Form* of 1936, or *Two Segments and Sphere* of 1935 (both reflective of her visit to Brancusi's studio in 1932–33).[45] Hepworth's perception of maternity, unlike that of her male contemporary Henry Moore, deals directly with her physiological and psychological awareness of it. Her vital abstracting images suggest an identification with a timeless idea, the relationship between mother and child, which she characterized as follows:

> So many ideas spring from an inside response to form; for example, if I see a woman carrying a child in her arms it is not so much what I see that affects me, but what I feel within my own body. There is an immediate transference of sensation, a response within to the rhythm of weight, balance and tension of large and small forms making an interior organic whole. The transmutation of experience is, therefore, organically controlled and contains new emphasis on forms. It may be that the sensation of being a woman presents yet another facet of the sculptural idea. In some respects it is a form of being rather than observing.[46]

Thus as a woman and an artist she perceives the crucial difference between man's experience of motherhood and woman's.

Lest we assume that all women artists react to maternity positively, let us turn to the work of the American surrealist painter Dorothea Tanning, whose identity in art has been subsumed by the fame accorded her German husband Max Ernst. *Maternity 1* (1946) gives an alarming vision of motherhood. Tanning shows a mother and infant dressed in identical clothing standing in a large yellow desert expanse, their bodies glued together. The mother's long white gown is torn in the abdominal area, a device often used by the artist to indicate ambivalence concerning sexual sensations and erotic emotions. Near the woman's feet and sharing the blanket on which she stands is a pekingese often identified with Max Ernst in her other work. This time, the dog is white and has the same face as the rosy-cheeked baby. We see an open door to the mother's left and another in the distance from which appears a biomorphic apparition constructed of tiny swollen sails. Despite the obvious power of Tanning's work, she, like the majority of surrealist women, has been ignored by the art historical establishment. Commenting on this, she said, "the place of women among Surrealists was no different from that which they occupied among the population in general."[47] On the basis of such analysis, we ought to question the claim of traditional art history to represent the whole of human culture. Indeed, even these women artists were all middle- or upper-class women, and therefore, privileged observers. Additionally, we need to be alert to the claims of feminist revisionists.

A careful examination of the "woman question" in the context of two traditional themes in art, eroticism and maternity, reveals the cultural imperialism of the discipline itself. Given the facts I have briefly outlined, the question still remains: "What is to be done?"

In an attempt to carry feminist theory into the realm of a working gynergenic critique of the discipline of art history, I have tried to give a fresh perspective in terms of meaningful interpretation. This has required making an active commitment to redefining my critical language in terms of a gynocentric perspective, one which does not continue to serve the purposes of patriarchal art history. In this context I should like to clarify a few points of difficulty inherent in formulating and practicing such a working gynergenic—rather than "feminist"—criticism. First, there is the difficulty of comprehending the larger sociopolitical, linguistic and economic dimensions of the problem. Second, one must consider finding a working definition for gynergenic criticism. Finally, one must deal with the implications of such a critique and what it tells us about culture and society. A gynergenic analysis may reveal not only the biases and inadequacies of traditional art history in regard to women artists, but may also suggest further critical questions which challenge not only the discipline but society as a whole.

In essence, all of the "feminist" artists and art historians I have chosen as examples are dealing with subject matter that is in some way threatening to established patriarchal ideas of what constitutes proper inquiry and conduct for women in our society. Doubtless, what is most disturbing to a sexist culture, in spite of the relatively limited nature of these attempts, is that they undermine the "ladylike" conduct expected of handmaidens of culture. Indeed, the fact that such women seem not to aspire to make art or art history that apes "masculine" tastes and values constitutes a primary danger. The vehement attacks on women-identified art and gynergenic criticism raise serious critical questions for us all. Such considerations as "is it art?" or "does it belong in a museum?" bring us to the more profound issues of who makes these decisions and on what grounds. Immediately, we are confronted with the sociopolitical nature of the established art system itself and its power when it comes to what is seen and read by the public. The entire nature of gynergenic activity requires a rethinking of our own relationship to old-style "feminism." What we need is not to meld into the established categories, but instead to construct alternatives to the disciplinary system which dominates patriarchal art consciousness. It is indeed difficult to do given the nature of art periodicals. Those among us willing to risk addressing such problems as "high art," "quality" and a host of others find that we are dealing with language as a tool of exclusion. The object of such definitions and values is to keep outsiders where they belong, safely on the marginal fringes of establishment culture, i.e., minority art. Thus a woman-centered perspective would appear to be a cutting edge of not only revisionist practice but revolutionary sociopolitical consciousness as well. A gynergenically oriented criticism facilitates a greater consciousness of basic inequities, not only in the art world, but in the "lived-in" world as well. What we are forced to recognize is that while ours is a shared and complimentary experience, sexists continue to ignore our part in it. Nor is it only men we have to fear; it is a simple fact of life that "feminists," too, discriminate. Our own inherent and conditioned biases prove that we are the products of our sex, class, and culture. The Chicago controversy is by no means an isolated incident of our own inherent conditioning.

In conclusion, while providing explanations for women's oppression in and out of art and art history we must also make an active commitment to strategies for change. We must be willing to pay the price that such challenges to patriarchal values currently demand. It is indeed difficult to make our language afresh when, for instance, the editor of a leading women's art magazine insists on retranslating one's new woman-centered language back into acceptable patriarchal syntax. The antagonism between old-fashioned "feminists" who merely wish to be accepted into a patriarchal establishment and thorough-going gynergenic revolutionaries who wish to provide radical alternatives constitutes the dynamic of a new dialectic. While it seems to me that there are compelling reasons to give that "other experience," the woman's experience, the same respect and representation that male modes of seeing have always received in our society, it also appears that there are equally compelling reasons for insisting on a gynergenic interpretation of these experiences. The crucial question is whether alternatives can be created if our own "feminist" journals provide no outlet for this new perspective. How then do gynergenic critics get their message across? Must they continue to compromise themselves merely to be heard while speaking the enemy's language?

Notes

1. Mary Garrard, "Status of Women in Ph.D. Granting Art Departments' Statistical Summaries," *CAA Newsletter* 6, 1 (April 1981): 7–9; Barbara Ehrlich White, "A 1974 Perspective: Why Women's Studies in Art and Art History?," *Art Journal* 36, 4 (Summer 1976): 240–44; Ann Sutherland Harris, "Women in College Departments and Museums," *Art Journal* 32, 4 (1973): 417–18; B.E. White and L.S. White, "Survey on the Status of Women in College Art Departments," *Art Journal* 32, 4 (Summer 1973): 420–22; Pat Hills, "Art History Text Books: Hidden Persuaders," *Artforum* 14 (June 1976): 58–61; Gloria Orenstein, "Art History," *Signs* 1, 2 (Winter 1975): 505–25.

2. A few resources which cover this crucial dialectic are: Susan Griffin's *Woman and Nature* (New York: Harper Colophon, 1980); Juliet Mitchel's *Women's Estate* (New York: Pantheon, 1971); Adrienne Rich's *A Wild Patience Has Taken Me This Far* (New York: W.W. Norton & Co., 1981); Lillian S. Robinson's *Sex, Class and Culture* (Bloomington and London: Indiana Univ. Press, 1977); and Dorothy L. Sayers's classic *Are Women Human?* (Michigan: William B. Eerdman's Pub. Co., 1971).

3. Elizabeth Fries Lummis Ellet, *Women Artists in All Ages and Countries* (New York: Harper & Co., 1859); Clara Erskine Clement, *Women in the Fine Arts* (Boston and New York: Houghton, Mifflin & Co., 1904); Walter Shaw Sparrow et al., *Women Painters of the World* (London: Hodder and Stoughton, 1905); Eleanor Tufts, *Our Hidden Heritage: Five Centuries of Women Artists* (New York and London: Paddington Press, Ltd., 1974); Karen Petersen and J.J. Wilson, *Women Artists: Recognition and Reappraisal* (New York: Harper and Row, 1976); Ann Sutherland Harris and Linda Nochlin, *Women Artists: 1550–1950* (New York: Knopf, 1976); Elsa Honig Fine, *Women and Art* (Montclair, New Jersey: Abner Schram, 1978); Germaine Greer, *The Obstacle Race: The Fortunes of Women Painters and Their Work* (New York: Farrar, Straus & Giroux, 1979); Eleanor Munro, *Originals: American Women Artists* (New York: Simon & Schuster, 1979).

4. Cassandra L. Langer, "Emerging Feminism and Art History," *Art Criticism* 1, 2 (Winter 1979/80): 66–83. I wish to thank the editors of *Art Criticism* for permission to reprint parts of my article concerning some of the literature cited above.

5. Ibid., p. 81. I am hardly alone in forming such notions. Writers such as Adrienne Rich, Susan Griffin, and Lillian Robinson, to mention only a few, are pursuing gynergenic approaches to intellectual inquiry. Of these writers the most provocative in formulating new language appears to me to be Mary Daly in her *Gyn/Ecology* (Boston: Beacon Press, 1978). Throughout this discourse I have used the Daly/Culpepper term (p. 12) "gynergy," which I have transformed for the purposes of this essay into "gynergenic," to characterize a working woman-centered critique. I have used this term as a replacement for "feminist" throughout the article, and I referred to a gynocentric perspective as one which actively seeks to critique any field from a woman-centered point of view.

6. Kate Chopin, *The Awakening,* ed. M. Culley (New York: W.W. Norton Co., 1976), p. 114.

7. Evelyn Reed, *Women's Evolution from Matriarchal Clan to Patriarchal Family* (New York: 1975), p. 53. My thanks to Sarah Slavin Schramm for directing me to this resource.

8. In note 1, I mentioned M. Garrard's CAA statistical comments. She makes the point that we have come a short way and are daily losing ground. This is especially evident in salaries, where "the 1979 National Research Council report revealed that the gap between male and female earnings in art history was greater than in any other humanistic discipline."

9. *The Chronicle of Higher Education* 23, 15 (December 1981)—Georgia's Dinnan Case. This is a perfect example of sexism hiding behind a cloak of academic freedom while doing an axe job on an uncontrollable woman's libber.

10. Christine Havice, WCA Newsletter (Spring 1981): 13, notes that Wayne Thiebaud "provided a startling reminder that we have not come a long way, baby. For, in a witty, low-key, and generally admirable discussion of art as an unsettling and revitalizing force in educational programs that are often lifeless or self-satisfied, he cited artists and works that provided stimulating examples of the range of human creativity and invention. And not one in the list of 20 to 25 artists from the Renaissance to the present was a woman! . . . [I]t remained to reflect in sad astonishment that it is still so easy and so acceptable to revert to the pre-feminist status quo." One might also reflect on the failure of "feminists" to really affect male consciousness after well over ten years of energetic effort. It may explain the emergence of gynocentric criticism.

11. Adrienne Rich, "Diving into the Wreck," *Diving into the Wreck* (New York: W.W. Norton, 1973), p. 24.

12. See note 3. Further references may be found in notes 2 and 5.

13. *Art Criticism,* p. 68. See note 4.

14. *Art Criticism,* pp. 69–70.

15. Susan Conrad, *Perish the Thought: Intellectual Women in Romantic America* (New York: Oxford, 1973), pp. 119–20.

16. One example would be Mrs. Ellet. See Sandra L. Langer, "Women Artists in All Ages and Countries: Reviewed," *Women's Art Journal* 1, 2 (1980/81): pp. 55–58. Another instance would be the case of Ann Sutherland Harris, educated at the Courtauld Institute of Art, University of London, B.A. (honors, first class), 1961, and Ph.D., 1965.

17. Bobbi Rothstein, "Book Review Digest," *Best Seller* 39, 35 (December 1979): 501.

18. Ibid., Linda Nochlin, Lucy Lippard. In all fairness to Nochlin, one must certainly cite her as a seminal figure in "feminist" theory in the arts, but nowhere in her prose does one find the emergence of a new language.

19. Robinson, *Sex, Class and Culture.* An excellent example of how one might practice a gynocentrically oriented criticism is her "Woman under Capitalism: The Renaissance Lady," pp. 150–77. This is one of the best examples I know of gynergenic methodology.

20. Discussions of these problems may be found in Mary Daly's *Gyn/Ecology,* Adrienne Rich's *A Wild Patience Has Taken Me This Far; On Lies, Secrets, and Silence; The Dream of a Common Language;* and *Twenty-One Love Poems,* and Susan Griffin's *Woman and Nature.*

21. Robinson, *Sex, Class and Culture,* pp. 3–21, "Dwelling in Decencies: Radical Criticism and the Feminist Perspective."

22. For further discussion of this highly complex problem, see Juliet Mitchel's *Women's Estate* and Robinson's *Sex, Class and Culture.*

23. Mitchel, pp. 85–86. Ellen Willis's impressions in Mitchel's book are revealing: "Take it off!" "Take her off the stage and fuck her!" or the instance from Paris, at Vincennes, the enclave of the May Revolutionaries: "Here were 'movement' men shouting insults at us: 'Lesbians,' 'Strip,' 'What you need is a good fuck. . . .'"

24. Jane Rule, *Outlander* (Florida: The Naiad Press, 1981), pp. 151–54, "Sexuality in Literature."

25. Adrienne Rich, *A Wild Patience Has Taken Me This Far*, p. 3.

26. Naomi Weisstein, " 'How can a little girl like you teach a great big class of men?' the Chairman Said, and Other Adventures of a Woman in Science," In *Working It Out*, ed. Sara Ruddick and Pamela Daniels (New York: Pantheon Books, 1977), p. 249.

27. Daly, *Gyn/Ecology*, pp. 20–21.

28. Carol Duncan, "Virility and Domination in Early 20th Century Vanguard Painting," *Artforum* (December 1973): 30–39; Duncan, "The Esthetic of Power in Modern Erotic Art," *Heresies* 1, 1 (January 1977): 46–50.

29. Nochlin's postcard featured a well-endowed young woman wearing a garter belt, pearls, and high-heeled boots. She presented a tray of apples upon which her full, rounded breasts were also displayed. The caption read "Buy some apples?"

30. Alessandra Comini, "Titles Can Be Troublesome: Misinterpretations in Male Art Criticism," *Art Criticism* 1, 2 (Winter 1979/80): 50–54.

31. Edward Lucie-Smith, *Eroticism in Western Art* (New York: Praeger, 1972), pp. 134–35.

32. Much as one does not wish to deal with the issue of class privilege and the results of conditioning, Judy Chicago's *Dinner Party* serves as a perfect example of why constant vigilance is required of "feminists." This is a case in point of party line ideology but delinquency when it comes to realities of sexism (viz. the volunteer status of women workers), racism (particularly as regards the Sojourner Truth plate), and classism in terms of historical choices which placed emphasis on middle- or upper-class women. Chicago's Cultural Imperialism serves notice on us all that we have a long way to go in throwing off our social conditioning and becoming sensitive to classes and races outside our own.

33. Daly, p. 29. A piece that traces the lives of female saints or revolutionaries.

34. Judy Chicago, *The Dinner Party* (New York: Anchor Press/Doubleday, 1979), p. 57. This is again a case of genitally oriented thinking when it comes to symbols which stand for women. Susan Griffin (p. 22) points out that males named all the species according to their sexual parts. It appears to me that Chicago's depictions are almost as limiting and vulgar as male personifications and identifications of women as "clits," "cunts," "holes" and "cracks." Is not Chicago simply following patriarchal tradition in using the vagina in depicting her heroines? Griffin, Daly, and Rich offer far more complex and thoughtful metaphoric images of women.

35. Ibid., pp. 95–97.

36. O'Keeffe herself has consistently denied genitally oriented readings of her works. These were apparently fostered by her husband and by the emergence of Freudian symbolism in the first decades of this century. It is indeed perplexing that "feminist" critics have not yet considered examining Ms. O'Keeffe's art in some other light given the artist's insistence that others are hanging meanings on her images which she herself never put there.

37. Carol Duncan, "Happy Mothers and Other Ideas in French Painting," *The Art Bulletin* (December 1973): 570–83.

38. Adelyn Breeskin, *Mary Cassatt: A Catalogue Raisonné of Oils, Pastels, Watercolors, and Drawings* (Washington, D.C.: Smithsonian Institution Press, 1979).

39. Daly, pp. 25–26.

40. *The Letters and Journals of Paula Modersohn-Becker*, trans. and annotated by J. D. Radyck (New Jersey and London: The Scarecrow Press, Inc.).

41. Gillian Perry, *Paula Modersohn-Becker* (New York: Harper & Row, 1979), p. 57.

42. Martha Kearns, *Kathe Köllwitz: Woman and Artist* (New York: The Feminist Press, 1976), pp. 55–60.

43. Ibid., p. 68.

44. Ibid., p. 107.

45. These illustrations may be found in Ronald Alley, *Barbara Hepworth—Tate Gallery, 3 April– 19 May 1968* (New York: Arno Press, 1968), p. 13.

46. Barbara Hepworth, *Carvings and Drawings* (London: Lund Humphries & Co., 1952), pp. 135–36.

47. Elsa Fine, *Women and Art,* p. 212. I am indebted to Fine's book for this description and quote.

Aesthetic and Feminist Theory:
Rethinking Women's Cinema

Teresa de Lauretis

When Silvia Bovenschen in 1976 posed the question "Is there a feminine aesthetic?" the only answer she could give was, yes and no: "Certainly there is, if one is talking about aesthetic awareness and modes of sensory perception. Certainly not, if one is talking about an unusual variant of artistic production or about a painstakingly constructed theory of art."[1] If this contradiction seems familiar to anyone even vaguely acquainted with the development of feminist thought over the past fifteen years, it is because it echoes a contradiction specific to, and perhaps even constitutive of, the women's movement itself: a two-fold pressure, a simultaneous pull in opposite directions, a tension toward the positivity of politics, or affirmative action in behalf of women as social subjects, on one front, and the negativity inherent in the radical critique of patriarchal, bourgeois culture on the other. It is also the contradiction of women in language, as we attempt to speak as subjects of discourses which negate or objectify us through their representations. As Bovenschen put it, "we are in a terrible bind. How do we speak? In what categories do we think? Is even logic a bit of virile trickery? . . . Are our desires and notions of happiness so far removed from cultural traditions and models?" (p. 119).

Not surprisingly, therefore, a similar contradiction was also central to the debate on women's cinema, its politics and its language, as it was articulated within Anglo-American film theory in the early 1970s in relation to feminist politics and the women's movement, on the one hand, and to artistic avant-garde practices and women's filmmaking, on the other. There, too, the accounts of feminist film culture produced in the mid-to-late seventies tended to emphasize a dichotomy between two concerns of the women's movement and two types of film work that seemed to be at odds with each other: one called for immediate documentation for purposes of political activism, consciousness-raising, self-expression, or the search for "positive images" of woman; the other insisted on rigorous, formal work on the medium—or better, the cinematic apparatus, understood as a social technology—in order to analyze and disengage the ideological codes embedded in representation.

Thus, as Bovenschen deplores the "opposition between feminist demands and artistic production" (p. 131), the tug of war in which women artists were caught between the movement's demands that women's art portray women's activities, document demonstrations, etc., and the formal demands of "artistic activity and its concrete work with material and media"; so does Laura Mulvey set out two successive moments of feminist film culture. First, she states, there was a period marked by the effort to change the *content* of cinematic representation (to present realistic images of women, to record women talking about their real-life experiences), a period "characterized by a mixture of consciousness-raising and propaganda."[2] This was followed by a second moment in which the concern with the language of representation as such became predominant, and the "fascination with the cinematic process" led filmmakers and critics to the "use of and interest in the aesthetic principles and terms of reference provided by the avant-garde tradition" (p. 7).

In this latter period, the common interest of both avant-garde cinema and feminism in the politics of images, or the political dimension of aesthetic expression, made them turn to the theoretical debates on language and imaging that were going on outside of cinema, in semiotics, psychoanalysis, critical theory, and the theory of ideology. Thus it was argued that, in order to counter the aesthetic of realism, which was hopelessly compromised with bourgeois ideology, as well as Hollywood cinema, avant-garde and feminist filmmakers must take an oppositional stance against narrative "illusionism" and in favor of formalism. The assumption was that "foregrounding the process itself, privileging the signifier, necessarily disrupts aesthetic unity and forces the spectator's attention on the means of production of meaning" (p. 7).

While Bovenschen and Mulvey would not relinquish the political commitment of the movement and the need to construct other representations of woman, the way in which they posed the question of expression (a "feminine aesthetic," a "new language of desire") was couched in the terms of a traditional notion of art, specifically the one propounded by modernist aesthetics. Bovenschen's insight that what is being expressed in the decoration of the household and the body, or in letters and other private forms of writing, is in fact women's aesthetic needs and impulses, is a crucial one. But the importance of that insight is undercut by the very terms that define it: the "*pre*-aesthetic realms."

After quoting a passage from Sylvia Plath's *The Bell Jar*, Bovenschen comments: "Here the ambivalence once again: on the one hand we see aesthetic activity deformed, atrophied, but on the other we find, even within this restricted scope, socially creative impulses which, however, have no outlet for aesthetic development, no opportunities for growth. . . . [These activities] remained bound to everyday life, feeble attempts to make this sphere more aesthetically pleasing. But the price for this was narrowmindedness. The object could never leave the realm in which it came into being, it remained tied to the household, it could never break loose and initiate communication'' (pp. 132–33). Just as Plath laments that Mrs. Willard's beautiful home-braided rug is not hung on the wall but put to the use for which it was made, and thus quickly spoiled of its beauty, so would Bovenschen have "the object" of artistic creation leave its context of production and use value in order to enter the "artistic realm" and so to "initiate communication"; that is to say, to enter the museum, the art gallery, the market. In other words, art is what is enjoyed publicly rather than privately, has an exchange value rather than a use value, and that value is conferred by socially established aesthetic canons.

Mulvey, too, in proposing the destruction of narrative and visual pleasure as the foremost objective of women's cinema, hails an established tradition, albeit a radical one: the historic left avant-garde tradition that goes back to Eisenstein and Vertov (if not Méliès) and through Brecht reaches its peak of influence in Godard, and on the other side of the Atlantic, the tradition of American avant-garde cinema. "The first blow against the monolithic accumulation of traditional film conventions (already undertaken by radical film-makers) is to free the look of the camera into its materiality in time and space and the look of the audience into dialectics, passionate detachment."[3] But much as Mulvey and other avant-garde filmmakers insisted that women's cinema ought to avoid a politics of emotions and seek to problematize the female spectator's identification with the on-screen image of woman, the response to her theoretical writings, like the reception of her films (co-directed with Peter Wollen), showed no consensus. Feminist critics, spectators, and filmmakers remained doubtful. For example, Ruby Rich: "According to Mulvey, the woman is not visible in the audience which is perceived as male; according to Johnston, the woman is not visible on the screen. . . . How does one formulate an understanding of a structure that insists on our absence even in the face of our presence? What is there in a film with which a woman viewer identifies? How can the contradictions be used as a critique? And how do all these factors influence what one makes as a woman filmmaker, or specifically as a feminist filmmaker?"[4]

The questions of identification, self-definition, the modes or the very possibility of envisaging oneself as subject—which the male avant-garde artists and theorists have also been asking, on their part, for almost one hundred years, even as they work to subvert the dominant representations or to challenge their hegemony—are fundamental questions for feminism. If identification is "not simply one physical mechanism among others, but the operation itself whereby the human subject is constituted," as Laplanche and Pontalis describe it, then it must be all the more important, theoretically and politically, for women who have never before represented ourselves as subjects, and whose images and subjectivities—until very recently, if at all—have not been ours to shape, to portray, or to create.[5]

There is indeed reason to question the theoretical paradigm of a subject-object dialectic, whether Hegelian or Lacanian, that subtends both the aesthetic and the scientific discourses of Western culture; for what that paradigm contains, what those discourses rest on, is the unacknowledged assumption of sexual difference: that the human subject, Man, is the male. As in the originary distinction of classical myth reaching us through the Platonic tradition, human creation and all that is human—mind, spirit, history, language, art, or symbolic capacity—is defined in contradistinction to formless chaos, *phusis* or nature, to something that is female, matrix and matter; and on this primary binary opposition, all the others are modeled. As Lea Melandri states,

> Idealism, the oppositions of mind to body, of rationality to matter, originate in a twofold concealment: of the woman's body and of labor power. Chronologically, however, even prior to the commodity and the labor power that has produced it, the matter which was negated in its concreteness and particularity, in its "relative plural form," is the woman's body. Woman enters history having already lost concreteness and singularity: she is the economic machine that reproduces the human species, and she is the Mother, an equivalent more universal than money, the most abstract measure ever invented by patriarchal ideology.[6]

That this proposition remains true when tested on the aesthetic of modernism or the major trends in avant-garde cinema from visionary to structural-materialist film, on the films of Stan Brakhage, Michael Snow, or Jean-Luc Godard, but is not true of the films of Yvonne Rainer, Valie Export, Chantal Akerman, or Marguerite Duras, for example; that it remains valid for the films of Fassbinder but not those of Ottinger, the films of Pasolini and Bertolucci but not Cavani's, and so on, suggests to me that it is perhaps time to shift the terms of the question altogether.

To ask of these women's films: what formal, stylistic, or thematic markers point to a female presence behind the camera?, and hence to generalize and universalize, to say: this is the look and sound of women's cinema, this is its language—finally only means complying, accepting a certain definition of art, cinema, and culture, and obligingly showing how women can and do "contribute," pay their tribute, to "society." Put another way, to ask whether there is a feminine or female aesthetic, or a specific language of women's cinema, is to remain caught in the master's house and there, as Audre Lorde's suggestive metaphor warns us, to legitimate the hidden agendas of a culture we badly need to change. "The master's tools will never dismantle the master's house"; cosmetic changes, she is telling us, won't be enough for the majority of women—women of color, black women, and white women as well; or in her own words, "assimilation within a solely western-european herstory if not acceptable."[7] It is time we listened. Which is not to say that we should dispense with rigorous analysis and experimentation on the formal processes of meaning production, including the production of narrative, visual pleasure, and subject positions, but rather that feminist theory should now engage precisely in the redefinition of aesthetic and formal knowledge, much as women's cinema has been engaged in the transformation of vision.

Take Akerman's *Jeanne Dielman* (1975), a film about the routine, daily activities of a Belgian middle-class and middle-aged housewife, and a film where the pre-aesthetic is already fully aesthetic. This is not so, however, because of the beauty of its images, the balanced composition of its frames, the absence of the reverse shot, or the perfectly calculated editing of its still-camera shots into a continuous, logical and obsessive narrative space; but because it is a woman's actions, gestures, body, and look that define the space of our vision, the temporality and rhythms of perception, the horizon of meaning available to the spectator. So that narrative suspense is not built on the expectation of a "significant event," a socially momentous act (which actually occurs, though unexpectedly and almost incidentally, one feels, toward the end of the film), but is produced by the tiny slips in Jeanne's routine, the small forgettings, the hesitations between real-time gestures as common and "insignificant" as peeling potatoes, washing dishes or making coffee—and then not drinking it. What the film constructs— formally and artfully, to be sure—is a picture of female experience, of duration, perception, events, relationships and silences, which feels immediately and unquestionably true. And in this sense the "pre-aesthetic" is *aesthetic* rather than *aestheticized,* as it is in films like Godard's *Two or Three Things I Know about Her,* Polanski's *Repulsion,* or Antonioni's *Eclipse.* To say the same thing in another way, Akerman's film addresses the spectator as female.

The effort, on the part of the filmmaker, to render a presence in the feeling of a gesture, to convey the sense of an experience that is subjective yet socially coded (and therefore recognizable), and to do so formally, working through her conceptual (one could say, theoretical) knowledge of film form, is averred by Chantal Akerman in an interview on the making of *Jeanne Dielman:*

> I *do* think it's a feminist film because I give space to things which were never, almost never, shown in that way, like the daily gestures of a woman. They are the lowest in the hierarchy of film images. . . . But more than the content, it's because of the style. If you choose to show a woman's gestures so precisely, it's because you love them. In some way you recognize those gestures that have always been denied and ignored. I think that the real problem with women's films usually has nothing to do with the content. It's that hardly any women really have confidence enough to carry through on their feelings. Instead the content is the most simple and obvious thing. They deal with that and forget to look for formal ways to express what they are and what they want, their own rhythms, their own way of looking at things. A lot of women have unconscious contempt for their feelings. But I don't think I do. I have enough confidence in myself. So that's the other reason why I think it's a feminist film—not just what it says but *what* is shown and *how* it's shown.[8]

This lucid statement of poetics resonates with my own response as a viewer and gives me something of an explanation as to why I recognize in those unusual film images, in those movements, those silences and those looks, the ways of an experience all but unrepresented, previously unseen in film, though lucidly and unmistakably apprehended here. And so the statement cannot be dismissed with commonplaces such as authorial intention or intentional fallacy. As another critic and spectator points out, there are "two logics" at work in this film, "two modes of the feminine": character and director, image and camera, remain distinct yet interacting and mutually interdependent positions. Call them femininity and feminism, the one is made representable by the critical work of the other; the one is kept at a distance, constructed, "framed," to be sure, and yet "respected," "loved," "given space" by the other.⁹ The two "logics" remain separate: "the camera look can't be construed as the view of any character. Its interest extends beyond the fiction. The camera presents itself, in its evenness and predictability, as equal to Jeanne's precision. Yet the camera continues its logic throughout; Jeanne's order is disrupted, and with the murder the text comes to its logical end since Jeanne then stops altogether. If Jeanne has, symbolically, destroyed the phallus, its order still remains visible all around her."¹⁰ Finally, then, the space constructed by the film is not only a textual or filmic space of vision, in frame and off—for an off-screen space is still inscribed in the images, although not sutured narratively by the reverse shot but effectively reaching toward the historical and social determinants which define Jeanne's life and place her in her frame. But beyond that, the film's space is also a critical space of analysis, a horizon of possible meanings which includes or extends to the spectator ("extends beyond the fiction") insofar as the spectator is led to occupy at once the two positions, to follow the two "logics," and to perceive them as equally and concurrently true.

In saying that a film whose visual and symbolic space is organized in this manner *addresses its spectator as a woman*, regardless of the gender of the viewers, I mean that the film defines all points of identification (with character, image, camera) as female, feminine, or feminist. However, this is not as simple or self-evident a notion as the established film-theoretical view of cinematic identification, namely, that identification with the look is masculine and identification with the image is feminine. It is not self-evident precisely because such a view—which indeed correctly explains the working of dominant cinema—is now accepted: that the camera (technology), the look (voyeurism), and the scopic drive itself partake of the phallic and thus somehow are entities or figures of a masculine nature.

How difficult it is to "prove" that a film addresses its spectator as female is brought home time and again in conversations or discussions between audiences and filmmakers. After a recent screening of *Redupers* in Milwaukee (January 1985), Helke Sander answered a question about the function of the Berlin wall in her film and concluded by saying, if I may paraphrase: "but of course the wall also represents another division that is specific to women." She did not elaborate but, again, I felt that what she meant was clear and unmistakable. And so does at least one other critic and spectator, Kaja Silverman, who sees the wall as a division other in kind from what the wall would divide—and can't, for things do "flow through the Berlin wall (TV and radio waves, germs, the writings of Christa Wolf)" and Edda's photographs show the two Berlins in "their quotidian similarities rather than their ideological divergences." "All three projects are motivated by the desire to tear down the wall, or at least to prevent it from functioning as the dividing line between two irreducible opposites. . . . *Redupers* makes the wall a signifier for psychic as well as ideological, political, and geographical boundaries. It functions there as a metaphor for sexual difference, for the subjective limits articulated by the existing symbolic order both in East and West. The wall thus designates the discursive boundaries which separate residents not only of the same country and language, but of the same partitioned space."[11] Those of us who share Silverman's perception must wonder whether in fact the sense of that other, specific division represented by the wall in *Redupers* (sexual difference, a discursive boundary, a subjective limit) is in the film or in our viewers' eyes.

Is it actually there on screen, in the film, inscribed in its slow montage of long takes and in the stillness of the images in their silent frames; or is it rather in our perception, our insight, as—precisely—a subjective limit and discursive boundary (gender), a horizon of meaning (feminism) which is projected into the images, onto the screen, around the text? I think it is this other kind of division that is acknowledged in Christa Wolf's figure of "the divided heaven," for example, or in Virginia Woolf's "room of one's own": the feeling of an internal distance, a contradiction, a space of silence, which is there alongside the imaginary pull of cultural and ideological representations without denying or obliterating them. Women artists, filmmakers, and writers acknowledge this division or difference by attempting to express it in their works. Spectators and readers think we find it in those texts. Nevertheless, even today, most of us would still agree with Silvia Bovenschen.

"For the time being," writes Gertrud Koch, "the issue remains whether films by women actually succeed in subverting this basic model of the camera's construction of the gaze, whether the female look through the camera at the world, at men, women and objects will be an essentially different one."[12] Posed in these terms, however, the issue will remain fundamentally a rhetorical question. I have suggested that the emphasis must be shifted away from the artist behind the camera, the gaze or the text as origin and determination of meaning, toward the wider public sphere of cinema as a social technology: we must develop our understanding of cinema's implication in other modes of cultural representation, and its possibilities of both production and counterproduction of social vision. I further suggest that, even as filmmakers are confronting the problems of transforming vision by engaging all of the codes of cinema, specific and nonspecific, against the dominance of that "basic model," our task as theorists is to articulate the conditions and forms of vision for another social subject, and so to venture into the highly risky business of redefining aesthetic and formal knowledge.

Such a project evidently entails reconsidering and reassessing the early feminist formulations or, as Sheila Rowbotham summed it up, "look[ing] back at ourselves through our own cultural creations, our actions, our ideas, our pamphlets, our organization, our history, our theory."[13] And if we now can add "our films," perhaps the time has come to rethink women's cinema as the production of a feminist social vision. As a form of political critique or critical politics, and through the specific consciousness that women have developed to analyze the subject's relations to sociohistorical reality, feminism has not only invented new strategies or created new texts, but more importantly it has conceived a new social subject, women: as speakers, writers, readers, spectators, users, and makers of cultural forms, shapers of cultural processes. The project of women's cinema, therefore, is no longer that of destroying or disrupting man-centered vision by representing its blind spots, its gaps, or its repressions. The effort and challenge now are how to effect another vision: to construct other objects and subjects of vision, and to formulate the conditions of representability of another social subject. For the time being, then, feminist work in film seems necessarily focused on those subjective limits and discursive boundaries that mark women's division as gender-specific, a division more elusive, complex, and contradictory than can be conveyed in the notion of sexual difference as it is currently used.

The idea that *a film may address the spectator as female,* rather than portray women positively or negatively, seems very important to me in the critical endeavor to characterize women's cinema as a cinema for, not only by, women. It is an idea not found in the critical writings I mentioned earlier, which are focused on the film, the object, the text. But rereading those essays today, one can see, and it is important to stress it, that the question of a filmic language or a feminine aesthetic has been articulated from the beginning in relation to the women's movement: "the new grows only out of the work of confrontation" (Mulvey, p. 4); women's "imagination constitutes the movement itself" (Bovenschen, p. 136); and in Claire Johnston's nonformalist view of women's cinema as counter-cinema, a feminist political strategy should reclaim, rather than shun, the use of film as a form of mass culture: "In order to counter our objectification in the cinema, our collective fantasies must be released: women's cinema must embody the working through of desire: such an objective demands the use of the entertainment film."[14]

Since the first women's film festivals in 1972 (New York, Edinburgh) and the first journal of feminist film criticism (*Women and Film,* published in Berkeley from 1972 to 1975), the question of women's expression has been one of both self-expression and communication with other women, a question at once of the creation/invention of new images and of the creation/imaging of new forms of community. If we rethink the problem of a specificity of women's cinema and aesthetic forms in this manner, in terms of address—who is making films for whom, who is looking and speaking, how, where, and to whom—then what has been seen as a rift, a division, an ideological split within feminist film culture between theory and practice, or between formalism and activism, may appear to be the very strength, the drive, and productive heterogeneity of feminism. In their introduction to the recent collection, *Re-Vision: Essays in Feminist Film Criticism,* Mary Ann Doane, Patricia Mellencamp, and Linda Williams point out:

> If feminist work on film has grown increasingly theoretical, less oriented towards political action, this does not necessarily mean that theory itself is counter-productive to the cause of feminism, nor that the institutional form of the debates within feminism have simply reproduced a male model of academic competition. . . . Feminists sharing similar concerns collaborate in joint authorship and editorships, cooperative filmmaking and distribution arrangements. Thus, many of the political aspirations of the women's movement form an integral part of the very structure of feminist work in and on film."[15]

The "re-vision" of their title, borrowed from Adrienne Rich ("Re-vision—the act of looking back, of seeing with fresh eyes," writes Rich, is for women "an act of survival" [p. 6]), refers to the project of reclaiming vision, of "seeing difference differently," of displacing the critical emphasis from "images of" women "to the axis of vision itself—to the modes of organizing vision and hearing which result in the production of that 'image'."[16] I agree with the *Re-Vision* editors when they say that over the past decade feminist theory has moved "from an analysis of difference as oppressive to a delineation and specification of difference as liberating, as offering the only possibility of radical change" (p. 12). But I believe that radical change requires that such specification not be limited to "sexual difference," that is to say, a difference of women from men, female from male, or Woman from Man. Radical change requires a delineation and a better understanding of the difference of women from Woman, and that is to say as well, *the differences among women.* For there are, after all, different histories of women. There are women who masquerade and women who wear the veil; women invisible to men, in their society, but also women who are invisible to other women, in our society.[17]

The invisibility of black women in white women's films, for instance, or of lesbianism in mainstream feminist criticism, is what Lizzie Borden's *Born in Flames* (1983) most forcefully represents, while at the same time constructing the terms of their visibility as subjects and objects of vision. Set in a hypothetical near-future time and in a place very much like lower Manhattan, with the look of a documentary (after Chris Marker) and the feel of contemporary science fiction writing (the post-new-wave s-f of Samuel Delany, Joanna Russ, Alice Sheldon, or Thomas Disch), *Born in Flames* shows how a "successful" social democratic cultural revolution, now into its tenth year, slowly but surely reverts to the old patterns of male dominance, politics as usual, and the traditional Left disregard for "women's issues." It is around this specific gender oppression, in its various forms, that several groups of women (black women, Latinas,

lesbians, single mothers, intellectuals, political activists, spiritual and punk per-
formers, and a Women's Army) succeed in mobilizing and joining together: not
by ignoring but, paradoxically, by acknowledging their differences.

Like *Redupers* and *Jeanne Dielman,* Borden's film addresses the spectator
as female, but it does not do so by portraying an experience which feels immediately one's own. On the contrary, its barely coherent narrative, its quick-paced
shots and sound montage, the counterpoint of image and word, the diversity of
voices and languages, and the self-conscious science-fictional frame of the story
hold the spectator across a distance, projecting toward her its fiction like a bridge
of difference. In short, what *Born in Flames* does for me, woman spectator, is
exactly to allow me "to see difference differently," to look at women with eyes
I've never had before and yet my own; for, as it remarks the emphasis (the words
are Audre Lorde's) on the "interdependency of different strengths" in feminism,
the film also inscribes the differences among women as *differences within women.*

Born in Flames addresses me as a woman and a feminist living in a particular moment of women's history, the United States today. The film's events and
images take place in what science fiction calls a parallel universe, a time and
a place elsewhere that look and feel like here and now, yet are not, just as I (and
all women) live in a culture that is and is not our own. In that unlikely, but not
impossible universe of the film's fiction, the women come together in the very
struggle that divides and differentiates them. Thus what it portrays for me, what
elicits my identification with the film and gives me, spectator, a place in it, is
the contradiction of my own history and the personal/political difference within
myself.

"The relationship between history and so-called subjective processes," says
Helen Fehervary in a recent discussion of women's film in Germany, "is not
a matter of grasping the truth in history as some objective entity, but in finding
the truth of the experience. Evidently, this kind of experiential immediacy has
to do with women's own history and self-consciousness."[18] That, how, and why
our histories and our consciousness are different, divided, even conflicting, is
what women's cinema can analyze, articulate, reformulate. And, in so doing,
it can help us create something else to be, as Toni Morrison says of her two
heroines: "Because each had discovered years before that they were neither white
nor male, and that all freedom and triumph was forbidden to them, they had set
about creating something else to be."[19]

In the following pages I will refer often to *Born in Flames,* discussing some
of the issues it has raised, but it will not be with the aim of a textual analysis.
Rather I will take it as the starting point, as indeed it was for me, of a series
of reflections on the topic of this essay.

Again it is a film, and a filmmaker's project, that bring home to me with greater
clarity the question of difference, this time in relation to factors other than gender,
notably race and class—a question endlessly debated within Marxist feminism

and recently rearticulated by women of color in feminist presses and publications. That this question should reemerge urgently and irrevocably now, is not surprising, at a time when severe social regression and economic pressures (the so-called feminization of poverty) belie the self-complacency of a liberal feminism enjoying its modest allotment of institutional legitimation. A sign of the times, the recent crop of commercial, man-made "woman's films" (*Lianna, Personal Best, Silkwood, Frances, Places in the Heart,* etc.) is undoubtedly "authorized," and made financially viable, by that legitimation. But the success, however modest, of this liberal feminism has been bought at the price of reducing the contradictory complexity—and the theoretical productivity—of concepts such as sexual difference, the personal is political, and feminism itself to simpler and more acceptable ideas already existing in the dominant culture. Thus, to many today, "sexual difference" is hardly more than sex (biology) or gender (in the simplest sense of female socialization) or the basis for certain private "life styles" (homosexual and other nonorthodox relationships); "the personal is political" all too often translates into "the personal instead of the political"; and "feminism" is unhesitantly appropriated, by the academy as well as the media, as a discourse—a variety of social criticism, a method of aesthetic or literary analysis among others, and more or less worth attention according to the degree of its market appeal to students, readers, or viewers. And, yes, a discourse perfectly accessible to all men of good will. In this context, issues of race or class must continue to be thought of as mainly sociological or economic, and hence parallel to but not dependent on gender, implicated with but not determining of subjectivity, and of little relevance to this "feminist discourse" which, as such, would have no competence in the matter but only, and at best, a humane or "progressive" concern with the disadvantaged.

The relevance of feminism (without quotation marks) to race and class, however, is very explicitly stated by those women of color, black, and white who are not the recipients but rather the "targets" of equal opportunity, who are outside or not fooled by liberal "feminism," or who understand that feminism is nothing if it is not at once political and personal, with all the contradictions and difficulties that entails. To such feminists it is clear that the social construction of gender, subjectivity, and the relations of representation to experience, do occur within race and class as much as they occur in language and culture, often indeed across languages, cultures, and sociocultural apparati. Thus not only is it the case that the notion of gender, or "sexual difference," cannot be simply accommodated into the preexisting, ungendered (or male-gendered) categories by which the official discourses on race and class have been elaborated; but it is equally the case that the issues of race and class cannot be simply subsumed under some larger category labelled femaleness, femininity, womanhood or, in the final instance, Woman. What is becoming more and more clear, instead, is that all the categories of our social science stand to be reformulated *starting from* the notion of gendered social subjects. And something of this process of reformulation—revision, rewriting, rereading, rethinking, "looking back at *ourselves*"—is what I see inscribed in the texts of women's cinema but not yet sufficiently focused in feminist film theory or feminist critical practice in general. This point, like the relation of feminist writing to the women's movement, demands a much lengthier discussion than can be undertaken here. I can do no more than sketch the problem as it strikes me with unusual intensity in the reception of Lizzie Borden's film and my own response to it.

What *Born in Flames* succeeds in representing is this feminist understanding: that the female subject is engendered, constructed and defined in gender across multiple representations of class, race, language, and social relations; and that, therefore, differences among women are differences *within* women, which is why feminism can exist despite those differences and, as we are just beginning to understand, can only continue to exist because of them. The originality of this film's project is its representation of woman as a social subject and a site of differences; differences which are not purely sexual or merely racial, economic, or (sub)cultural, but all of these together and often enough in conflict with one another. What one takes away after seeing this film is the image of a heterogeneity in the female social subject, the sense of a distance from dominant cultural models and of an internal division within women that remain, not in spite of but concurrently with the provisional unity of any concerted political action. Just as the film's narrative remains unresolved, fragmented, and difficult to follow, heterogeneity and difference within women remain in our memory as the film's narrative image, its work of representing, which cannot be collapsed into a fixed identity, a sameness of all women as Woman, or a representation of Feminism as a coherent and available image.

Other films, in addition to the ones already mentioned, have effectively represented that internal division or distance from language, culture, and self that I see recur, figuratively and thematically, in recent women's cinema (it is also represented, for example, in Gabriella Rosaleva's *Processo a Caterina Ross* and in Lynne Tillman and Sheila McLaughlin's *Committed*). But *Born in Flames* projects that division on a larger social and cultural scale, taking up nearly all of the issues and putting them all at stake. As we read on the side of the (stolen) U-Haul trucks which carry the free women's new mobile radio transmitter, reborn as Phoenix-Regazza (girl phoenix) from the flames that destroyed the two separate stations, the film is "an adventure in moving." As one reviewer saw it, "An action pic, a sci-fi fantasy, a political thriller, a collage film, a snatch of the underground: *Born in Flames* is all and none of these. . . . Edited in 15-second bursts and spiked with yards of flickering video transfers . . . *Born in Flames* stands head and shoulders above such Hollywood reflections on the media as *Absence of Malice, Network,* or *Under Fire*. This is less a matter of its substance (the plot centers on the suspicious prison 'suicide,' à la Ulrike Meinhoff, of Women's Army leader Adelaide Norris) than of its form, seizing on a dozen facets of our daily media surroundings."[20] The words of the last sentence, echoing Akerman's emphasis on form rather than content, are in turn echoed by Borden in several printed statements.

She, too, is keenly concerned with her own relation as filmmaker to filmic representation ("Two things I was committed to with the film were questioning the nature of narrative . . . and creating a process whereby I could release myself from my own bondage in terms of class and race").[21] And she, too, like Akerman, is confident that vision can be transformed because hers has been: "whatever discomfort I might have felt as a white filmmaker working with black women has been over for so long. It was exorcized by the process of making the film." Thus, in response to the interviewer's (Anne Friedberg) suggestion that the film is "progressive" precisely because it "demands a certain discomfort for the audience, and forces the viewer to confront his or her own political position(s) (or lack of political position)," Borden flatly rejects the interviewer's implicit assumption: "I don't think the audience is solely a white middle-class audience. What was important for me was creating a film in which that was *not* the only audience. The problem with much of the critical material on the film is that it assumes a white middle-class reading public for articles written about a film that they assume has only a white middle-class audience. I'm very confused about the discomfort that reviewers feel. What I was trying to do (and using humor as a way to try to do it) was to have various positions in which everyone had a place on some level. Every woman—with men it is a whole different question—would have some level of identification with a position within the film. Some reviewers over-identified with something as a privileged position. Basically, none of the positioning of black characters was *against* any of the white viewers but more of an invitation: come and work with us. Instead of telling the viewer that he or she could *not* belong, the viewer was supposed to be a repository for all these different points of view and all these different styles of rhetoric. Hopefully, one would be able to identify with one position but be able to evaluate all of the various positions presented in the film. Basically, I feel this discomfort only from people who are deeply resistant to it."[22]

This response is one that, to my mind, sharply outlines a shift in women's cinema from a modernist or avant-garde aesthetic of subversion to an emerging set of questions about filmic representation to which the term "aesthetic" may or may not apply, depending on one's definition of art, one's definition of cinema, and the relationship between the two. Similarly, whether or not the terms "postmodern" or "postmodernist aesthetic" would be preferable or more applicable in this context, as Craig Owens has suggested of the work of other women artists, is too large a topic to be discussed here.[23] At any rate, as I see it, there has been a shift in women's cinema from an aesthetic centered on the text and *its* effects on the viewing or reading subject—whose certain, if imaginary, self-coherence is to be fractured by the text's own disruption of linguistic, visual and/or narrative coherence—to what may be called an aesthetic of reception, where the spectator is the film's primary concern—primary in the sense that it is there from the beginning, inscribed in the filmmaker's project and even in the very making of the film.[24] An explicit concern with the audience is of course not new in either art or cinema, since Pirandello and Brecht in the former, and always conspicuously present in Hollywood and TV. What is new here, however, is the particular conception of the audience, which now is envisaged in its heterogeneity and otherness from the text.

That the audience is conceived as a heterogeneous community is made apparent, in Borden's film, by its unusual handling of the function of address. The use of music and beat in conjunction with spoken language, from rap singing to a variety of subcultural lingos and nonstandard speech, serves less the purposes of documentation or cinema vérité than those of what in another context might be called characterization: they are there to provide a means of identification of and with the characters, though not the kind of psychological identification usually accorded to main characters or privileged "protagonists." "I wanted to make a film that different audiences could relate to on different levels—if they wanted to ignore the language they could," Borden told another interviewer, "but not to make a film that was antilanguage."[25] The importance of "language" and its constitutive presence in both the public and the private spheres is underscored by the multiplicity of discourses and communication technologies—visual, verbal, and aural—foregrounded in the form as well as the content of the film. If the wall of official speech, the omnipresent systems of public address, and the very strategy of the women's takeover of a television station assert the fundamental link of communication and power, the film also insists on representing the other, unofficial social discourses, their heterogeneity, and *their* constitutive effects vis-à-vis the social subject.

In this respect, I would argue, both the characters and the spectators of Borden's film are positioned in relation to social discourses and representations (of class, race, and gender) within particular "subjective limits and discursive boundaries" that are analogous, in their own historical specificity, to those which Silverman saw symbolized by the Berlin wall in *Redupers*. For the spectators, too, are limited in their vision and understanding, bound by their own social and sexual positioning, as their "discomfort" or diverse responses suggest. Borden's avowed intent to make the spectator a locus ("a repository") of different points of view and discursive configurations ("these different styles of rhetoric") suggests to me that the concept of a heterogeneity of the audience also entails a heterogeneity of, or in, the individual spectator.

If, as claimed by recent theories of textuality, the Reader or the Spectator is implied in the text as an effect of its strategy—either as the figure of a unity or coherence of meaning which is constructed by the text ("the text of pleasure"), or as the figure of the division, dissemination, incoherence inscribed in the "text of jouissance"—then the spectator of *Born in Flames* is somewhere else, resistant to the text and other from it. This film's spectator is not only *not* sutured into a "classic" text by narrative and psychological identification; nor is it bound in the time of repetition, "at the limit of any fixed subjectivity, materially inconstant, dispersed in process," as Stephen Heath aptly describes the spectator intended by avant-garde (structural-materialist) film.[26] What happens is, this film's spectator is finally not liable to capture by the text. Yet one is engaged by the film's powerful erotic charge, one responds to the erotic investment that its female characters have in each other, and the filmmaker in them, with something that is neither pleasure nor jouissance, oedipal or pre-oedipal, as the terms have been defined for us, but with something that is again (as in *Jeanne Dielman*) a recognition, unmistakable and unprecedented. Again the textual space extends to the spectator, in its erotic and critical dimensions, addressing, speaking-to, making room, but not (how very unusual and remarkable) cajoling, soliciting, seducing. These films do not put me in the place of the female spectator, do not assign me a role, a self-image, a positionality in language or desire. Instead, they make a place for what I will call me, knowing that I don't know it, and give "me" space to try to know, to see, to understand. Put another way, by addressing me as *a* woman, they do not bind me or appoint me as Woman.

The "discomfort" of Borden's reviewers might be located exactly in this dis-appointment of spectator and text: the disappointment of not finding oneself, not finding oneself "interpellated" or solicited by the film, whose images and discourses project back to the viewer a space of heterogeneity, differences and fragmented coherences that just do not add up to one individual viewer or one spectator-subject, bourgeois or otherwise. There is no one-to-one match between the film's discursive heterogeneity and the discursive boundaries of any one spectator. We are at once invited in and held at a distance, addressed intermittently and only insofar as we are able to occupy the position of addressee; for example when Honey, the Phoenix Radio disk jockey, addresses to the audience the words: "Black women, be ready. White women, get ready. Red women, stay ready, for this is our time and all must realize it."[27] Which individual member of the audience, male or female, can feel singly interpellated as spectator-subject or, in other words, unequivocally addressed?

There is a famous moment in film history, something of a parallel to this, which not coincidentally has been "discovered" by feminist film critics in a woman-made film about women, Dorothy Arzner's *Dance Girl, Dance:* it is the moment when Judy interrupts her stage performance and, facing the vaudeville audience, steps out of her role and speaks to them as a woman to a group of people. The novelty of this direct address, feminist critics have noted, is not only that it breaks the codes of theatrical illusion and voyeuristic pleasure, but that it demonstrates that no complicity, no shared discourse can be established between the woman performer (positioned as image, representation, object) and the male audience (positioned as the controlling gaze); no complicity, that is, outside the codes and rules of the performance. By breaking the codes, Arzner revealed the rules and the relations of power that constitute them and are in turn sustained by them. And sure enough, the vaudeville audience in her film showed great discomfort with Judy's speech.

I am suggesting that the discomfort with Honey's speech is also to do with codes of representation (of race and class as well as gender) and the rules and power relations that sustain them—rules which also prevent the establishing of a shared discourse, and hence the "dream" of a common language. How else could viewers see in this playful, exuberant, science-fictional film a blueprint for political action which, they claim, wouldn't work anyway? ("We've all been through this before. As a man I'm not threatened by this because we know that this doesn't work. This is infantile politics, these women are being macho like men used to be macho. . . .")[28] Why else would they see the film, in Friedberg's phrase, "as a *prescription* through fantasy"? Borden's opinion is that "people have not really been upset about class and race. . . . People are really upset that the women are gay. They feel it is separatist."[29] My own opinion is that people are upset with all three, class, race, and gender—lesbianism being precisely the demonstration that the concept of gender is founded across race and class on the structure which Adrienne Rich and Monique Wittig have called, respectively, "compulsory heterosexuality" and "the heterosexual contract."[30]

The film-theoretical notion of spectatorship has been developed largely in the attempt to answer the question posed insistently by feminist theorists and well summed up in the words of Ruby Rich already cited (above): "how does one formulate an understanding of a structure that insists on our absence even in the face of our presence?" In keeping with the early divergence of feminists over the politics of images, the notion of spectatorship was developed along two axes: one starting from the psychoanalytic theory of the subject and employing concepts such as primary and secondary, conscious and unconscious, imaginary and symbolic processes; the other starting from sexual difference and asking questions like, how does the female spectator see? with what does she identify? and so on. Arzner's infraction of the code in *Dance, Girl, Dance* was one of the first answers in this second line of questioning, which now appears to have been the most fruitful by far for women's cinema. *Born in Flames* seems to me to work out the most interesting answer to date.

For one thing, the film assumes that the female spectator may be black, white, red, middle-class, or not middle-class, and wants her to have a place within the film, some measure of identification—"identification with a position," Borden specifies. "With men [spectators] it is a whole different question," she adds, obviously without much interest in exploring it (though later suggesting that black male spectators responded to the film "because they don't see it as just about women. They see it as empowerment").[31] In sum, the spectator is addressed as female in gender and multiple or heterogeneous in race and class; which is to say, here too all points of identification are female or feminist, but rather than the "two logics" of character and filmmaker, like *Jeanne Dielman, Born in Flames* foregrounds their different discourses.

Secondly, as Friedberg puts it in one of her questions, the images of women in *Born in Flames* are "unaestheticized": "you never fetishize the body through masquerade. In fact the film seems consciously deaestheticized, which is what gives it its documentary quality."[32] Nevertheless, to some, those images of women appear to be extraordinarily beautiful. If this were to be the case for most of the film's female spectators, however socially positioned, we would be facing what amounts to a film-theoretical paradox, for in film theory the female body is construed precisely as fetish or masquerade.[33] Perhaps not unexpectedly, the filmmaker's response is amazingly consonant with Chantal Akerman's, though their films are visually quite different and the latter's is in fact received as an "aesthetic" work. Borden: "The important thing is to shoot female bodies in a way that they have never been shot before. . . . I chose women for the stance I liked. The stance is almost like the gestalt of a person."[34] And Akerman (cited above): "I give space to things which were never, almost never, shown in that way. . . . If you choose to show a woman's gestures so precisely, it's because you love them."

The point of this crossreferencing of two films that have little else in common beside the feminism of their makers is to remark the persistence of certain themes and formal questions about representation and difference which I *would* call aesthetic, and which are the historical product of feminism and the expression of feminist critical-theoretical thought. Like the works of the feminist filmmakers I have referred to, and many others too numerous to mention here, *Jeanne Dielman* and *Born in Flames* are engaged in the project of transforming vision by inventing the forms and processes of representation of a social subject, women, who until now has been all but unrepresentable; a project already set out (looking back, one is tempted to say, programmatically) in the title of Yvonne Rainer's *Film about a Woman Who* . . . (1974), which in a sense all of these films continue to reelaborate.

The gender-specific division of women in language, the distance from official culture, the urge to imagine new forms of community as well as to create new images ("creating something else to be"), and the consciousness of a "subjective factor" at the core of all kinds of work—domestic, industrial, artistic, critical, or political work—are some of the themes articulating the particular relations of subjectivity, meaning, and experience which engender the social subject as female. These themes, encapsulated in the phrase "the personal is political," have been formally explored in women's cinema in several ways: through the disjunction of image and voice, the reworking of narrative space, the elaboration of strategies of address that alter the forms and balances of traditional representation. From the inscription of subjective space and duration inside the frame (a space of repetitions, silences, and discontinuities in *Jeanne Dielman*) to the construction of other discursive social spaces (the heterogeneous but intersecting spaces of the women's "networks" in *Born in Flames*), women's cinema has undertaken a redefinition of both private and public space that may well answer the call for "a new language of desire" and may actually have met the demand for the "destruction of visual pleasure," if by that one alludes to the traditional, classical, and modernist canons of aesthetic representation.

So, once again, the contradiction of women in language and culture is manifested in a paradox: most of the terms by which we speak of the construction of the female social subject in cinematic representation bear in their visual form the prefix "de-" to signal the deconstruction or the destructuring, if not destruction, of the very thing to be represented. We speak of the deaestheticization of the female body, the desexualization of violence, the deoedipalization of narrative, and so forth. Rethinking women's cinema in this way, I may provisionally answer Bovenschen's question thus: there is a certain configuration of issues and formal problems that have been consistently articulated in what we call women's cinema. The way in which they have been expressed and developed, both artistically and critically, seems to point less to a "feminine aesthetic" than to a feminist *deaesthetic*. And if the word sounds awkward or inelegant to you. . . .

Notes

I am very grateful to Cheryl Kader for generously sharing with me her knowledge and insight from the conception through the writing of this essay, and to Mary Russo for her thoughtful critical suggestions.

1. Silvia Bovenschen, "Is There a Feminine Aesthetic?," trans. by Beth Weckmueller, *New German Critique* 10 (Winter 1977): 136. [Originally published in *Aesthetik und Kommunikation* 25 (September 1976).] Hereafter, references to this work will be cited in text.

2. Laura Mulvey, "Feminism, Film and the Avant-Garde," *Framework* 10 (Spring 1979): 6. Hereafter, references to this work will be cited in text. See also Christine Gledhill's account, "Recent Developments in Feminist Film Criticism," *Quarterly Review of Film Studies* 3, no. 4 (1978).

3. Laura Mulvey, "Visual Pleasure and Narrative Cinema," *Screen* 16, no. 3 (Autumn 1975): 18.

4. B. Ruby Rich, in "Women and Film: A Discussion of Feminist Aesthetics," *New German Critique* 13 (Winter 1978): 87.

5. J. Laplanche and J.-B. Pontalis, *The Language of Psycho-Analysis*, trans. by D. Nicholson-Smith (New York: W.W. Norton, 1973), p. 206.

6. Lea Melandri, *L'infamia originaria* (Milano: Edizioni L'Erba Voglio, 1977), p. 27; my translation. For a more fully developed discussion of semiotic theories of film and narrative, see Teresa de Lauretis, *Alice Doesn't: Feminism, Semiotics, Cinema* (Bloomington: Indiana University Press, 1984).

7. See Audre Lorde, "The Master's Tools Will Never Dismantle the Master's House" and "An Open Letter to Mary Daly," in *This Bridge Called My Back: Writings by Radical Women of Color*, ed. by Cherríe Moraga and Gloria Anzaldúa (New York: Kitchen Table Press, 1983), p. 96. Both essays are reprinted in Audre Lorde. *Sister Outsider: Essays and Speeches* (Trumansburg, N.Y.: The Crossing Press, 1984).

8. "Chantal Akerman on *Jeanne Dielman*," *Camera Obscura* 2 (1977): 118–19.

9. In the same interview, Akerman said: "I didn't have any doubts about any of the shots. I was very sure of where to put the camera and when and why. . . . I *let* her [the character] live her life in the middle of the frame. I didn't go in too close, but I was not *very* far away. I let her be in her space. It's not uncontrolled. But the camera was not voyeuristic in the commercial way because you always knew where I was. . . . It was the only way to shoot that film—to avoid cutting the woman into a hundred pieces, to avoid cutting the action in a hundred places, to look carefully and to be respectful. The framing was meant to respect the space, her, and her gestures within it" (Ibid., p. 119).

10. Janet Bergstrom, "*Jeanne Dielman, 23 Quai du Commerce, 1080 Bruxelles* by Chantal Akerman," *Camera Obscura* 2 (1977): 117. On the rigorous formal consistency of the film, see also Mary Jo Lakeland, "The Color of Jeanne Dielman," *Camera Obscura* 3–4 (1979): 216–18.

11. Kaja Silverman, "Helke Sander and the Will to Change," *Discourse* 6 (Fall 1983): 10.

12. Gertrud Koch, translated essay.

13. Sheila Rowbotham, *Woman's Consciousness, Man's World* (Harmondsworth: Penguin Books, 1973), p. 28.

14. Claire Johnston, "Women's Cinema as Counter-Cinema," in *Notes on Women's Cinema*, ed. by Claire Johnston (London: SEFT, 1974), p. 31. See also Gertrud Koch, "Was ist und wozu brauchen wir eine feministische Filmkritik," *frauen und film* 11 (1977).

15. Mary Ann Doane, Patricia Mellencamp, and Linda Williams, eds., *Re-Vision: Essays in Feminist Film Criticism* (Los Angeles: The American Film Institute, 1984), p. 4. Hereafter, references to this work will be cited in text.

16. Adrienne Rich, *On Lies, Secrets, and Silence* (New York: W.W. Norton, 1979), p. 35.

17. See Barbara Smith, "Toward a Black Feminist Criticism," in *All the Women Are White, All the Blacks Are Men, But Some of Us Are Brave: Black Women's Studies*, ed. by Gloria T. Hull, Patricia Bell Scott, and Barbara Smith (Old Westbury, N.Y.: The Feminist Press, 1982).

18. Helen Fehervary, Claudia Lenssen, and Judith Mayne, "From Hitler to Hepburn: A Discussion of Women's Film Production and Reception," *New German Critique* 24–25 (Fall/Winter 1981–82): 176.

19. Toni Morrison, *Sula* (New York: Bantam Books, 1975), p. 44.

20. Kathleen Hulser, "Les Guérillères," *Afterimage* 11, no. 6 (January 1984): 14.

21. Anne Friedberg, "An Interview with Filmmaker Lizzie Borden," *Women and Performance* 1, no. 2 (Winter 1984): 43. On the effort to understand one's relation as a feminist to racial and cultural differences, see Elly Bulkin, Minnie Bruce Pratt, and Barbara Smith, *Yours in Struggle: Three Feminist Perspectives on Anti-Semitism and Racism* (Brooklyn, N.Y.: Long Haul Press, 1984).

22. Interview in *Women and Performance*, p. 38.

23. Craig Owens, "The Discourse of Others: Feminists and Postmodernism," in *The Anti-Aesthetic: Essays in Postmodern Culture*, ed. Hal Foster (Port Townsend, Wash.: Bay Press, 1983), pp. 57–82. See also Andreas Huyssen, "Mapping the Postmodern," *New German Critique* 33 (Fall 1984): 5–52.

24. Borden's nonprofessional actors, as well as her characters, are very much part of the film's intended audience: "I didn't want the film caught in the white film ghetto. I did mailings. We

got women's lists, black women's lists, gay lists, lists that would bring different people to the Film Forum. . . .'' (Interview in *Women and Performance*, p. 43.)

25. Betsy Sussler, "Interview," *Bomb* 7 (1983): 29.

26. Stephen Heath, *Questions on Cinema* (Bloomington: Indiana University Press, 1981), p. 167.

27. The script of *Born in Flames* is published in *Heresies* 16 (1983): 12–16. Borden discusses how the script was developed in conjunction with the actors and according to their particular abilities and backgrounds in the interview in *Bomb*.

28. Interview in *Bomb*, p. 29.

29. Interview in *Women and Performance*, p. 39.

30. Adrienne Rich, "Compulsory Heterosexuality and Lesbian Existence," *Signs* 5, no. 4 (Summer 1980): 631–60; Monique Wittig, "The Straight Mind," *Feminist Issues* (Summer 1980): 103–11.

31. Interview in *Women and Performance*, p. 38.

32. Ibid., p. 44.

33. See Mary Ann Doane, "Film and the Masquerade: Theorising the Female Spectator," *Screen* 23, no. 3–4 (Sept./Oct. 1982): 74–87.

34. Interview in *Women and Performance*, pp. 44–45.

Towards a Feminist
Theory of Art Criticism

Joanna Frueh

Like Marxism and structuralism, which receive due attention, feminism has altered the content and constructs of art history over the past 15 years and continues to do so. However, many art historians, like their compatriots in other academic disciplines, view the adoption of a feminist perspective with suspicion. Simply put, detractors claim that feminist art historians and critics are narrow and self-indulgent and that they distort and polemically misread images and material, thereby undermining art history.

Actually, feminists serve both art and art history: by seeking knowledge about the overlooked meanings of art; by examining our own unacknowledged assumptions and biases and those of previous and contemporary art historians and critics; and by developing ways to write about art that will serve as new models for art critical discourse.

Art history and criticism are frequently divorced: you practice one or the other. Basically, the myth is that art historians aim for objectivity by gathering data that will prove the "truth" about various aspects of an artist's life and career or of a particular period's aesthetic mentality. By keeping their distance, art historians supposedly maintain intellectual neutrality.

Traditionally, art critics, whose function and pleasure is primarily writing about the art of their own time, also seek "truth." However, many of the best critics have been, and are, highly subjective. For Diderot, the first modern art critic, criticism was an empathetic occupation. In fact, he demanded passion from art so that he could feel it. In 1766 he wrote, "move me, surprise me, rend my heart; make me tremble, weep, shudder, outrage me; delight my eyes afterwards if you can."[1]

Traditional art historical methodology answers certain questions about art: Who made it? When? Where? How? Whys are often unsatisfactorily answered through stylistic analyses or investigations of iconography and patronage.

Whys also demand analyses and interpretations of social and conceptual contexts. Because it involves discernment, criticism is a more inclusive activity than historical study that focuses on the recording, analysis, and interpretation of events. Pursuing old questions in new ways, as feminism does, extends art historical methodology and makes connections between historical context and culture. Such a pursuit turns the historian into a critic.

Feminist art critics join the supposedly incompatible modes of art historical and art critical practice, wedding deep responsiveness to art with factual information, such as biography, sources of an individual artist's work, and stylistic connections with other artists and movements. Many traditionalists find such a marriage wanting in intellectual neutrality, but feminist historian/critics like Arlene Raven believe in intimacy with art. As Raven writes in the first sentence of an essay on Harmony Hammond, "I enter Harmony Hammond's works."[2] Raven is speaking of complete identification: being at one with the art, and through it, the creator, another woman. Thus, subject, Raven, and object, the art works and another human being, are not detached at all. The object no longer exists. In this kind of criticism, the term art object does not make sense, and a subject to subject relationship replaces the standard subject to object one.

Utter involvement without loss of self is the outcome of this new critic-to-art connection, which is discourse as intercourse: entry into another's body (of art). Feminist criticism of this order belongs to an art criticism of overtly personal engagement, which has waxed and waned in appeal during the past two centuries. After a period of disfavor, for most of the twentieth century, it is now on the upswing. In a 1979 issue of *Art in America,* Nancy Marmer wrote about "the . . . critic's openly subjective interpretation of art" and stated that "the expressive possibilities of a personalist prose have once again become highly attractive."[3]

Moreover, Marmer noted that "such criticism weaves the fabric of its content out of the critic's subjective, psychological response to the work—thus absorbing the artist into the critic's mental universe."[4] Feminist critics do this and more, for a penetrating study of art, being physical as well as mental, requires that the penetrator, as poet and thinker Robin Morgan has said in *The Anatomy of Freedom,* "feel with the brain and think through the body."[5] Penetration, then, should not be viewed as phallic, an insertion of self into other (subject into object). Rather, penetration may be understood in terms of mutuality, a diffusion of (my)self into (your)self into (my)self. In this way, the study of art becomes even more empathetic than it was for Diderot.

Although it has some exemplary practitioners, such as Carol Duncan, Lucy Lippard, Roszika Parker, Griselda Pollock, and Arlene Raven, feminist art criticism is woefully unevolved. Far more sophisticated than feminist theory and scholarship is feminist literary criticism. Consequently its development in the 1970s and methodology serve as useful models for an understanding of feminist art criticism.

Three "critical" stages exist in recent feminist literary criticism. The first has been a resurrection of lost or ignored women writers and works. Concurrently, feminists in art have been rediscovering women artists and works. H. W. Janson's classic survey text does not mention one woman artist. Therefore, scholars such as Eleanor Tufts, in *Our Hidden Heritage: Five Centuries of Women Artists,* and Linda Nochlin and Ann Sutherland Harris, in *Women Artists 1550–1950,* redress this omission. Also, through such a comparison as Artemisia Gentileschi's and Caravaggio's versions of Judith beheading Holofernes, in which a woman boldly treats the same subject as the man from whom her style of dramatic realism derives, feminist critics can prove that women, unlike what male-engendered myth would have us believe, are fertile and productive in other ways than simply as sexual creatures and mothers.

First-stage scholarship has been important, by showing that women are a part of art history and thereby providing women artists with a sense of belonging. Also, unlike traditional art history, which generally examines "major" monuments by venerated "masters," first-stage feminism shifts the focus of study to "minor" works by artists whose skill has not been deemed consummate. Dealing with "secondary" artists and objects fleshes out the skeletal "truth" of art history, encouraging us to create new bodies of knowledge. Such "bodybuilding" strengthens art history.

Despite the accomplishments of first-stage efforts, they are often reformist rather than truly re-visionist; for they exemplify scholars' interest in new subjects, but with a continuing employment of standard art historical tools. As Roszika Parker and Griselda Pollock write in *Old Mistresses,* the "determination to relocate women in art history on the discipline's own terms" is "subscrib[ing] to a slightly modified, but none the less conventional notion of art history; its system of values and criteria of significance . . . a radical reform, if not a total deconstruction of the present structure of the discipline is needed in order to arrive at a real understanding of the history of women and art."[6]

Second-stage critics have considered the possibility of a women's tradition either counter or related to the male literary tradition. They have examined a "female imagination," their counterparts in art a "female sensibility." When we think of Eva Hesse's and Sol LeWitt's minimalist sculptures, can we say that the pieces reveal the sex of their creators? Is Hesse more involved in a visceral response to materials, indicative of women's perhaps socialized awareness of their bodies, both inside and out? Is LeWitt more concerned with rationalizing the materials, ordering them in an evenly systematic fashion?

These questions and their implicit answers are simplistic. Nonetheless, in the mid-1970s female sensibility was a burning issue, and the following hypothesis, among others, was presented: women's art is obsessive and often characterized by central core imagery. But are Alfred Jensen's works any less obsessive than Joyce Kozloff's? Or are Barnett Newman's voids any less symbolic of a central core (a cunt, a womb) than many of Georgia O'Keeffe's flowers or Judy

Chicago's *Dinner Party* plate images?

Despite the superficiality of such hypotheses, they were significant attempts to think about the differences between female and male art. Perhaps Newman sees the central core as a void (as a gross generalization: for the male, the womb is empty, the vagina something to be filled), whereas O'Keeffe and Chicago see the central core as full (for the female, the inside of her body is complete in itself).

Second-stage questioning also revealed the class aspect of art world sexism in the distinction between high (men's) and low (women's) art. Crafts and decorative objects made by women were reconsidered as fine art, proving the absurdity of labeling Mondrian's or Rothko's paintings as high art and, say, a reductively composed and colored Amish quilt as low art, for all are examples of nonobjective design.

However, because the first two existed within the avant-garde, intellectualized framework of modernism and the quilt was created for use in the everyday world, the paintings could be praised for their denial of merely decorative (in other words, frivolous) effects and for their absolute aesthetic integrity. Indeed, it is their "immaculate" conception that assured their value to viewers and critics.

The exposure of classism also opened the way for women and men to make use of pattern and decoration in their art, and Miriam Schapiro's deliberate use of fabric and floral and geometric designs in many works of the late 1970s demonstrates a "low" art, "feminine" aesthetic transferred to a "high" art context; for Schapiro exhibits and is written about in the art world dominated by male-identified authority figures.

Third-stage feminism is more theoretical than the first two and centers on gender analysis of literature or art, and thereby the interconnections among text or object, historical context, and culture. Here, critics reassess the values placed on art in regard to content as well as function. What would previously have been viewed as just "feminine" sentimentality in, for example, the heart motif of some of Schapiro's "femmages," is reinterpreted in several ways: society has relegated women to the degraded sphere of emotion; feeling, however, is powerful and beautiful; sentiment, then, can expose the heart of the matter (of life), which is Love; and Love emerges from and leads to both intellectual and emotional exploration.

Third-stage critics also reappraise men's art, the gender implications of which have been either ignored or considered innocently intentioned because of the creator's supposed pure, serious, commitment to Art. Most art critics and historians, however, fail to discuss the power of images to inform and educate the viewer.

A feminist perspective does not replace traditional art historical methodology. Rather, the new complements and amplifies the old, for fresh analyses and interpretations of style and iconography show that art is not value-free and that previous scholarship has not taken this into consideration.

Feminist art criticism is significant and necessary because it challenges what feminist literary critic Annette Kolodny calls the "dog-eared myth of intellectual neutrality.''[7] Such neutrality presupposes the neuter status of the mind; as if gender imbalances did not exist in scholarship. For the most part, male-identified minds study art, and as feminist philosopher Mary Daly understands, the sexist products of such intellects affirm what she terms Methodolatry, which is the worship of method, the devotion and faith in ''the rite of right re-search.''[8]

I turn again to the model of feminist literary criticism, in Kolodny's article ''Dancing through the Minefield: Some Observations on the Theory, Practice and Politics of a Feminist Literary Criticism,'' for an argument against Methodolatry. Kolodny offers three pertinent propositions. (I have substituted art terms for literary ones): (1) Art history (and with that the historicity of art) is a fiction; (2) insofar as we are taught to see, what we engage are not objects but paradigms; and, finally, (3) that since the grounds upon which we assign aesthetic value to objects are never infallible, unchangeable, or universal, we must reexamine not only our aesthetics but as well, the inherent biases and assumptions informing the critical methods which (in part) shape our aesthetic responses.[9]

Kolodny is proposing what Adrienne Rich calls re-vision; and feminist art critics re-view and re-vise by looking at well-known works in fresh ways and seeing what art historical ''authority'' has taken for granted or made invisible. Even those mainstays of traditional art history—style, iconography, and patronage—can illuminate a work from a re-visionist perspective.

Embedded in Gustave Courbet's *The Source* (1868), for instance, is the deep-rooted notion that woman is nature. Both the subject—a naked woman at a spring—and the theme—woman as origin of life—are conventional, but Courbet's conflation of woman and nature is unusually deft. A fleshy woman sits by a stream. One hand holds onto a branch, seems almost molded to it, as if she herself were part of the tree; and her contours, from the buttocks up, are eaten by shadows, so that nature absorbs her flesh, is actually one with it. Her lower left leg and right foot are submerged, so that she and the water are also one; more so, because Courbet creates an equivalent sensuousness between her dimpled thighs and the rippling water. Woman and nature literally mirror one another for the material of the female body is the material world.

Not only does this equation cast woman as body, as opposed to man as mind, which, of course, is analogous to culture; but also, because Courbet is a master at making paint read as the texture of whatever it describes, landscape and woman reverberate with one another's physicality. Water feels like flesh, dense, smooth, heavy; and flesh feels like water—surely it would ''give'' with pressure. Courbet elaborates this bonding in various ways: the spring gushes from the dark vegetation much as the nude emerges from it; the water pours over her left hand, and light dapples skin and liquid; lush greenery reads as a metaphor for the lushness of the body.

All in all, woman symbolizes fecundity and lack of consciousness. But who is this nude? She is the single, anonymous woman who represents all women, not as a social group, but as Woman—Female of the Species in one aspect of the Eternal Feminine: Earth Mother/Mother Earth. This myth of Woman is not necessarily repugnant. However, it is only a fragment of reality, an ideology through which we should not expect to see what any individual woman genuinely is.

Courbet painted *Woman with White Stockings* (1861) for Khalil Bey, a wealthy one-time Ottoman ambassador in St. Petersburg, who settled in Paris. In the painting a seated young woman pulls a stocking over a bare foot balanced on an already stockinged, raised knee. The view, from below, angles up, making her genitals a focal point. Patronage indicates where aesthetic, economic, and political power lies, bluntly, who can "own" people and things. The artist owns the image as a creation, but the buyer owns the art as an object of aesthetic and/or monetary value and the image as an object of desire.

Most likely, Khalil Bey did not want the painting primarily because, as Jack Lindsay writes, "This is a masterpiece in its organization of form, making of the nude a compact unity without parallel."[10] According to Lindsay, Khalil Bey "kept it locked in a sort of tabernacle or cabinet."[11] An image of power resonates: Khalil Bey as purchaser of two "sacred" objects: the painting and the woman, who he "has" (to himself). She, of course, is woman, whose being is locked up in *her* tabernacle, the genitals. Lindsay disengages her from any selfness, for she is only "a brilliantly original piece of patterning, with the body a single solid mass, yet with the limbs clearly articulated in a rhythmic structure balanced on the slit of the genitals."[12] That slit! It is the pivotal point: not only of a composition, but also of the myth that Woman is a cunt and no more.

If feminism is about freedom, then feminist art criticism strives for the accomplishment of mental freedom. I use the word mental rather than intellectual because the latter is generally thought to be the power of rational thought as distinguished from the power to feel or to will, and the former relates to the total emotional and intellectual response of an individual to an environment.

Notions of intellect discount the possibility that knowledge can be gained through the body, the emotions, or wishes. Consequently, intellect, alone, confines the critic by denying not only the usefulness, but also the worth and relevance of his desire to use himself fully. Exclusive emphasis on intellect denies a critic's being, the fact that she lives: on many levels and in many modes, and in an aggregate of social and cultural conditions.

From Duchamp's *Bicycle Wheel* to Johns's *Painted Bronze (Beer Cans)* to Chicago's *Menstruation Bathroom,* modern and contemporary art have dealt with, to paraphrase Robert Rauschenberg, the gap between art and life. The interplay between the two, demanded by their disparity, involves the feminist critic as much as the artist. It is as a participant in this interplay that she can truly penetrate the art and it her, that she can know it as subject.

I imagined someone writing me a letter after reading a recently published article of mine. "Joanna, your ideas are interesting, and you state them with some passion, but why is the structure so tight, the style so dry? I'm familiar with your criticism, and I've seen it be personal and engaging. I would like more of you and less of the objective observer."

I reply.

Thanks. You caught me in an act of validation through conventional logic. Not long ago, some keepers of the art wor(l)d told me that my thinking was disorganized, my writing pointless. I was hurt and angry. I loved my vagrant mind; but I needed to prove that I could think in a "professional" mode.

I confess, I dislike the airtight cases that the scholar wants to build. They do not let me breathe. Most art history and criticism coming from a so-called feminist perspective are conventionally academic and uninspiring. Inspire derives from the Latin *inspirirare,* to breathe, which is akin to *spiritus,* breath, from which the English "spirit" comes. I've wondered, where's the spirited criticism I expect from feminists in art? Why haven't they incorporated (given body through language to) the work of women who have been joining feminist theory and practice in their writing?

One of the answers is that feminists in art, like feminists in other fields, want to be acceptable. Their choice of scholarly argument says so. "Prove it," demands the logocentric system that the art historian worships. "Prove that you still love me." As writer Marguerite Duras says, "There are many women who write as they think they should write—to imitate men and make a place for themselves in literature."[13] Or art criticism.

So some feminists become feminist thinker Mary Daly's Methodolaters, worshipping methodology, fearful of being wrong, of believing in false idols, or, more likely, of desiring no idols at all.

My imagined letter writer has accused me of what French feminist Chantal Chawaf calls "fleshless academicism."[14] However, I am an iconoclast, and, as novelist Monique Wittig writes in *The Lesbian Body,* "m/y heart is in m/y mouth."[15] So I will feel my way through this paper, as I give voice to a body inseparable from a mind. The pulse will be a chorus of possibilities, not a drone of proofs.

> The frightful masculine fashion of speaking always surprises me. Speaking in order to be right—how ridiculous! In fact, to put someone else in the wrong. Speaking to nail the listener's trap shut.
> Xavière Gauthier[16]

A fellow art historian advised me that revisionists in our field want to convince others of rightness. Daly's "rite of right re-search" came to mind: knowing is being right. I was not interested in this kind of persuasion, an intellectual erection.

An ideal structure for presenting knowledge resembles bricks cemented, row after row, higher and higher. We think this edifice (for edification) has a firm foundation, that it's built to last. Higher and higher, thrusting into the sky, Tower of Babel, ivory towers of babble.

Castles in the air, imagined by minds whose dreams have come true.

I know I am made from this earth, as my mother's hands were made from this earth, as her dreams came from this earth and all that I know, I know in this earth, the body of the bird, this pen, this paper, these hands, this tongue speaking, all that I know speaks to me through this earth. . . .

Susan Griffin[17]

Griffin uses a way of knowing that differs from my colleague who believes that to convince is to arm yourself with reason(s), so that you can win some battle. Knowing-as-defense is a weapon. For Griffin, however, knowing is being, and it exists on and in solid ground, the earth itself, which she equates with the body. Both are matter.

Art criticism, like other disciplines that privilege the intellect, is generally deprived of the spontaneous knowing of intuition—of knowledge derived from the senses and experience as well as the mind. Nerves connect throughout the body, conduct sensations, bits of knowledge to the brain. Blood pumping to and from the heart flows everywhere inside us. Knowing is being alive, wholly, not just intellectually. It is a recognition of human being, the intelligence of the body. The intellectual may feel enslaved in matter. If only she could escape from the body. But the mind will not fly unless we embrace the body as a path to freedom.

And we learn . . .
that our speech is unholy.

Susan Griffin[18]

"And the Word was made flesh, and dwelt among us. . . ."

God embodied his mind and will in Christ. The Father and Son are holy (words), the Son is a sacred body, of words, a sacred text.

What about mother and daughter? They remain cunts, idolized and idealized, yet unholy holes. The phallic tongue has penetrated the silent vault of the mouth, and many feminists have discussed the idea that women are linguistically colonized. There is no Mother Tongue, only the Word(s) of the Father.

As art critics, we have lost our tongues when we write jargon, words such as great, master, and genius that carry much weight but are simultaneously meaningless through overuse. They have become generic art words, interchangeable and indistinguishable from one another. The solution is not devising some means through which we can give the Word. Rather, a solution is to pass the word that the art gospel need not exist.

Once a woman owns her body, she will speak a different language. When the organ in her mouth belongs to her, we will know that all tongues, all words are flesh.

Isn't the final goal of writing to articulate the body? For me the sensual juxtaposition of words has one function: to liberate a living paste, to liberate matter. Language through writing has moved away from its original sources: the body and the earth. Too often GOD was written instead of LIFE.

Chantal Chawaf[19]

One of the GODS that has taken the LIFE out of writing is logocentrism. The point is not to set up a countersystem, say, somacentrism, but rather, to pursue the difficult task of inventing, in Hélène Cixous's words "another thinking as yet not thinkable."[20]

> Woman's desire most likely does not speak the same language as man's desire, and it probably has been covered over by the logic that has dominated the West since the Greeks. . . . In this logic, the prevalence of the gaze, discrimination of form, and individualization of form is particularly foreign to female eroticism.
>
> Luce Irigaray[21]

The penis stands out, the vagina does not. The first is proof, the second possibility. Logically, then, that which is evident can be used as evidence of reality. Art historians rely on documents, formalists on what they see; the connoisseur's discriminating eye is valued; and the monograph on a single artist, that individuates him or her from others stylistically, is a standard art historical product. However, that which is "invisible" is unsightly, and for an art critic to write about his feelings or an artist's or about sexual content (when it is not apparent or documented) is suspect.

According to Irigaray and others, language—for the art critic, the way he as the viewer handles the viewed, the way viewer and viewed may unite—bears a strong relationship to erotic impulse. Writing as process and text is pleasure, running the gamut from seduction to orgasm, rather than being persuasion, convincing. Fascinating . . . convince derives from the Latin *convincere,* to conquer. Feminist discourse is not involved in gaining power over others. Rather it is an empowering process, of (be)coming.

> Thought has always worked by opposition,
> Speech/Writing
> High/Low . . .
> And all the couples of oppositions are *couples.* Does this mean something? Is the fact that logocentrism subjects thought—all of the concepts, the codes, the values—to a two-term system, related to "the" couple man/woman?
>
> Hélène Cixous[22]

The two-term system is nonprocess oriented, for in it, everything is taken care of. The opposition(s) are in constant struggle, but the conflict is nonetheless always resolved. We have good and bad painting, major and minor works. The battle of the sexes, the battle between the geniuses and the mediocrities. The two-term system, in which one term is usually "better" than the other, promotes hierarchy and conflict while simultaneously keeping the latter in check.

From now on, if anyone asks me why feminists point out the differences between women and men, I will tell her about the two-term system, whose falsifications have already polluted our minds. Feminists try to find a way out of the bind by distinguishing its parts, not by stiffening them further. In Monique Wittig's words, "[M]ay you lose the sense of morning and evening of the stupid duality that flows therefrom.''[23]

> Her language does not contain, it carries; it does not hold back, it makes possible.
>
> Hélène Cixous[24]

System and hierarchy. They withhold (information). Everything in its place. Discuss an artist's work chronologically. Picasso was more influential than Braque. "Straight" thinking.

Feminist thinking is the curves, bends, angles, and irregularities of thought, departures from prescribed patterns of art historical logic. To be "straight" is to be upright-erect-phallic-virtuous-heterosexual, but feminists turn away from the straight and narrow. Deviants without their heads on straight.

Logocentrism produces closure, tight arguments. It sews up the fabric(ations) of discourse.

Feminists with loose tongues embroider, patch new and worn pieces together, re-fabricate.

> Their distinguishing feature is one of contiguity. They touch (*upon*).
>
> Luce Irigaray[25]

Irigaray notes the contiguity of female genitalia and connects it with the contiguity of a woman's language. It comes from feeling as well as thinking and treats its subjects accordingly. It moves from point to point without the rigor (mortis) of logocentric discourse. (Academics praise intellectual rigor.)

Contiguity allows for fragmented structure(lessness), abhorrent to users of logocentric systems. Structure(lessness) may seem to some like nonsense, but it is a new sense; coming to one's senses.

Xavière Gauthier says that "we can *make audible* that which agitates within us, suffers silently in the *holes of discourse,* in the unsaid, or in the non-sense."[26] The holes of discourse are not, as I see it, just a vaginal language of some sort, but rather the voids left by the "sensible" systems of logocentrism, which, according to many feminists, is a product of phallocentrism. A new language of the body will fill in the blanks, do away with the blankness and blandness of logo/phallocentric lingo. Contiguous fragments of discourse form a whole that does not describe or explain, but that is natural, like the earth, like the body.

> The women say that they perceive their bodies in their entirety. They say that they do not favour any of its parts on the grounds that it was formerly a forbidden object. They say that they do not want to become prisoners of their own ideology.
>
> Monique Wittig[27]

In *The Lesbian Body* Wittig brings the female body back from the dead. The point of focusing on the body, and all of its parts, is to reclaim the whole of a lost and defiled home(land).

A woman without a body, dumb, blind, can't possibly be a good fighter.

Hélène Cixous[28]

Possessing the body empowers us with new sight, speech, and hearing. Moreover, self-possession helps us to shoulder responsibility, stomach criticism, stand on our own two feet, head into the fray.

They say, let those who call for a new language first learn violence.

Monique Wittig[29]

It is necessary to violate the status quo if change is to occur. Challenging language radicalizes thought. Threatening style and structure disrupt outworn ideologies.

So take the blade of your intelligence, and bleed away the lie. Begin with the body.

A gash is a long, deep cut and a slit is a long, narrow one. In slang, you are a gash and a slit because you have labia and a vagina. Slang suggests that you belong to the walking wounded and that you have been mutilated or punished.

One derivation of gash is the Greek *charassein,*

to sharpen (a gash has wit),

to cut into furrows (a gash knows how to plant her seed),

to engrave (a gash will make the mark she chooses),

to carve (a gash shapes the world).

One derivation of slit is the Lithuanian *skelti,*

to split (a slit breaks the bonds of conventional discourse).

Yoko Ono gave John Lennon a knife to cut away his troubles.

A knife, or athame, is a witch's tool.

Practice magic.

Cut their arguments. Make them so thin that they fade away.

Cut it out. You are the surgeon removing the diseased organs. You are the healer who tells the patient to stop poisoning himself.

You are a cut-up. Enjoy your unruliness.

Cut a swathe. We want to see and hear you.

In fact, why don't you bite, rip, and snarl? Why are you so nice?

Nice derives from the Latin *nescire,* not to know. Choosing to be ignorant is choosing to be nicey-nicey.

The opposite of a nicey-nicey is a bitch, who does bite (take hold of an issue), rip (attack a problem without delay), and snarl (use threatening language).

They say that they foster disorder in all its forms. Confusion troubles violent debates disarray upsets disturbances incoherences irregularities divergences complications disagreements discords clashes polemics discussions contentions brawls disputes conflicts routs débâcles cataclysms disturbances quarrels agitation turbulence conflagrations chaos anarchy.

Monique Wittig[30]

Rupture to achieve rapture.

> I drift, I dream, I rave, I lust.
>
> Xavière Gauthier[31]

Gauthier's statement gives an idea of how free writing can be. The self is present, as personality. In logocentrism the I, as excited dreamer, mental vagrant, manic sensualist, is absent. The free writing of feminist criticism is a relationship *with,* not *to,* art. Being with art is like being with a lover, for bodies and minds are pleasurably and demandingly engaged. For the critic Stendhal, the pursuit of both art and love was an ideal, not to be taken on by "moderately passionate people."[32] The feminist art critic assumes the challenge, but in unabashedly showing that she is an "art lover," she risks the charge of intellectual promiscuity; because she supposedly mixes methodologies, ways of writing, and body and mind indiscriminately. Such promiscuity, however, is the mental freedom whose ultimate aim is freedom itself. That goal is so subtle and dramatic, and we are so unfree, that we can barely imagine what freedom is. And yet . . . feminist art criticism is one way to invent that future.

> They say, If I take over the world, let it be to dispossess myself of it immediately, let it be to forge new links between myself and the world.
>
> Monique Wittig[33]

Notes

1. Denis Diderot, quoted in Anita Brookner, *The Genius of the Future: Studies in French Art Criticism; Diderot, Stendhal, Baudelaire, Zola, the Brothers Goncourt, Huysmans* (London: Phaidon, 1971), 21.

2. Arlene Raven, "Harmonies: An Essay on the Work of Harmony Hammond" (Chicago: Klein Gallery, 1982), 1.

3. Nancy Marmer, "The Performing Critic," *Art in America* 67.8 (December 1979): 71.

4. Ibid., 71.

5. Robin Morgan, *The Anatomy of Freedom: Feminism, Physics, and Global Politics* (Garden City: Anchor/Doubleday, 1982), 247.

6. Roszika Parker and Griselda Pollock, *Old Mistresses: Women, Art and Ideology* (New York: Pantheon, 1981), 46, 47–48.

7. Annette Kolodny, "Dancing through the Minefield: Some Observations on the Theory and Practice of a Feminist Literary Criticism," *Feminist Studies* 6.1 (Spring 1980): 21.

8. Mary Daly, *Beyond God the Father: Toward a Philosophy of Women's Liberation* (Boston: Beacon, 1973), 11; and Mary Daly, *Gyn/Ecology: The Metaethics of Radical Feminism* (Boston: Beacon, 1978), 23.

9. Kolodny, 8.

10. Jack Lindsay, *Gustave Courbet: His Life and Art* (New York: Harper & Row, 1973), 217.

11. Ibid., 217.

12. Ibid., 217.

13. Marguerite Duras, "From an Interview," trans. Susan Husserl-Kapit, *New French Feminisms,* ed. Elaine Marks and Isabelle de Courtivron (New York: Schocken, 1981), 174.

14. Chantal Chawaf, "Linguistic Flesh," trans. Yvonne Rochette-Ozzello, Marks and de Courtivron, 178.

15. Monique Wittig, *The Lesbian Body,* trans. David Le Vay (New York: Avon, 1976), 35.

16. Xavière Gauthier, "Why Witches?," trans. Erica M. Eisinger, Marks and de Courtivron, 200.

17. Susan Griffin, *Woman and Nature: The Roaring Inside Her* (New York: Harper & Row, 1978), 227.

18. Ibid., 19.

19. Chawaf, 177.

20. Hélène Cixous, "Sorties," trans. Ann Liddle, Marks and de Courtivron, 93.

21. Luce Irigaray, "This Sex Which Is Not One," trans. Claudia Reeder, Marks and de Courtivron, 101.

22. Cixous, "Sorties," 90, 91.

23. Wittig, *The Lesbian Body,* 143.

24. Hélène Cixous, "The Laugh of the Medusa," trans. Keith Cohen and Paula Cohen, Marks and de Courtivron, 260.

25. Irigaray, 103.

26. Xavière Gauthier, "Is There Such a Thing as Women's Writing?" trans. Marilyn A. August, Marks and de Courtivron, 163.

27. Monique Wittig, *Les Guérrillères,* trans. David Le Vay (New York: Avon, 1973), 57.

28. Cixous, "The Laugh of the Medusa," 250.

29. Wittig, *Les Guérrillères,* 85.

30. Ibid., 93.

31. Gauthier, "Why Witches?," 203.

32. Quoted in Brookner, 54.

33. Wittig, *Les Guérrillères,* 107.

Women Artists and the Politics of Representation

Whitney Chadwick

Woman's place in the history of Western art is nowhere more clearly articulated than in Johann Zoffany's group portrait, *The Academicians of the Royal Academy* (1772). Painted for King George III on the occasion of the opening of new drawing studios for the Royal Academy school, it depicts the Royal Academicians in the life drawing studio. Among the founding members of the Academy in 1768 were two women: the painters Angelica Kauffmann and Mary Moser. Kauffmann, elected to the prestigious Academy of Saint Luke in Rome in 1765, hailed as the successor to Van Dyke on her arrival in London, and credited, along with Gavin Hamilton and Benjamin West, with popularizing Neoclassicism in England, was one of the most successful artists of her day. Moser, whose reputation at the time rivalled Kauffmann's, was one of only two floral painters accepted into the Academy. Yet there is no place for Kauffmann and Moser in Zoffany's painting. Neither is shown among the artists casually grouped around the male model learnedly discussing the nude, the study of which formed the basis for all academic training and representation from the sixteenth to the nineteenth centuries. Women were prohibited from the presence of the nude model, barred from the training that opened the door to artistic success in France and England and, after Kauffmann and Moser, barred from membership in the Royal Academy itself until 1922 when Annie Louisa Swynnerton became an Associate Member. Thus Zoffany, whose painting is as much about the ideal of the academic aritst as it is about the Royal Academicians, has inserted them into art history *as representation,* as the objects of art rather than as its producers.[1]

Zoffany's painting reiterates woman's marginal place in the history of western painting and sculpture and her traditionally passive role as the object of male contemplation in a history of art commonly traced through "Old Masters" and

Part of this material is derived from the introduction and first chapter of a forthcoming book of the same title (scheduled for publication in 1989 by Thames and Hudson, Ltd., London).

Johann Zoffany, *The Academicians of the Royal Academy*, 1771–72
Oil on canvas, 39¾" × 58".
(*Courtesy the Royal Collection. Copyright reserved to Her Majesty Queen
Elizabeth II*)

"masterpieces." In the early 1970s, feminist artists, critics, and historians began to question the masculinist claim for the universal values of a history of heroic art produced by men which had so systematically excluded women's productions from its mainstream, and so powerfully transformed the image of woman into one of possession and consumption. The resulting reexamination of women's lives as artists during the 1970s proceeded amidst debates about the relationship between gender, culture, and creativity. Why had art history chosen to ignore the work of almost all women artists? Were successful women artists exceptional (perhaps to the point of deviance) or merely the tip of a hidden iceberg, submerged by patriarchal culture's demand that women produce children, not art, and confine their activities to the domestic, not the public, sphere? Could, and should, women artists lay claim to "essential" gender differences that might be linked to the production of certain kinds of imagery? Could the creative process, and its results, be viewed as androgynous or genderless? Finally, what was the relationship between the "craft" and "fine" arts traditions for women?

Feminism in the arts grew out of the contemporary women's movement and its first investigations relied heavily on sociological and political methodology. Early feminist analyses focused new attention on the work of remarkable women artists *and* on unequalled traditions of domestic and utilitarian production by women. They also revealed the way that women and their productions have been presented in a negative relation to creativity and high culture.[2] It is now a commonplace of feminist analysis that high art locates value in the fact that it is not "decorative," "precious," "minor," "sentimental," etc.; that is, that it glories in not being "feminine." Presented as outside culture and history, women and their art have provided a set of negative characteristics against which to oppose "high" art. Economically, legally, and politically powerless throughout much of western history, women have been linked to nature and the unknowable through metaphors of the body while the masculine has signified culture and mental activity.

As the inadequacies of methodologies based on the ideological and political conviction that women were more unified by the fact of being female than by the specifics of race, class, and historical moment were exposed, many academic feminists began to turn to structuralism, psychoanalysis, and semiology for theoretical models. Through a growing understanding of the ways in which the assumed inferiority of women's productions have been used to "prove" the superiority of art produced by men, we have also become aware of the extent to which the history of women's participation in the production of art has been shaped by social and cultural forces different from those affecting men. One result has been changes in the ways many feminist art historians think about art history itself. Michel Foucault's distinction between "total" and "general" history in his *Archeology of Knowledge* (1972) allowed for a "general" history which does not focus on a single meaning. The reliance of "general" history on "series, segmentations, limits, difference of level, time-lags, anachronistic survivals, possible types of relation," seemed to many women applicable to the feminist problematic of formulating a history which was responsive to women's specific experiences without positing a parallel history uniquely feminine and existing outside dominant culture.

As some art historians began to question the ahistoricity of writing about women artists as if gender were a more significant point of connection between women artists than was their relationship to either their contemporaries or the particular historical circumstances in which they worked, others found the isolation in which many women artists have worked, and their exclusion from the major movements that conventionally plot the course of Western art, insurmountable barriers to their reinscription into art history. It now appears that the availability of more information about the lives and work of women artists has had little apparent effect on the writing of art history generally. The inclusion of a few more women artists in recent editions of standard art history surveys like H. W. Janson's *History of Art* (1986), long notorious for its omission of *all* women from the canon, has done little to define new roles for women in the history of art. Janson's contentious remark in 1978 that ". . . I have not been able to find a woman artist who clearly belongs in a one-volume history of art," merely reaffirmed the position of many conservative art historians.[3]

Again and again attempts to reevaluate the work of women artists and to reassess the actual historical conditions under which they worked have come in conflict with art history's identification of art with the wealth, power, and privilege of the individuals and groups who commissioned or purchased it. If, on the one hand, the issue of "quality" in art produced by women has refused to submit to feminist demands that we abandon the biased designations of "genius" and "masterpiece," it is equally true, on the other, that much art by women remains inaccessible to the constant comparative connoisseurship through which art history continues to be written. When work by women, even well-known artists, is in museum collections it is often isolated in storage areas rather than displayed in galleries where it could be easily examined in relation to other work produced at the same time. And, one is sadly forced to conclude, much of the work by women which has found its way to sales rooms and auction houses has done so under the names of their better-known, and higher-priced, male colleagues.

There remains a relatively small body of work in the history of Western art since the Renaissance that can, with any certainty, be firmly identified with specific women artists. This lack of artistic oeuvre, the basis of all traditional art historical scholarship, suggests that we may *never* be able to fully integrate women's art with that of their male contemporaries and colleagues despite all arguments that gender is irrelevant to "great" art. Feminist critiques of feminist art history, particularly those of the English art historians Lisa Tickner, Roszika Parker, and Griselda Pollock, have elucidated the shortcomings of attempts to reabsorb or "annex" women artists to art history as the discipline is currently practiced.[4] In addition, the work of many women artists has perished due to their lack of adequate technical preparation and training.[5] Moreover, attempts to juggle domestic responsibilities with artistic production have often resulted in smaller bodies of work, and often smaller works. Yet art history continues to privilege prodigious output and monumental scale or conception over the selective and the intimate. Finally, the historical and critical evaluation of that work has proved inseparable from ideologies which define woman's place in Western culture generally.

The origins of art history's focus on the personalities and work of exceptional individuals can be traced back to an early Renaissance desire to celebrate Italian cities and their achievements by focusing on the remarkable men whose talents were nurtured in these urban contexts. The result was a view of art as the aggregate of the work of particularly gifted individuals.[6] Modern art historical scholarship, beginning in the nineteenth century, has been closely aligned with the kind of connoisseurship which built great private collections, often through dubious attribution to "named" artists. Reassembling an oeuvre for a woman artist requires painstaking connoisseurship as well as a risk of devaluation often at odds with art market aspirations. The number of women artists, well-known in their own day, for whom *no* work now exists is a tantalizing indication of the vagaries of artistic attribution.[7] It now seems possible that many deserving women artists may not be returned to the art historical canon because they will never acquire bodies of work comparable to those of their male contemporaries. Moreover, feminist art history's quite legitimate demand that art historians turn their attention from issues of artistic genius and "masterpiece" to explorations of the cultural conditions under which art is produced stands in direct opposition to the conservative traditions of connoisseurship and attribution by which artistic oeuvres are slowly and carefully assembled. Reviewing attribution problems in the work of selected women artists identified by feminist art historians working during the 1970s clearly reveals both the reasons why feminist art historians' attempts to reinsert women artists into history have been so disappointing to date and why it is art history and its established canons which must continue to be the focus of our investigations.

Let us briefly consider three "case studies." They are Marietta Robusti, the sixteenth-century Venetian painter; Judith Leyster, the seventeenth-century Dutch painter; and a group of women artists who figured prominently in the circle of Jacques-Louis David, the eighteenth-century French painter. First, their stories elucidate the way that art history's emphasis on individual genius has distorted our understanding of workshop procedures and the nature of collaborative artistic production. Second, they illustrate the extent to which art history's close alliance with art market economics has affected the attribution of women's art. And third, they offer a dramatic set of examples as to the ways that expectations about gender affect the ways we literally *see* works of art.

Marietta Robusti was the eldest daughter of Tintoretto, the Venetian painter named Jacopo Robusti. Her birth, probably in 1560,[8] was followed by those of three brothers and four sisters. Her sister Ottavia became a skilled needlewoman in the Benedictine nunnery of S. Amia di Castello; Marietta and her brothers Domenico and Marco (and possible Giovanni Battista) entered the Tintoretto workshop as youths. It is known that Robusti worked there more or less full-time for fifteen years, that she was, like many young Renaissance women of her class, a skilled musician as well as painter, and that her fame as a portrait painter spread as far as the courts of Spain and Austria. Her likeness of Jacopo Strada, Emperor Maximilian's antiquarian, so impressed the emperor that she was invited first to his court as painter and subsequently to the court of Philip II of Spain. Her father refused and instead found her a husband, Jacopo d'Augusta, the head of the Venetian silversmith's guild, to whom she was betrothed on condition that she not leave Tintoretto's household in his lifetime. Four years later, at age 30, she died in childbirth.

Marietta Robusti lived at a moment when the model of artistic production was shifting from that of crafts produced by skilled artisans to that of the work of art inspired by the genius of an individual creator. In the sixteenth century the family was still a unit of production (as well as consumption) in many parts of Europe and family businesses of all sorts were a typical feature of Renaissance Venice. Tintoretto's workshop, organized around the members of his immediate family, would have been classified in general economic life as a craft under guild regulation. Similar to the dynastic family workshops of artists like Veronese and Bellini in Venice, Pollaiuolo, Rossellino, and della Robbia in Florence, it provides the context within which to examine Robusti's career (or what little we know of it).

Marietta Robusti's social and economic autonomy would have been no greater than those of other women of the artisan class. Nevertheless, remarks by Tintoretto's biographer Carlo Ridolfi about her musical skills and deportment, published in 1648, suggest that she was part of a changing ideal for the artist from that of artisan to gentleman/gentlewoman. At the same time, art historical accounts of Tintoretto and his workshop offer a series of paradoxes with regard to a daughter whose hand was apparently indistinguishable from that of her father, whose painting was of sufficient quality to be confused with his, and whose fame had spread to the courts of Spain and Austria.

Marietta Robusti, like her brother Domenico, who inherited the workshop on Tintoretto's death and with it a degree of art historical attention as the new "master," learned to paint portraits in her father's grand manner.[9] Like most well-known women artists of the sixteenth to the nineteenth centuries, she was the daughter of a painter and trained by her father. The commonly held assumption that her achievements were largely due to the overriding influence of her father, however, might be questioned in the light of the limitations imposed on her potential career and her development as an independent painter by his refusal to relinquish control of her life. Although Ridolfi mentions portraits by Robusti of all the members of the silversmith's guild, modern scholars have attributed only a single work to her, the portrait *Old Man and Boy* (undated), now in the

Marietta Robusti (Attributed to Tintoretto), *Old Man and Boy* (n.d.)
Oil on canvas, 24 cm. × 30 cm.
(*Courtesy of the Kunsthistorisches Museum, Vienna*)

Kunsthistorisches Museum, Vienna. Long considered one of Tintoretto's finest portraits, it was only in 1920 that the work was found to be signed with Robusti's monogram. Even so, the attribution has been subsequently questioned.[10]

Tintoretto's secretiveness and refusal to admit visitors to his studio, along with an almost complete lack of documentation concerning the everyday activities of the workshop, have proved difficult obstacles to scholarship. Nevertheless, the workshop's prodigious output has served to help define the artistic genius of its Master. Tintoretto scholars, though many acknowledge the problems of attribution in the workshop, generally embrace a model of almost superhuman production and use it to help build an image of "greatness" for the artist.[11] Hans Tietze has proposed a "Tintorettesque style" to encompass the varied hands at work. "The Tintorettesque style is not only an impoverishment," he suggests, "but also an enrichment of the style of Tintoretto; it enters into innumerable combinations with the personal style, makes transitions and mixtures possible, increases the master's scope, augments his effectiveness, and affords opportunity for trying out on a larger scale artistic principles which in reality are his own personal property."[12] Thus the Tintorettesque proves Tintoretto, leading inexorably to Tietze's conclusion that, "Works in which pupils certainly had a considerable share—as for instance the two mighty late works in San Giorgio Maggiore—are among his most important and most personal creations."[13] In the case of the many extant Tintoretto portraits, Tintoretto's production is often identified with "uneven quality" and an "amazing variability of brushstroke,"[14] but even these observations have not led to new interpretations of workshop production that differ significantly from conventional views of individual creation. It is widely assumed that Robusti assisted in the preparation of large altarpieces, as did all workshop assistants. Yet surely we should question Francesco Valcanover's assertion that in the 1580s, "assistants were largely confined to working on less important areas of the canvas, not only because of the family tie and the submission that could be expected but also because of the imperiousness of the recognized master that Tintoretto has by now become . . . . What responsibility they may have been allowed must therefore have been partial and at best modest."[15] It is clear from Robusti's renown by that decade that she had achieved status as an independent painter although we do not know precisely what that meant. Nor do we know how it related to her continuing participation in the workshop.

The imposition of contemporary views of originality and artistic individuality on workshop production obscures the actual development of painters like Robusti and her brother Domenico by subsuming them entirely under the name Tintoretto despite contemporary evidence of independent achievement. Although it is clear that Robusti's position would have been subservient in every way to that of her father as a female member of his household, while her short life span would have resulted in limited production, it is modern scholarship which has buried her life under that of her father and brother. Rather than exploring the dynamics of the workshop as a site of varied production, it has redefined it as a place in which lowly assistants painted angels' wings while a "master" artist breathed life into the Madonna's features. Even Ridolfi's remark about the slackening of Tintoretto's "fury for work" upon Robusti's death in 1590, which he and others have attributed solely to a father's grief at the death of a beloved daughter, demands rereading in the light of the loss of so capable an assistant.

Questions of attribution have colored most attempts to write about women artists in history. The fact that the monetary value of works of art is inextricably bound up in their attribution to "named" artists has subsumed the work of many women artists. At the same time the number of Venetian sixteenth-century portraits of women on the market as Marietta Robusti's is as legion as eighteenth-century misattributions to Madame Vigée LeBrun or obscure Cremonese portraits to Sofonisba Anguissola. To reassemble the oeuvre of the eighteenth-century Venetian painter Giulia Lama, Germaine Greer reports, scholars were forced to borrow from the work of Federico Bencovich, Tiepolo, Domenico Maggiotto, Francesca Capella, Antonio Petrini, Jan Lyss, and even Zurbaran.[16] Thus it comes as no surprise that Judith Leyster, one of the best-known painters of seventeenth-century Holland, was almost completely lost from history from the end of the seventeenth-century until 1893, when Cornelius Hofstede de Groot discovered her monogram on a painting titled *The Happy Couple* (1630) which had just sold as a Frans Hals.[17]

Judith Leyster, the daughter of a Flemish brewer, was born in Haarlem in 1609. In 1628 she moved with her family to Vreeland, near Utrecht. Her early work shows the influence of Hendrick Terrbrugghen and the Utrecht Caravaggisti. The family returned to Haarlem in 1629 and it is probably at this time that she entered the studio of Frans Hals. She was admitted to the Guild of St. Luke in Haarlem in 1633 and in 1636 married the genre painter Jan Molenaer, with whom she had three children. The fact that in 1635 Leyster is recorded as having three male pupils is a good index of her status as an artist, as is her inclusion in Ampzing's description of the city of Haarlem in 1627; thirty years later she appears to have been completely forgotten.

As early as the seventeenth century, when Sir Luke Schaub acquired her painting, *The Jolly Companions* (now in the Louvre), as a Hals, her work had already begun to disappear into the oeuvres of Gerard Van Honthorst and Molenaer, as well as Hals. Prices for Dutch painting remained painfully low until the latter part of the nineteenth century when the emergence of "modern" art with its painterly surfaces and sketchlike finish, the aesthetic tastes of the English Royal family, and the appearance of wealthy private collectors all contributed to a burgeoning demand for Dutch paintings. As late as 1854 connoisseur Gustav Waager could write of Hals that, "the value of this painter has not been sufficiently appreciated"; by 1890 demand outpaced supply. In 1875 the Kaiser-Friedrich Museum in Berlin had purchased a Leyster *Jolly Toper* as a Hals; another work sold in Brussels in 1890 bore her monogram crudely altered to read as an interlocking F. H. Another *Jolly Toper*, acquired by Amsterdam's Rijksmuseum

Judith Leyster, *The Jolly Toper*, 1629
Oil on canvas, 89 cm. × 85 cm.
(*Courtesy the Rijksmuseum-Stichting, Amsterdam*)

in 1897, and one of "Hals's" best-known works, bears her distinctive monogram and the date 1629.[18]

In the 1890s, a time when Hals prices were rising dramatically, Leyster's name was known, but no work by her hand had been identified. Hofstede de Groot's dramatic discovery in 1893 that the Louvre's *Jolly Companions* belonged to Leyster led to the reattribution of seven paintings to her.[19] Her emergence as an artist in her own right, however, was blurred in turn by the many copies after Hals subsequently attributed to her. The attributions in Julian Harms's series of articles on her published in 1927 have more recently been challenged by Frima Fox Hofrichter, author of a forthcoming *catalogue raisonée*.

Leyster's work, though similar to that of Hals, is not the same. Nevertheless, the ease with which her works have been sold as his in an art market eager for Hals at any price offers a sober warning to art historians committed to a view of women's productions as obviously and inevitably inferior to those of men. "Some women artists tend to emulate Frans Hals," noted James Laver in 1964, "but the vigorous brushstrokes of the master were beyond their capability. One has only to look at the work of a painter like Judith Leyster to detect the weakness of the feminine hand."[19] Yet many have looked and not seen.

That there is a direct relationship between what we see and what we expect to see is nowhere clearer than in the case of three well-known "David" paintings in American museum collections. The Metropolitan Museum of Art's *Portrait of Mademoiselle Charlotte du Val d'Ognes* (ca.1800) was purchased as a David for two hundred thousand dollars in 1922 under the terms of a bequest. In 1952 the Frick Collection purchased a *Portrait of Antonio Bruni* (1804) through Knoedler & Co., and in 1943 the Fogg Art Museum at Harvard University acquired a *Portrait of Dublin-Tornelle* from a bequest. All three were believed to be by David. The three paintings in fact belong to a large group of portraits in the manner of David produced in the years after the French Revolution.

David, chronicler of the Revolution and painter to Emperor Napoleon, was France's foremost artist from the 1780s until his exile in 1816. As a popular teacher at a time when reforms initiated by the Revolution had opened salons to unrestricted participation by women (the number of exhibiting women artists increased dramatically from twenty-eight in 1801 to sixty-seven in 1822), David left his imprint on the work of a number of women artists. Moreover, he encouraged these women pupils to paint both portraits and history subjects, and to submit them regularly to the Salon. George Wildenstein's publication of a list of all the portraits exhibited in Paris at the salon between 1800 and 1826 has greatly aided attempts to wort out the profusion of portraits executed in the Davidian style. It contributed directly to the reattribution of the *Portrait of Mademoiselle Charlotte du Val d'Ognes* to Constance Marie Charpentier in 1951, the *Portrait of Antonio Bruni* to Césarine Davin-Mirvault in 1962, and that of *Dublin-Tornelle* to Adélaïde Labille-Guiard in 1971.[20] All three women were followers or pupils of David

Constance Marie Charpentier (Attributed to), *Portrait of Mademoiselle Val d'Ognes,*
ca. 1800
Oil on canvas, 63½″ × 50⅝″.
(*Courtesy the Metropolitan Museum of Art, New York, Bequest of Isaac D. Fletcher,
1917. Mr. and Mrs. Isaac D. Fletcher Collection*)

Césarine-Henriette-Flore Davin-Mirvault, *Portrait of Antonio Bruni*, 1804
Oil on canvas, 50⅞″ × 37¾″.
(*Photo copyright the Frick Collection, New York*)

and their portraits, like the works by David which inspired them, are characteristic by the powerful presence of the sitter against a simple, often dark background, a clarity of form, academic finish, and forthright definition of character.

The finding during reattribution to lesser known artists that works of art are "simply not up to the high technical standards" of the Master is common. More revealing, and more questionable, is a shifting language that accompanies changes in attribution in which gender is an issue. Speaking of the Metropolitan's *Portrait of Mademoiselle Charlotte du Val d'Ognes,* Charles Sterling noted that the "treatment of the skin and fabric is gentle" and "the articulation lacks correctness." Finally, he stripped the work entirely of its former stature, concluding that: "Its poetry literary rather than plastic, its very evident charms and cleverly concealed weaknesses, its ensemble made up of a thousand subtle artifices all seem to reveal the feminine spirit."[21] Not only is one forced to wonder how such characterizations will hold up in the light of recent allegations that the work is not, in fact, by Charpentier after all and may well have been painted by either Gérard or Pierre Jeuffrain, a pupil of David, but also how André Maurois's characterization of the painting as "a perfect picture" and the Metropolitan Museum's own identification of it as exemplary of "the austere taste of the time" so quickly turned to "cleverly concealed weaknesses" in the eyes of the beholder.[22]

The cases of Marietta Robusti, Judith Leyster, and the "Davids" reveal the roles played by modern assumptions about individual genius, market economics, and aesthetic expectations in the valuing of works of art. The existence of these and other falsely attributed works by women artists in major museum collections continues to challenge easy assumptions about "quality." It has led art historians like Roszika Parker and Griselda Pollock to argue that the hierarchies within which we range the visual productions of both men and women over the centuries have been created for us by art history.[23] It has prompted others to challenge the canons of art history by directing attention to the ways that dominant ideologies are reinforced through representation. And it has encouraged still others to question whether there is any significant place for women artists in art history as it is presently written. Nevertheless, we must guard against the tendency to solve these complex problems by returning the issue of women artists to one of representation, taking them out of the studio, as Zoffany did in *The Academicians of the Royal Academy,* and framing them on a wall defined by current theoretical preoccupations.

Today, as we seek to locate our investigations within the theoretical framework of postmodernism, views of feminism as an active political force working for change in the world often seem to come in conflict with the academic discourses of "postfeminism." Recent scholarly writing—deriving its theoretical structure and its methodology from disciplines as diverse as literary criticism, semiotics, and psychoanalytic theory—appears to be shifting attention away from "art" and "artist" to broader issues concerning ideologies of gender, sexuality, and power. There is an increasing tendency to see femininity and masculinity

Adélaïde Labille-Guiard, *Portrait of Dublin-Tornelle,* ca. 1799
Oil on canvas, 28½″ × 22½″.
*(Courtesy of The Harvard University Art Museums [Fogg Art Museum], Cambridge,
Massachusetts. Bequest of Grenville L. Winthrop)*

as constructed patterns of sexuality and behavior which are imposed by social and cultural norms and reinforced through representation. As the writings of Roland Barthes and others have challenged long-cherished views of the writer or artist as a unique individual creating in the image of divine creation in an unbroken chain that links father and son (as Michelangelo's God touches life into a recumbent Adam in the Sistine Chapel fresco of 1508–12), new attitudes toward the relation of artist and work have begun to emerge. Many of them have important implications for feminist analysis. Now artistic intention can be seen more clearly as just one of many often conflicting strands—ideological, economic, social, and political—that make up the work of art, whether literary text, painting, or sculpture. Philosopher Louis Althusser has contributed a more sophisticated understanding of the way ideology functions. For Althusser, ideology is a series of representations and images reflecting the beliefs a society holds about "reality." In the end, they are nothing more than the myths by which a culture lives and in which it believes as if they were true reflections of some natural and verifiable "reality."

As a result of these and other theoretical developments, feminism and gender studies now offer a multiplicity of approaches to issues of women, art, and representation. One of the functions of a feminist art history has come to be seen as the exploration of the ways the techniques of visual representation operate to construct certain images of women and ideas of femininity which are then "naturalized" through ideology. It must also account for the paradoxes of patriarchal ideology in relation to the woman artist. For example, in the nineteenth century the valorization of domestic space as a sign of bourgeois affluence and control both affirmed woman's "natural" place in the home *and* made the domestic interior a legitimate subject for painting. On the one hand, many women were confined to the home and excluded from professional life; one the other, Impressionists like Berthe Morisot and Mary Cassatt were able to base their work on domestic imagery.

A current preoccupation with European, particularly French, psychoanalytic writings has focused attention on women, not as producers of art, but as signifiers for male power and privilege. The writings of Jacques Lacan and his followers have been concerned with a psychoanalytic explanation as to how the subject is constructed in language and, by extension, in representation. The place assigned woman by Lacan is one of absence, of "otherness." Lacking the penis which signifies phallic power in patriarchal society and provides a speaking position for the male child, she also lacks access to the symbolic order which structures language and meaning. In the view of psychoanalyst Jacques Lacan, she is destined "to be spoken" rather than to speak. This position of otherness in relation to language and power poses serious challenges to the woman artist who wishes to assume the role of speaking subject rather than submit to that of object. Yet Lacan's views have proved important for feminists interested in clarifying the positioning of woman in relation to dominant discourses and have provided the theoretical base for the work of a number of contemporary women artists.

The implications of these new ways of thinking about gender and representation have yet to be fully articulated and understood. Nevertheless, for many contemporary women artists, as well as art historians, they pose complex questions about the relationship between making images out of the experience of one's life and theorizing their meaning, or lack of meaning. As feminist teaching programs in the arts have closed or moved outside the university in recent years, often in response to economic and political changes in the Reagan-Thatcher years, and as many women artists have sought support and community in the professional art world rather than in the academy, earlier alliances between feminist art historians/critics and artists seem to be breaking down. Although many of us continue to believe that a feminist art history which is not rooted in the actual experience of women artists has lost its political *raison d'être*, others have come to distrust the very subject of women artists.

At the present moment the ways we talk about women and art are showing signs of falling into categories of feminist/postfeminist, replicating the current modernist/postmodernist paradigm. In the face of the complex relationship of women artists to the mainstream traditions of painting and sculpture, it may be tempting to relegate them to the category of historical curiosity. From the standpoint of a continuing analysis of art's relationship to broader issues of history and culture, however, we cannot afford to lose sight of the very real contributions which women artists have made to the history of visual culture. Dividing feminist art history/criticism into developmental stages reiterates modernism's view of an avant-garde set in opposition to the outworn, discarded directives of the past.[24] Privileging gender in representation rather than in production raises the danger of overlooking the valid steps women artists have taken toward defining authentic positions within which to explore through representation that which is unique to woman's experience of the world.

The gradual integration of women's productions with recent theoretical developments can only be achieved by reexamining the woman artist's relationship to dominant modes of production *and* representation in the light of a growing body of literature concerning the production and intersection of gender and representation. Only an art history that continues to concern itself with women's productions, as well as with woman's place in a system of signification for male power and privilege, can remain faithful both to the history of women in the visual arts and to the ongoing political and intellectual critique which must continue to inform feminist scholarship.

Notes

1. For a fuller discussion of the implications of this painting for feminist art history, see Roszika Parker and Griselda Pollock, *Old Mistresses: Women, Art and Ideology* (New York: Pantheon Books, 1981), pp. 87–90.

2. The literature on which this study is based, and without which it could not have been written, is too extensive to cite in its entirety. It includes: Eleanor Tufts, *Our Hidden Heritage: Five Centuries of Women Artists* (London: Paddington Press Ltd., 1974); *Women Artists: 1550–1950*.

Exhibition catalog. Los Angeles County Museum of Art, December 1976–March 1977. Catalog essays by Ann Sutherland Harris and Linda Nochlin; Karen Petersen and J. J. Wilson, *Women Artists: Recognition and Reappraisal, from the Early Middle Ages to the Twentieth-Century* (New York: Harper and Row, 1976); Elsa Honig Fine, *Women and Art: A History of Women Painters and Sculptors from the Renaissance to the Twentieth-Century* (Montclair, N. J.: Allanheld and Schram, 1978); Germaine Greer, *The Obstacle Race: The Fortunes of Women Painters and Their Work* (New York: Farrar Straus Giroux, 1979); Eleanor Munro, *Originals: American Women Artists* (New York: Simon and Schuster, 1979); Roszika Parker and Griselda Pollock, *Old Mistresses: Women, Art and Ideology* (New York: Pantheon Books, London, 1981); and Norma Broude and Mary Garrard, eds., *Feminism and Art History: Questioning the Litany* (New York: Harper and Row, 1982).

3. Eleanor Dickinson, Typescript of an interview with H. W. Janson, Washington, D.C., February 1, 1975.

4. See, for example, Griselda Pollock, "Vision, Voice and Power: Feminist Art History and Marxism," *Block* 6 (1982): 6–9, and *passim.*

5. Greer, *The Obstacle Race,* p. 133; the disproportionate amount of work by women artists which is in private, rather than public, collections has also contributed to the problem of access.

6. Mark Roskill, *What Is Art History* (London: Thames and Hudson, 1976); Roskill's discussion includes issues of attribution.

7. Among them Lucrezia Quistelli della Mirandola, the Anguissola sisters, Margaretha van Eyck, Antonia Uccello, Suor Plautilla, Onorata Rodiani, Suor Luisa Capomazza, Tommasina del Fiesco, St. Catherine de Pazzi, Sabina von Steinback, and Irene of Spilimbergo; see Greer, *The Obstacle Race,* pp. 130–50.

8. Her date of birth is listed as early as 1552 (Hans Tietze, *Tintoretto* [London: Phaidon Press, 1948]); the 1560 date proposed by E. Tietze-Conrat, "Marietta, Fille du Tintoret," *Gazette des Beaux-Arts* 12 (December 1934): 59, is more likely. Domenico's probable birth between 1560 and 1562 has also created confusion as both children worked in the Tintoretto workshop. For a good discussion of the situation, see P. Rossi, *Iacopo Tintoretto, I Ritratti* (Venice, 1974), pp. 138–39.

9. *Le Meraviglie dell-Arte* (1648) (Rome: Societa Multigrafica Editrice Somu, 1965) II: 78–80; for a discussion of artists and class in the Renaissance, see Griselda Pollock, "Vision, Voice and Power," pp. 2–21; and Peter Burke, *Culture and Society in Renaissance Italy* (London: B. T. Batsford, 1972).

10. Tietze-Conrat, "Marietta, Fille du Tintoret," pp. 259–62; for a discussion of Domenico's career, see Francesco Valcanover, *Tintoretto* (New York: Harry N. Abrams, 1985).

11. See Valcanover, "The Assistance of the Workshop," in *Tintoretto,* p. 49 and *passim;* also, M. Suida, "Clarifications and Identifications of Works by Venetian Painters," *Art Quarterly* 9 (1946): 288–98; John Paoletti, "The Venetian School: Problems and Suggestions," *Apollo* (December 1968): 420–22.

12. Tietze, *Tintoretto,* p. 58.

13. Ibid.

14. Suida, "Clarifications," p. 290.

15. Valcanover, *Tintoretto,* p. 49.

16. Greer, *The Obstacle Race,* pp. 136–40; see also, Nochlin and Harris, *Women Artists,* p. 137.

17. Cornelis Hofstede de Groot, "Judith Leyster," *Jahrbuch der Koniglich preussischen Kunstsammlungen* 14 (1893): 190–98.

18. "Judith Leyster, ihr Leben und ihr Werk," *Oud-Holland* 44 (1927): 88–96, 112–26, 145–54, 221–42, 275–79; I am grateful to Frima Fox Hofrichter, who is currently preparing a *catalogue raisonée* for Judith Leyster's work, for her assistance in sorting out the Leyster/Hals attributions.

19. Hofstede de Groot, "Women Painters," *Saturday Book* (1964): 19.

20. See Charles Sterling, "A Fine 'David' Reattributed," *The Metropolitan Museum of Art Bulletin* 9, no. 5 (1951): 121–32; George Wildenstein, "Un Tableau attribué à David et rendu à Mme. Davin-Mirvault: 'Le Portrait du Violiniste Bruni' (Frick Collection)," *Gazette des Beaux-Arts* 59 (1962): 93–98; Amy Fine, "Césarine Davin-Mirvault: *Portrait of Bruni* and Other Works by a Student of David," *Woman's Art Journal* 4 (Spring/Summer 1983): 15–20; Andrew Kagan, "A Fogg 'David' Reattributed to Madame Adélaïde Labille-Guiard," *Fogg Art Museum Acquisitions, 1969–1970* (Cambridge: Harvard University, 1971), pp. 31–40.

21. Sterling, "A Fine 'David,' " p. 124.

22. *The Bulletin of the Metropolitan Museum of Art* 13 (1918): 59.

23. Parker and Pollock, *Old Mistresses*, pp. 50–78 and *passim*.

24. Thalia Gouma-Peterson and Patricia Mathews, "The Feminist Critique of Art History," *The Art Bulletin* 69, no. 3 (Fall 1987): 326–57. Those stages include a feminist phase covering initial commitments to exhuming the histories of long-neglected women artists, exploring the implications of women's marginalization in Western culture as manifested in representation, and developing systems of active critical and curatorial support for contemporary women artists, and a "postfeminism." The latter, arising from fears of intellectual inadequacy among academic women and a perceived need for more rigorous analytic and theoretical models, is concerned primarily with the cultural construction of gender and the politics of representation as it has situated women in relation to the dominant discourses of patriarchy. The danger is that, at the moment of Foucault's criticism of linear history, they reduce feminist art criticism and art history to any historical chronology and developmental paradigm which fails to account for a pluralism of approaches.

"Portraying Ourselves": Contemporary Chicana Artists

Shifra Goldman

The Chicana struggle is not an off-shoot of the Chicano movement, but is the next step within the movement to bring Chicanos and Chicanas even more closely together to form an even stronger unidad. To accomplish this unity Chicanas need to be able to share, need to be listened to, but most of all, need to see themselves . . . in works done by other Chicanas. La Chicana needs to come to know the many-faceted woman that she is.

Rita Sánchez, "Imágenes de la Chicana"

Wearing My Critical Hat—The One I Never Take Off

Writing art criticism and history in the field of modern Latin American art in general, and Chicana(o) art specifically, is an exercise in second-class citizenship (vis-à-vis U.S. mainstream publications) similar to the conditions suffered by the artmakers themselves in both the art world and the political, economic, and social worlds. In 1986, while living in Los Angeles (a city with the greatest number of Mexicans outside Mexico City, and a growing population of Central Americans numbering close to half a million), I had the opportunity to spend considerable time in New York enquiring into the status of Latin American artists on the other coast. Many Latin American artists reside there because of the art market, because of forced political exile, or due to a more propitious social climate for creative production. Not to my great surprise, I discovered that their situation in terms of recognition and acceptance is marginal. Though some "stars" have little difficulty exhibiting and selling in mainstream galleries, and might occasionally be invited to a museum exhibit, the great majority of talented artists have to overcome the "stigma" of being Latin American before they are accepted on equal terms with their peers.

This is even more pointedly true for the two colonized populations in the U.S.—the Puerto Ricans of New York and the Chicanos, some of whose ancestors lived in the Southwest before it was militarily added to United States territory. And the situation has been even further exacerbated for women of these groups. Discrimination on the basis of gender, in their case, was added to that based on race, ethnicity, and class.

I have found that art professionals dedicated to writing about modern Latin American art are also treated as second-class: their contributions are usually considered with indifference or rejected by major art magazines because of subject matter. The few exceptions serve to prove the rule. What is sad but certain is that no body of knowledgeable criticism can develop since no systematic coverage (as is the case with European movements or regional U.S. movements) has been built into the policy of mainstream art magazines. Thus it can be said that better coverage exists about Latin Americans and Latino-descent artists living in the U.S. in prestigious journals of Europe and Latin America, or alternative magazines in this country, than can be found in the most widely circulated art publications of the United States. The net result of such exclusionary policies based on disinterest is a distorted view of the whole of modern art, generally, and the scope of art from the Americas in particular.

A century dominated not only by modernism, but its corollary art-for-art's sake ideology—from Clive Bell to Clement Greenberg—and by the linear history of art constructed by Alfred H. Barr, Jr., and his successors at the New York Museum of Modern Art, not only excluded most women in the history of modern art but also most modern Latin Americans, Africans, and Asians; and inevitably led to a formalist art history and art criticism that was both male-dominated and Eurocentric in its focus. From these imperatives I prefer to distance myself.

I imagine that I share problems with feminist critics. In the same way that feminist artists and critics saw fit to establish their own exhibition structures and publications, so did the two Latin American communities previously mentioned. A similar situation is doubtless true for other artists of color (Native Americans, Blacks, Asians, etc.) and the critics who write about their work.

One qualifier is necessary: this second-class status adheres specifically to those critics who share the views and respect the sensibilities of the rejected groups on a consistent basis: who take an ''advocacy'' position. Lucy Lippard defines an ''advocate critic'' so succinctly, so appropriately, that I would like to quote it here. She says:

> An advocate critic . . . works from a communal base to identify and criticize the existing social structures as a means to locate and evaluate the social and aesthetic effect of the art. Ideally such a critic avoids star making or promoting a single style; openly supports art that is openly critical of, or openly opposed to, the political powers that be; and perhaps most importantly, tries to innovate the notion of ''quality'' to include the unheard voices, the unseen images, of the unconsidered people.[1]

Advocacy criticism should suggest broad endorsement and support for "minority" voices—those whom the ideology of hegemonic forces have marginalized in the interests of domination—without relinquishing the right and responsibility to be critical, *within* that advocacy, of individual works of art as well as ideological formulations. The role of the critic should always include the large view, the societal and global views which give dimension and placement to art production. Our role is to assert, and reassert, that the art of women and of peoples of the Third World (women and men) are crucial elements in the construction of the history of art.

*   *   *

The first and most important thing that can be said about Chicana artists is that they *are* artists. The second fact concerns the number of women today who can be counted in their ranks, whether in the fields of literature, drama, dance, or the visual arts. The third matter to be considered are the multiple oppressions Chicanas had to confront and conquer before they could achieve the first state: that of being artists. The pith and essence of what is presented by Chicana artists derives from a specific social history, the lived experiences of that history, and the matured reflections made *on* that history by artists born Chicana in "occupied America."

The Chicano socio-political movement (as differentiated from the Mexican and Mexican American movements preceding it) began in 1965, as a result of the grape pickers' strike in Delano, California, that triggered the imagination of a whole generation of young people of Mexican descent. It was followed in 1966 by a demonstration in Albuquerque, New Mexico; by the founding of the Crusade for Justice in Denver, Colorado, the same year; by the courthouse raid on behalf of land grant rights in northern New Mexico in 1967; by the founding in 1967 of campus organizations throughout the Southwest, and the consequent birth of terms like "Chicano" and "*chicanismo*"; by the formation in 1967 of the Raza Unida Party in El Paso, Texas; by the 1968 student "blowouts" from East Los Angeles high schools and the Third World strike at San Francisco State University; by the anti-Vietnam war demonstration of 1969 and the Chicano Moratorium of 1970, both in Los Angeles. These and many other economic and political events in the Southwest and the Midwest, were accompanied by a cultural explosion with a sufficient number of unifying symbols and characteristics to be considered a cultural *movement*—one that articulated the Chicano experience in the United States.

The Chicano experience was not a simple one to express, beginning with its self-designation. Mexicans in the United States have called themselves by a variety of names corresponding to historical and social pressures faced by a colonized people. Variously the terms have included Spanish American and

Hispanic (the latest "fashionable" term, rejected by many because it ignores the Indian component so important to the Chicano movement); Mexicano, Mexican, Mexican American, Raza (the "Race", or "the people"), and Chicano. In their search for a national denominator, Chicanos faced other problems of diversity: not all were brown, not all were Catholic, not all were Spanish-surnamed, not all were Spanish-speaking. Many identified equally as Native American and Mexican. There were also regional diversities, and, finally, the question of sexual differentiation.

Mexican and Chicana women have traditionally faced a series of stereotypes, misconceptions, and restrictions from society at large, and from within their own communities. Many of these are similar to those shared by women in general; some are specific to a so-called Latin American ethos. According to various studies, Latin American women, continentally, were expected to be gentle, mild, sentimental, emotional, intuitive, impulsive, fragile, submissive, docile, dependent, and timid; while men were supposed to be hard, rough, cold, intellectual, rational, farsighted, profound, strong, authoritarian, independent and brave. The Mexican family, in particular, was purportedly founded on the supremacy of the father (*machismo*), the total sacrifice of the mother (*hembrismo*), the elders having authority over the young, and the men over the women. Chicano men were seen as dominating their wives and overprotecting their daughters—and expecting passive compliance from both.[2] In actuality, the Chicana is a product of two cultures: the traditional Mexican culture experienced at home in diluted forms, and the dominant North American culture (with its own share of sexism, but a greater liberty for women) outside the home. But the final point to be made is that Chicanas, like women everywhere, have never conformed to the stereotypes manufactured about and for them by male historians, psychologists, and other apologists or contributors to female oppression. Chicana and Chicano historians and sociologists are revising the history of Mexican women in the United States and Mexico: reexamining the legends, discovering and publishing the names and deeds of writers, intellectuals, labor leaders and social reformers, as well as thousands of unnamed working women whose combined actions have shaped history.

There is no question that Chicanas living in North America were also influenced by the feminist movement whose modern reincarnation was almost simultaneous with that of the Chicano movement (both products of the turbulent and reforming sixties). Though women played a prominent role in the Chicano movement, they felt the need for a clearer articulation of their own role in society. The movement called for an end to oppression—discrimination, racism, and poverty—goals which Chicanas supported unequivocally, but it did not propose basic changes in male-female relations or the status of women. A commonly expressed attitude on woman's role was, "It is her place and duty to stand behind and back up her Macho."[3] As Martha Cotera has pungently pointed out, when the men (and even some of the women—those she calls the "chickie-babies" and the "groupies" of the movement) spoke of liberation, "you found that they literally meant liberation for men, and they couldn't care peanuts about you or your little girls or your little sisters, or your own mother."[4] However, precisely through strong, perceptive, and outspoken feminists like Cotera and Inés Hernándes Tovar of Texas, Alicia Escalante and Francisca Flores of California, and many others, Chicanas began to sense their power and speak out on their own behalf. They established organizations like the Mexican American Women's Organization, the Comisión Femenil Mexicana, the Mexican American Business and Professional Women, the Hijas de Cuauhtémoc, and the Concilio Mujeres. In Texas, the art group Mujeres Artistas del Suroeste (MAS: Southwestern Women Artists) organized exhibits for Chicana and Latina women. Publications like *Encuentro femenil, Regeneración, Popo femenil,* and *La razón mestiza* appeared. The relations of Chicanas with the main groupings of white, middle-class U.S. feminists were not always cordial. Racism and classism within these movements often came under attack. "We are an integral part of [the feminist] movement," says Dorinda Moreno, "but the often brutal clashing of ideas have made the building of that bridge to be a sometimes painful encounter."[5] As Third World women discovered in Mexico City at the 1975 International Women's Year, their differences with the U.S. movement were sometimes irreconcilable. For these women and for Third World women in the United States, there is more to the question of women's rights than equality with men. While insisting on their right to be equal and have the same opportunities for advancement as men, they are dedicated, by necessity, to liberating their whole people from the injustices of the dominant society which oppresses both men and women. Sexism, for Chicana women, is coupled with racism and economic exploitation. The direction of Chicana feminism, therefore, has particularly stressed issues affecting the victimization of women due to their color, national origin, and poverty, as well as their sex. Organizations have dealt with problems of welfare, battering, birth control, involuntary sterilization of genocidal proportions, inadequate health care, lack of child care facilities, unequal pay, unemployment, and lack of meaningful education and educational opportunities. For Chicanas in, or aspiring to the middle class (which includes most artists), the priority toward upward mobility was often in competition not only with men, but also with white women.

In conclusion: Chicanas participated from the beginning in the struggles and accomplishments of the Chicano movement, including its cultural expression. In addition to questions of identity as a people, Chicanas also wished to clarify their identity as women with its special problems and concerns. It was necessary to confront the racism, classism, and sexism of society at large, and the sexism within their own ranks, in order to achieve full personhood. Simply becoming artists frequently involved breaking stereotypes within the patriarchal family (or the working class family that conceived no economic advantage to be derived from entering the arts); persisting within the educational system, especially in opposition to its insistence on "mainstream" culture and art forms; juggling duties as lovers, wives, mothers, and workers with the time for creative work; and finally, being sufficiently self-confident and assertive to obtain exhibition space or commissions.

The Many Facets of Chicana Art: New Needs, New Themes

A few historical notes are in order to position Chicanas in the cultural and economic worlds of work. During the Spanish colonial period, in the Río Grande Valley which today encompasses much of the states of New Mexico, Texas, and Colorado, women worked as tanners, weavers, and seamstresses in a primarily rural economy. They were also gardeners, midwives, servants, nurses, *curanderas* (healers), and even overseers of Indian women slaves. In more recent years, the artisanship which formerly supplied internally needed domestic and religious articles for the isolated colonizers of northern New Spain/Mexico, has been transformed into production for collectors, tourists, and the new Chicano middle class. In northern New Mexico, women are engaged in work as artisans, alone, or with husbands and families, in making ornamental tinwork, straw inlay, rawhide work, embroidery and quilting—as well as weaving and plastering adobe structures.[6]

By the 1920s, their numbers swelled by the great increase in Mexican migration to the United States resulting from the chaos of the Mexican revolution, women entered the wage labor force in large numbers because families could not survive on men's wages alone. The cooking, canning, weaving, and other work previously performed at home were transferred to industries like packing, canning, textiles, garment factories, laundries, restaurants, and domestic labor. By the time of World War II, Mexican Americans had been urbanized throughout the Southwest, and were migrating to the great industrial centers of the Midwest.

Insufficient research exists to ascertain the extent and kind of artistic activities in which Mexican Americans as a whole were engaged. We know that a certain number of men were designers, caricaturists, commercial photographers, and printers—especially for Spanish-language publications—while a smaller number were professional fine artists generally creating along mainstream guidelines. The information about women is even more sparse. Jacinto Quirarte's book on Mexican American artists mentions only two women, both born in the early years of this century.[7] However there is little doubt that Mexican American women exercised their creativity in a multitude of ways within their own homes. Extrapolating from the evidence that is slowly coming in, women decorated their homes, crocheted, embroidered, knitted, made lace, and painted on a variety of surfaces. Eighty-one-year-old Alicia Dickerson "Monte" Montemayor, whom I interviewed in 1980 at the home where she was born in Laredo, Texas, exemplified this artistic creativity. Monte's great-grandparents settled in Laredo before Texas became part of the United States. From her strong frontier grandmother, she absorbed family stories and folktales, including those about relations between the Mexican and Indian peoples. As Monte's family was growing up, she knitted afghans, crocheted, and made dolls for her children and for church sales. In 1973, when her husband became ill, Monte started painting gourds she raised in her garden to pass the time while she cared for him. She then transferred her work to canvas, on which she did still lifes of fruit and flowers, imaginary images, and fantastic landscapes. Monte's entry into painting corresponded with the florescence of the Chicano art movement; and the Chicana women's art organization, MAS of Austin, showed her work in galleries. Like the men, contemporary Chicana artists are a product of the struggles in the sixties and seventies that, to a certain degree, opened higher education to people of Mexican descent. The same period saw an efflorescence of a grassroots artistic movement within which some women made their appearance. Both trained and self-trained women, in small numbers, painted murals and made silkscreen posters. Not many of the self-trained remained in art due to the problems of economic survival and lack of a support structure geared to their needs. (Trained artists, men and women, have fallen away for the same reasons.) In general, the public phase of Chicano art—street murals and posters—which reached its production nadir in the midseventies, was not conducive to much female participation. The problems of working outdoors on a large scale, of being subject to the comments or harassments of the passing public, the strenuous nature of the work in light of how women are socialized for physical effort, militated against their participation.[8] Judith Baca, then director of the Mural Resource Center in Los Angeles, early recognized this problem and, in addition to her regular mural manual for art directors and neighborhood teams, produced and illustrated the *Woman's Manual: How to Assemble Scaffolding.*

Despite convention and the attitudes of their menfolk, some women entered into mural production, particularly in California where the even climate and the existence of stuccoed buildings (which offered excellent surfaces for the priming and painting of outdoor murals) resulted in the largest production of Chicano murals existing in any state of the nation. Women began to be active in muralism by 1970 when Baca (later recognized nationally for the *Great Wall of Los Angeles* project)[9] began to work on walls with teams of young gang members from East Los Angeles. By 1974, women became active as muralists in the San Francisco Bay area with the organization of the Mujeres Muralistas, a team including three Chicanas and a Venezuelan woman. Short-lived though the group was, it became seminal for women artists throughout the state who took courage from its example and even, with variations, adapted its name as their own.

The great surge of women artists, however, corresponded with the "privatization" of Chicano art in the later seventies—which itself corresponded to a diminution of the intense activism of earlier years. As the Chicano gallery structure expanded in many states of the Southwest and Midwest, and community and feminist galleries became aware of Chicanas, the possibilities for exhibitions of smaller, more intimate work also expanded. To these possibilities were later added college and university galleries, and certain museums. The aperture is not large, even for the men who were on the scene earlier, but it exists.[10]

Women's art (overwhelmingly representational in the Chicano art movement) has engaged many new themes and interpretations that reflect different realities and perceptions. From the beginning, positive images of active women began to appear. One of the most ubiquitous images in male art (derived from Mexican calendars) has been the sexy, often seminude figure of the Aztec princess from the Iztaccíhuatl/Popocatépetl legend, carried ''Tarzan-Jane'' fashion by a gloriously arrayed warrior prince. This Hollywoodized rendition epitomizes the notion of the passive woman protected by the active man. In its place, Chicana artists substituted heroines from the Mexican revolution (particularly those culled from the Agustín V. Casasola Archives), labor leaders, women associated with alternative schools and clinics, working women, women in protest, etc. In other words, active women who shape their lives and environments.

The single most influential source of imagery for all Chicano artists was the 1976 bilingual book *450 Años del pueblo chicano/450 Years of Chicano History in Pictures,* produced in Albuquerque, with a text by Elizabeth Sutherland Martínez.[11] Mexican peoples from both sides of the border, of all periods, ages, occupations, and activities appear in its pages and provide an iconography of struggle, work, and culture. The role of women in all these areas is clearly delineated in historical photographs.

If *450 Years* provided a rich vein of extroverted imagery, the life and art of Mexican painter Frida Kahlo provided an introverted model: woman focused on her interior life, on the cycles of birth and death, on pain and fortitude, on the sublimation of the self in art. The whole feminist movement was fascinated by Kahlo; but for Chicana artists she provided a needed role model. Not only was her art of great interest and beauty, not only did it incorporate or absorb the pre-Columbian and folk imagery of Mexico which were vital strands of Chicano cultural nationalism in the seventies, but her whole life, lived as a work of art, was intriguing. Kahlo's brilliant color, minute detail, exuberant use of plant forms, fusion of the pre-Columbian and the modern, and use of the self-portrait as a mode began to appear in many Chicana works.

Another source of female imagery and inspiration was the vernacular art of the Southwest: particularly home altars and the smaller *nichos* (religious niches) which are created and tended by women.[12] Reinforced by Mexican altars for the *Día de los muertos* (Day of the dead), the altar, as a cumulative sculptural object, passed into Chicano/a art in numerous variations. Other popular religious imagery includes the Virgin of Guadalupe—traditional and transformed; and the curandera (female faith healer) whose roots are older than Catholicism.

The first half of the 1970s was dominated by militant and pre-Columbian images denoting Indian ancestry; the second half was more nostalgic (or perhaps it has also been a search for roots, but closer to home and more familiar). This search is perhaps best symbolized by the Luis Valdez play and movie *Zoot Suit.* Many artists dipped into family photograph albums to recreate the Pachuco of the 1940s and older eras. (Interestingly enough, the Zoot Suit/Pachuco revival did not extend to the Pachuca: the female embodiment of cool, hip, and distinctive dress and behavior during World War II. In one of the rare cases where a woman artist refers to the Pachuco era, she does so in terms of a pair of "Stacies," the fashionable pointed shoes associated with some Pachuco males. See the "testimony" of Carolina Flores below.) So infused with *machismo* has the Pachuco revival been, that the Pachuca is almost completely lost from sight. Instead, women became interested in female ancestors and their activities, tracing back family members—especially in long-settled areas like New Mexico and Texas—as much as five generations. Others have revived the domestic arts, which owe a strong debt to Native American influence and intermarriage. Weaving, pottery-making, and *enjarrando* (the plastering of adobe constructions traditionally done by women), have long been practiced by Pueblo and Mexican women in New Mexico and southern Colorado. These crafts were revived in New Mexico in the 1920s and 1930s by Anglo artists and tourists and received federal patronage. In the 1970s, another revival occurred due to the impetus of the Chicano movement and the land grant struggle. New Mexican women engaged in these practices also pay tribute to their ancestors of several generations who have passed on these skills. In the more alienated urban areas, Chicana artists have also turned their attention to *barrio* (Mexican neighborhood) women: particularly the young *cholas* characterized by heavy dramatic make-up, chic barrio-style clothing, and tattoos, with the toughness and tenderness to survive in a difficult environment. Others have documented grandmothers, aunts, mothers and children, and the family affection (immediate and extended) that provides a support structure throughout the Southwest.

This is by no means a complete list of the concerns that occupy Chicana artists; it is intended merely as an indicator. By the same token, Chicana artists employ a wide range of styles and techniques, from traditional *retablos* (altarpieces) to the most avant-garde methods of manipulated photography, xerography, and book art. If there are unifying characteristics, they include the overwhelming concern with images of women, their condition, and their environment. Many works are directly or indirectly autobiographical; a certain number deal with sexuality. Another common denominator that has emerged is the tendency to use organic rather than geometric form: the rounded corner, the flowing line, the potlike shape shared by clay vessels, the pregnant body, and the adobe fireplace.

Testimonies

Teresa Archuleta-Sagel (Española, New Mexico)

I knew I wanted to be a *tejedora* (weaver) at an early age. My family was involved and supportive in every aspect. My father built my looms. My mother told me rich stories about great-grandfather Juan Manuel Velásquez. She remembered him at his loom weaving and singing, while the *abuelitas* (old women) sat together on evenings telling *chistes y cuentos, cardando e hilando lana* (jokes and stories, carding and spinning wool). My mother intrigued me with those wonderful stories of the past, stories that compelled me to seek spinning tools I had never seen, and scarcer still, good fleece. I also started experimenting with the *yerbas* (wild plants) that grow abundantly in the Río Arriba area.

I dreamt of *Electric Ikat* [a dyed wool blanket] on three separate occasions before actually starting to weave it. I believe the dreams guided and reassured me during the five months of working through an unfamiliar process.

Alicia Arredondo (*Austin, Texas*)

The techniques I use, finger weaving and macramé, are not unique; they come from ancient folk art and trade crafts. The work I am involved in I have named *tejidos en nudos* (knotted weavings). It is the tejidos that reflect my people, my culture, my personal experiences and a physical history of where I have been. The nudos (knots) symbolize the complexities of life—life as it is common to all people.

Santa Barraza (*Austin, Texas*)

My artwork [drawings and prints] has been influenced by the Chicano movement of the late sixties and early seventies, my culture, historical background, the Mexican muralists, and shamanism. At the beginning of my creative endeavor, I created art about my physical experiences and struggle for my Raza (people). Today I utilize images from the unconscious, working intrinsically to convey a personal, indiscernible, and emotional experience.

Liz Lerma Bowerman (*Mesa, Arizona*)

I was pregnant with my first child. I was impressed [as a ceramist] with my body's ability to change so easily. My belly was large and round. My skin was shiny and elastic. I just had to do something with my beautiful body.

The *Body Mask* series was cast by my husband Tom in six-week intervals: June 23, August 8, September 21, and November 8 (just two weeks before my daughter Roxana was born). The masks have lacings on the sides to allow people to tie them on and experience the volume of a pregnant body.

Barbara Carrasco (*Los Angeles, California, b. El Paso, Texas*)

The lithograph *Pregnant Woman in a Ball of Yarn* portrays an oppressed pregnant woman trapped by the fear of fighting her oppressors. Actually it was inspired by the effect my brother's chauvinism had on his wife (he has since changed for the better). Others who have viewed the lithograph see it as the unconscious message of forced sterilization, a present-day reality.

Isabel Castro (*Los Angeles, California, b. Mexico City*)

The body of work *Women under Fire* is a series of manipulated color slides transferred to color xerox. This high-technology process allows me to have instant feedback on the image. The work is processed and altered four times: once through the lens of the camera when the image was taken, the second through the lab slide processing, the third through direct manipulation of the slide itself (scratching, coloring, bleaching, tearing), and the last process through the lens of the camera again. In *Women under Fire,* I intended to contrast the calm look on the woman's face with the danger of the gunsight focused on her.

The images of women have always been of great interest to me. Women within the Chicano community have to be strong in order to survive. Such has been the experience in my particular family. But women outside their family structures have greater obstacles imposed on them by their communities and society in general.

Yreina Cervántez (*Los Angeles, California, b. Garden City, Kansas*)

My artwork is the strongest aspect of me. At its best, it is the most honest reflection of everything I want to say, not only in the subject matter, but through the colors I use, which have a voice of their own. Art for me has always been an intense experience and, I realize now, a spiritual experience also. I often use the traditional "Madonna" figure, and the indigenous concept of the *Nahual* which appears in the form of animal counterparts—jaguars, cats, birds, etc., all representing duality. Some of my most satisfying works are my self-portraits where I can relate my private feelings about myself as a Chicana and as a woman. My other concerns in art are of a political and social nature. At times there is conflict between the personal statement and the political content in my work.

Carolina Flores (*San Antonio, Texas; b. Fort Stockton, Texas*)

Los Stacies de Javier are a pair of shoes belonging to Javier Piña of Laredo, Texas. They are personal in nature—about Javier's personal rebellion against family, society, etc. They symbolize our own rebellion against two oppressive societies— Mexican and Anglo—in relation to Chicanos!

Mi abuela Francisca y su amiga Cruz is taken from an old photograph of my grandmother and her best friend Cruzita—as we knew her as children. This painting became part of a series of family portraits (taken from old photographs) which I did as a student at the University of Texas in Austin. They formed a link between the home and cultural environment of my west Texas hometown and the alienated rootless Anglo environment of the Austin campus.

Diane Gamboa (*Los Angeles, California*)

I was always interested in fashion from the time my aunt used to sell things at the swap meets and I played with the stuff. In the early 1960s, I went to elementary school in short white go-go boots and fishnet stockings. Later I became interested in hippie fashions and bought vintage clothes at thrift shops in East Los Angeles. I have always collected accessories, jewelry, and hats. I admired the Pachuca and Chola looks, but I wanted to dress unusually.

I started doing paper fashions in 1982 for a Día de los Muertos show with three male artists. Paper fashions are so unusual, very original, instant and spontaneous, like a *piñata* [paper-ribbon covered clay pot filled with sweets for blindfolded children who break it with a stick]: so beautiful, but destroyed later. *Leopard-Spotted* is a custom handmade paper dress, one of six from the *Lizard* line. These dresses are specifically designed for the cold-blooded.

Ester Hernández (*Oakland, California; b. Dinuba, California*)

I am an ex-farmworker of Yaqui-Mexican ancestry. I have worked in many media, but I consider myself a printmaker. My images are always those of *la mujer chicana* (the Chicana woman). My ideas and inspiration come from life itself—the beautiful as well as the gross. I made the print *Sun Mad* as a very personal reaction to my shock when I discovered that the water in my hometown, Dinuba, which is the center of the raisin-raising territory, had been contaminated with pesticides for 25 to 30 years. I realized that I had drunk and bathed in this water.

I have always enjoyed taking apart well-known images and transforming them to what I believe is their true nature. As a cultural worker, it is my way of moving people toward positive action.

Juanita M. Jaramillo (*Taos, New Mexico*)

My grandmother is a person who socializes easily and has a lucid memory for names and genealogical connections. Her mother and aunts are now remembered for the impact they had in northern New Mexico weaving, more specifically for the El Valle Style blanket, distinguished by the 8-pointed star. She provided me with a vivid network of my weaver ancestors, and the extended family, the *parentela*.

Visits with elders in the family reveal more and more, especially when they have gone back into their old storage trunks to bring out wonderful heirloom textiles, along with family stories that go with them. I began to spin and weave on the traditional loom in 1971. I also spent a brief period in Mexico City studying Mesoamerican art, including textiles. I could never continue my weaving without my research.

Adivinanza is a mixture of handspun and commercial wool singles. The colors are vegetal dyed. This work evolves out of change, working toward the finer yarns I have been spinning. The title points at innuendos in communication . . . *Adivinanza* is a riddle, a prophecy.

Yolanda López (San Francisco, California; born San Diego, California)

For many Chicanos [the Virgin of] Guadalupe still has a religious and spiritual force. But I suspect her real power exists as a symbol of our national pride. There is something also nostalgic in our attitude towards her. She is an image infused with a certain kind of sentimentality for us. I looked at Guadalupe as an artist, as an investigator of the power of images. I was interested in her visual message as a role model. Essentially she is beautiful, serene, passive. She has no emotional life or texture of her own. She exists within the realm of magical mythology sanctified as a formal entity by religious tradition. She remained the Great Mother, but her representation is as plastic as our individual fears and aspirations.

Because I feel living, breathing women also deserve the respect and love lavished on Guadalupe, I have chosen to transform the image. Taking symbols of her power and virtue, I have transferred them to women I know. My hope in creating these alternative role models is to work with the viewer in a reconsideration of how we as Chicanas portray ourselves. It is questioning the idealized stereotypes we as women are assumed to attempt to emulate.

Linda Martínez de Pedro (Chimayo, New Mexico; b. Denver, Colorado)

My retablos [in this case, painted wood panels] are considered traditional by some and nontraditional by others. I, however, believe being a Native Woman is a matter of perception rather than name, skin color, and birthplace. My ancestors have blessed me; of that there is no doubt.

Judy Miranda (Long Beach, California; b. Los Angeles, California)

My work, in this case, is nonsilver [photographic] printing [on a sheet, then quilted]. The process begins with sensitizing material with a light-sensitive chemical. The material is then exposed to light and developed. The images I have chosen for this quilt were taken from magazines, periodicals, nature, and previous photographs. These images reflect society, politics, and all the bullshit our culture tries to implant upon women.

Yolanda López, *Portrait of the Artist as the Virgin of Guadalupe,* 1978
Tableau vivant.
(*Photo by Susan Mogul*)

Celia Muñoz (Arlington, Texas; b. El Paso, Texas)

I call this series [of images made into an artist's book] *Enlightenment Stories* because they deal with aspects of reasoning. An experience is told as seen by a child's eyes in a deceptively simple prose. The enlightenment is actually my enlightenment when I realized that my experience, good or bad, could be material for my pieces. The bilingual and bicultural upbringing in the border town of El Paso is what I portray.

Anita Rodríguez (El Prado, New Mexico; b. Taos, New Mexico)

The *enjarradoras* (plasterers) of northern New Mexico are those women who have finished, embellished, and maintained the native architecture of the Río Grande Pueblo area since pre-Columbian times. Passed on by oral tradition, the technology of the enjarradoras represents the accumulated experience of centuries of adobe builders.

I have 18 years of experience as a professional enjarradora, and am skilled in all phases of enjarrando including fireplace construction. My fireplaces are functional sculptures, combining the use of modern materials with traditional New Mexican forms, and techniques learned in the earth-building countries of Mexico, China, and Egypt.

Patricia Rodríguez (San Francisco, California; b. Marfa, Texas)

Boxes were the beginning of a new medium for me. I had spent years painting murals in the community[13] and I felt the need for a smaller, more personal work. My first box experiments were masks of well-known Chicano artists. The latest boxes speak in more general terms about the religious aspects which influence the Mexican culture, and the conflict one experiences being a Chicana artist. *Dreams of My Ancestors* functions on two levels. On the lower level there are Indian dolls laid on foamlike cotton—they are dead and this is a level of earth which is underground. Psychologically it shows another level of death, that of another world. The upper world is the reality in which we live today. The hand in the piece is reaching out for bags being handed out by the ancestors but is not able to reach them. As the door of the box opens, the panel has a dollar bill locked behind it, signifying that we have been oppressed through the means of money. We have lost our identity, the original dreams of the ancestors. The bags are representative of precious secrets and mementos handed down through time.

Contemplation is personal and deals with my conflict over a decision between having a child and being a career woman. Both together are very difficult to achieve if you're a starving artist. There are fetuses, there is a heart, and there is a pomegranate which is a very beautiful natural thing that shrivels up and yet holds its shape, and it has nails driven through it. To the side are gears which

Anita Rodríguez, Fireplace of Plastered Adobe, 1983
Taos, New Mexico.
(*Photo courtesy of the artist*)

Mujeres Muralistas (Mural Group), 1974
Left to right: Irene Pérez, Consuelo Méndez of Venezuela, Patricia Rodríguez,
Graciela Carrillo.
(*Photo courtesy of Patricia Rodríguez*)

show energy, movement, and bravery. The whole refers to being brave enough to dive into something and complete yourself as a Chicana. The little section of ridges below are levels of time.

Camilla Trujillo (Española, New Mexico)

The clay I work with is dug from local hillsides. It is then cleaned, thoroughly dried, ground to a fine powder, and sifted together with water and a temper. After it has aged, it is ready to be worked. I use the coil technique to form my pots and figurines. My pottery is fired using the "pit method," outdoors, in a tin box covered all around with cedar wood which burns steadily for about one hour. I don't consider the clay to be inanimate material. I approach it with the same respect I would any living thing. Making pottery is a quiet process. I try to work with the laws of the clay, keeping lines simple and clean. I try to bring out the beauty and personality that lives within the clay. To me, good pottery evokes a feeling, a knowledge, that we are part of the earth.

*   *   *

Chicana art displays a great variety of motifs, forms, and techniques—a reflection of the multifaceted woman with which this essay opened.

> *birth and death hot in my thighs: I see*
> *death grin between my legs and my*
> *body holds back and I'm*
> *bursting*
> *to birth houses and trains and wheat and*
> *   coal and stars*
> *and daughters and trumpets and volcanoes*
> *   and hawks and*
> *sons and porpoises and roots and stones and worlds and*
> *   galaxies*
> *of humanity and life*
> *yet to be born . . .*[14]

Notes

1. Lucy Lippard, "Headlines, Heartlines, Hardlines: Advocacy Criticism as Activism," *Cultures in Contention,* edited by Douglas Kahn and Diane Neumaier (Seattle: The Real Comet Press, 1985), p. 243.

2. María Nieto Senour, "Psychology of the Chicana," in *Female Psychology: The Emerging Self,* Sue Cox (ed.) (New York: St. Martin's Press, 1981), p. 137.

3. Alfredo Mirandé and Evangelina Enríquez, *La Chicana: The Mexican American Woman* (Chicago: The University of Chicago Press, 1979), p. 235.

4. Martha P. Cotera, *The Chicana Feminist* (Austin: Information Systems Development, 1977), p. 31.

5. Dorinda Moreno, "Un paso adelante," *La razón mestiza* (June 20–22, 1980): 1.

6. See William Wroth (ed.), *Hispanic Crafts of the Southwest,* The Taylor Museum of the Colorado Springs Fine Arts Center, 1977.

7. Jacinto Quirarte, *Mexican American Artists* (Austin: University of Texas Press, 1973).

8. It was pointed out to me at a women artists' conference in 1986 that I should except lesbian women from this statement, and there may be some merit in this contention. However the point has to do with the way women (lesbian or not) were *socialized,* not with their sexual preferences. Among Chicanas, some of the women who went into street muralism were lesbians and some were not. For either, it took extraordinary social strength in the seventies for women to assume this role in what was, in any case, a very marginal art form for men *or* women. In addition, women had to learn the manual skills from which they were often persuaded to abstain from as children.

9. In 1976, Judith Baca painted with teams what was to be the longest mural in Los Angeles—possibly anywhere: *The History of California,* also known as *The Great Wall of Los Angeles,* and the *Tujunga Wash Mural. The Great Wall* was done in segments starting with 1000 feet, and continuing during the summers of 1978, 1980, 1981, and 1983 in 350-foot segments.

10. In the second half of the 1980s, a new national interest in Latin American artists living in the United States seems to be developing, advanced by funding from the National Endowments and some private foundations, including the Rockefeller. According to my information, the interest in promoting cultural exchange between Latin America and the United States through art shows was expressed in January 1986 at a meeting in Puerto Rico by Frank Hodsell of the National Endowment for the Arts. Considering the poor track record of the Reagan administration toward arts funding, one cannot help but speculate at this unusual interest in what has been considered, generally speaking, a marginal arts population. One also wonders whether there might be foreign policy considerations behind such offers: for example, counteracting opposition to U.S. activities in Central America among Latin American countries abroad, and Latino artists in the U.S.

11. *450 Años del pueblo chicano/450 Years of Chicano History in Pictures* (Albuquerque: Chicano Communications Center, 1976).

12. See Kay Turner, "Mexican American Home Altars: Towards Their Interpretation," *Aztlán: International Journal of Chicano Studies Research* 13 (Spring and Fall 1982): 309–26.

13. Patricia Rodríguez was one of the founding members of Mujeres Muralistas of San Francisco in 1974.

14. Excerpt from Alma Villanueva, *Blood Knot,* reprinted in *El Tecolote Literary Magazine* 13, No. 6 (March 1983): 8.

Aspects of Performance in the
Work of Black American Women Artists

Lowery Stokes Sims

In 1983, Lorraine O'Grady stated: "At the moment, individual black performance artists are still exotic oddities".[1] This observation was verified by the controversy and resistance that met a presentation by this writer in a panel discussion on contemporary black American artists in 1985 concerning black women doing performance art.[2] It was clear from the leery comments of the older guard of painters, sculptors, printmakers, and photographers that these art manifestations were somewhat suspect. But, the almost delirious relief expressed by younger women artists (who told tales of outright hostility from their professors) and the interest in performance and video art shown by older colleagues made it clear that performance and video art was certainly going to be a more prevalent form of expression among the younger generation of black artists, and especially among women.

In retrospect, I wonder if the uneasiness experienced by this circle of black American artists was due to something beyond the issue of genre. To be sure, given the socio-political and economic considerations that all black American artists have had to (and still have to) contend with, performance and video would be considered anomalies and anathemas, since they are still basically non-commodity-oriented in form and purpose. Also, these are not art forms that allow themselves to be easily displayed in traditional gallery and museum settings, or to be disseminated through more familiar marketing devices. In view of the resistance that black Americans face in the visual arts, a certain conservative approach—calculated to make the art more acceptable to an audience within both the white and black middle and upper classes—is to be expected.

The group of black American women artists who will be discussed in this essay—along with their male colleagues such as Houston Conwill, David Hammons, Noah Jemison, Lorenzo Pace, Charles Abramson, and Joe Lewis—have deliberately used performance work to enliven and broaden the context for their artistic expression. In the context of the political, economic, and social dialogs of the last twenty years, these artists have been concerned with reaching out to the "community" with their art, and have specifically seen their art as vehicles for political action. Performance art, in conjunction with video, serves as a bridge between the seclusion of the studio and the gallery to the "real" world, the street. It also reclaims for these black Americans a connection with the traditional African nuances of his or her task, whereby the art object was created to be used as part of a grand performance piece[3]—i.e., a ritual that addressed the needs of an entire community, rather than serving as some kind of trophy for a privileged, elite, art-consuming class.

The fact that it is mostly women who have been involved in performance art might have something to do with the suspect status that it has within black American art circles. There are two reasons for this. First, the overwhelmingly male focus of black American art might not be able to accommodate an expressive form that is dominated by women. The act of performing also plays provocatively into certain stereotypes about women, black women in particular. "Acting-out" was the exclusive province of black American women long before it was accepted as a creative strategy for women as a whole.[4] The image is a familiar one: given the appropriate provocation—be it anger, annoyance, defiance, or enjoyment—the body language of the black American woman shifts into gear. Hands go on hips (we "assume the position," as my friend and mentor, Daisy Voigt, would say), the head flings back, and the mouth opens to emit what is more often than not an eloquent and relentless stream of epithets or commentary befitting the situation. The prototypes for this are on the shelves of libraries and the archives of the entertainment industry: Mammy, Aunt Jemima, Beulah, Sapphire, Bess.[5] While these are stereotypes that have been codified by the white establishment, they (as do all stereotypes) encompass the passion and vitality of the real thing.[6] The suitability of "acting-out" as an expressive strategy for a class of individuals who have few accepted or sanctioned means of self-expression—and women of color in this society are particularly stymied in this regard—also comes into consideration here. This invariably gives the performance work of black American women an edge that is decidedly confrontational, particularly in the area of male-female relationships. This remains a sensitive political issue within the black community in the United States. The peculiar machismo of the civil rights and black-power movements were definitely at odds with the goals and aspirations of the concurrent women's movement. And, as Michele Wallace has eloquently shown, not a few black women of that generation got caught at cross-purposes.[7] That black women artists now address these ideas through the performance idiom has resulted in a decidedly confrontational presentation that challenges the status quo, not only of American society as a whole, but of the intraracial dynamics of the black American situation in this country as well.

The link that the work of these women provides between black, feminist, and social welfare political camps can be discerned in the oeuvre of an individual like Adrian Piper, whose performance work started in the early 1970s. Piper engaged a myriad of concerns in her performance works, and collectively they intervene between art and life in the most direct way.[8] The series of street events known as her *Catalyst* series involved the artist roaming New York City dressed in a disheveled manner, with her face and body disfigured in various nonsociable ways (e.g., having refuse on it, or being stuffed with bits of fabric). As she interacted with people in the subway, in the lobbies of buildings, etc., Piper provided an eerie foreshadowing of our current preoccupation with homeless and displaced people in our streets, individuals who challenge our tolerance and grip the edges of our daily consciousness. In examining this work at the recent twenty-year retrospective of Piper's work organized by the Alternative Museum in New York City,[9] one was struck by the similarity of this activity to the special feature done in 1987 by NBC-TV anchorwoman Pat Harper, who donned cast-off clothing, and—armed with only a suitcase—set out to live as one of the homeless for a few days in order to intensify and add veracity to her reportage on nightly news. Likewise, Piper's performance in drag as a black male in the *Mythic Being* events of the mid-1970s addressed the contemporary revival of societal witch-hunting of black males and the reactions to their mere physical presence in our lives. In one of the poster images created in this series Piper-as-black-male has inserted the challenge: "I embody everything you most hate and fear."

Piper was among the first black artists to deal with the performance idiom in a serious and concerted way. The women whose work will be discussed here have by and large gotten involved in performance since the late 1970s and early 1980s. While many are painters or sculptors who do performance work along with their "primary" disciplines—such as Faith Ringgold, Howardena Pindell, and Candace Hill-Montgomery—others come from backgrounds and training in other disciplines: literature, dance, theatre, well as the visual arts. My interviews with them[10] revealed that they all got involved with performance art as a result of their theoretical and technical dissatisfactions with what they perceived as the traditional limitations of their individual fields of endeavor. For Joyce Scott, for example, performance work came as her art moved out from and off the wall. Her paintings evolved into more relief sculptural forms, which then were extended through her creation of jewelry and customized clothing—art wear. One of her first performance works was a fashion show, done in collaboration with artist Linda De Palma who created the environment for the presentation of Scott's art apparel. Scott has also done some singing, so the performance medium seemed to naturally combine her myriad talents. Kaylynn Sullivan was trained in dance and theater; and she moved into performance wanting to experiment with the extension of the usual sensory engagements of these media to include olfactory impressions and nonnarrative sound. Lorraine O'Grady comes from a literary background. It was her contact with the work of Adrian Piper and her interest in Surrealist literature and art that were the impetus for her involvement in performance.

Painter, sculptor, quilt-maker, and puppeteer Faith Ringgold was, like Adrian Piper, an early experimenter with art presentations that can be called "performance." Ringgold was involved in the civil rights and women's movements within the art world as a member of the Art Worker's Coalition and WASABAL in the late 1960s and early 1970s. As a painter, she has created some of the most memorable icons of black political art. She began making soft sculpture in the 1970s in order to accommodate her artistic activity to the demands of family life.[11] Soft sculpture—and later quilting—allowed her to work while being engaged in social settings. Her adoption of fabric media eventually led to an adaptation of Oriental prayer hangings—tongas—which Ringgold transformed into political collage/poems that she did in collaboration with her seamstress mother Willi Posey in the mid-1970s.

The soft sculptures gradually emerged as performances because they inevitably suggested such a step. Ringgold was also doing fabric masks that showed a direct influence of African art. The ones created for her sculptural piece *Buba and Bene* (1974) demanded the addition of stuffed bodies. This ensemble was then set in a more elaborate environmental trapping to become the 1976 work *The Wake and Resurrection of the Bicentennial Negro.* When her daughters took to donning the masks, and improvising stories, Ringgold got the idea of presenting masks within a storytelling format. It was when she found herself without a slide projector during a lecture she was giving on a college campus that the modus operandi finally came together. She resourcefully improvised a performance with the figures and the masks, finding that she preferred the more direct contact with the audience that this format allowed her to the more formal atmosphere of a slide lecture. It was also conducive to audience participation, which then became an integral part of her public presentations.

By 1984 Ringgold's performances were no longer tied to her static works. She still used the masks and backdrops, but opened the program by telling and acting out the story as a masked commentator, like the masquerader in African society. Ringgold began to introduce autobiographical material in her *No Name Performance #2* of 1982, and invited the audience to tell their own stories within the context of the performance. Thus the performance format, as in the African context, became the media by which the audience (i.e., the community) experienced spiritual and aesthetic catharsis. Such an approach is the opposite of the more passive role that the audience tends to play in recent performance art presentations. This is a consideration that has engendered much dialog within the performance community over the appropriate way in which performance art should be disseminated into the world at large when individuals other than the artist and his or her collaborators are involved.

This issue is a special preoccupation of Candace Hill-Montgomery, who constantly evaluates the situation within which she will present her performance statements. She deliberately "sabotages" the predictability of the "performing" ritual, on occasion failing to show up in person for an announced event, sending instead

Faith Ringgold, *Mrs. Jones and Family*, 1973
Cloth sculpture, 60″ × 12″.
(Photo courtesy of the artist)

Faith Ringgold, *Wake and Resurrection of the Bicentennial Negro*, 1976
Fiber and mixed media installation.
(Photo by Karen Bell; courtesy of the Bernice Steinbaum Gallery)

a statement to be read to the assembled group. Her sense of presence and non-presence is tied into the distinction she makes between "performing" and her individual works as political acts intended to propel people to react to a specific idea, issue, event, etc. Hill-Montgomery admits to being greatly influenced by the work of David Hammons and Houston Conwill; and, along with Hammons and Joe Lewis, was an integral part of the radical artistic events—focused around Colab in downtown Manhattan, and Fashion Moda in the South Bronx—which ushered in the decade of the eighties.

Hill-Montgomery began doing art in the street in the late 1970s while she was an artist-in-residence at the Studio Museum in Harlem. As she has observed, this invariably became "performance" because the people passing by got involved in what she was doing by participating and offering critiques. Some of her work at this time focused on urban decay—a theme that could be observed in the projects of many of her colleagues. *Vacant Lot* of 1979 was the installation of an abandoned boat amid the rubble of a vacant lot in Harlem. The allegorical potential was rather sophisticated and this quality can be perceived in Hill-Montgomery's work despite her cultivation of calculated chaos and spontaneity. Her work is always topical to the extreme, and she is always working out of a current issue which is presented in a context that broadens the perception of that issue. Her use of a literal paroxysm of multimedia effects is meant to bring as much of the "outside" (i.e., "real") world into the gallery setting as possible. *Food for Thought,* an installation that was presented in 1980 both at the New Museum for Contemporary Art in New York and on a lawn across from the Department of Health and Human Services in Washington, D.C., was an early advocate of dealing with the problem of hunger in America. It presented cabinets of food arranged in a criss-cross diagonal configuration, rather like the stores of food hoarded by the post-World War II generation in this country during the height of the civil defense mania of the 1950s. A recent installation, *What's Knot in Fashion or Other Quick Changes,* presented in the exhibition "Race and Representation" at Hunter College Gallery in New York City, showed the artist's familar use of collages of poetry, new items, xeroxes, drawings, and watercolors in a wall-installation that exposed the paradox of Eurocentricity's simultaneous embrace of African cultural forms and rejection of African peoples (particularly in the context of South Africa and in the person of Nelson Mandela).[12] Hill-Montgomery has likened this approach to performance/installation as photojournalism with a poet's vision.

While the black middle class has rarely been perceived as an arena for creative exploration, either in the chronicling of its peculiar preoccupations or in its aesthetic cooption into the mainstream, it has successfully formed the focus of the work of both Faith Ringgold and Lorraine O'Grady, who has made the black middle class the thematic focus of her performance work. Ringgold's 1985 performance work, *The Bitter Nest,* is a particularly interesting work in that it focuses on the contentious relationship between black women of the middle and lower

Lorraine O'Grady in Performance, *Nefertiti/Devonia Evangeline*, 1981(?)
(Photo © Freda Leinwand)

classes. It concerns the ambitions of a mother for a daughter who repudiates her and yet repeats her history through the upbringing of her son. This son ultimately comes to fulfill the middle class aspirations of the grandfather. A similar theme of circular destinies is the focus of Lorraine O'Grady's *Nefertiti/Devonia Evangeline* performance work. O'Grady draws on the story of the rejection of the legendary Queen Nefertiti by her husband Akhnaton in favor of her sister and, later, her daughter. She uses this story to explore her own relationship with her sister, who died under tragic circumstances before O'Grady could resolve their relationship. O'Grady was able to exploit the uncanny physical resemblance of her sister to the Egyptian queen and the similarities of poses in the chronicles of everyday life on the wall-paintings in the tomb of King Tut to those assumed by O'Grady's family in casual snapshots. The artist used these similarities to explore the follies and farces of family life and sexual and social mores through the centuries. O'Grady has noted: "As an advantaged member of a disadvantaged group, I've lived my life on the rim—a dialectically privileged location that's helped keep my political awareness acute. But the main reason my art is 'political' is probably that anger is my most productive emotion."[13]

One of O'Grady's first apparitions was as Mlle. Bourgeoise Noire, who appeared at gallery and museum openings in New York in 1980, clad in a ball-gown made of white gloves and wearing a tiara and long gloves. Mlle. Bourgeoise Noire circulated among the opening-night crowds distributing flowers from a bouquet of cat-o-nines. When she finished handing out the flowers, she then stood in the middle of the reception area and began to whip herself with the cat-o-nines, all the while declaring a manifesto of liberation for black artists:

> No more boot-lickin
> No more ass-kissing
> No more buttering up
> No more Posturing
> of superass . . . imulates
> BLACK ARTISTS MUST TAKE MORE RISKS.[14]

O'Grady directly communicated the frustrations of black artists who were struggling with the dilemma of trying to assimilate into the art world while largely being excluded from the "mainstream."

Writing in 1984, O'Grady provided a cogent paradigm for performance art in her description of her work as "situational interventions that rejects the widely held view of contemporary black art as either 'primitivist' or 'conventionally derivative.' "[15] She has been concerned with taking these ideas to the black community to demonstrate that avant-garde black art can be relevant. Towards this end she conceived her work *Art Is,* a float that was staged within the context of the annual West Indian Day Parade along Eastern Parkway in Brooklyn, New York. O'Grady wanted to see if art with a "capital A" could compete with and complement the floats and costumes inspired by the carnival tradition in the Caribbean. A phalange of dancers in white circulated among the paraders, holding frames up to their faces and the faces of random spectators along the parade route. Their "home" float consisted of a huge gold frame that isolated successive views of reality as it made its way along the parade route, declaring everything in its wake as "art"—with a "capital A."

The quiet violence underlying middle-class and middle-American life has also provided a focus for the work of Kaylynn Sullivan. In *Victims,* a work conceived in 1980, Sullivan retells the events of domestic violence that was visited upon her own family, as the preparation of food forms a continuity for the action. The role of food and its preparation, along with the attendant sounds and smells, are typical of Sullivan's preoccupation with expanding the sensory commitment of spectators at performance events to those arenas where more subliminal memories and associations are located within our psyches. This particular slant is the result of Sullivan's intensive study of the incidence of domestic murders and batterings which were immediately followed by the preparation and consumption of food. In a subsequent work, *Diminished Capacity* of 1983, Sullivan examined the role of junk food in two murders which occurred some twenty years apart. (In the 1950s, Charles Starkweather and Carol Fugate consumed large quantities of soft drinks, sweets, and salted food before and after murdering her family and then embarked on an eight-day murder spree through the state of Nebraska. In 1978, when Dan White was accused of murdering Mayor Moscone and gay activist Harvey Milk in San Francisco, the lawyer for his defense successfully got him a more lenient sentence by pleading "diminished capacity" for his client who was said to have consumed Twinkies and soft drinks the night before the murder: the "Twinkie Defense.") In her performance Sullivan takes the role of Carol Fugate and a fellow actor that of Charles Starkweather and together they eat junk food while watching video reenactments of the murders of 1958 and 1978.[16]

Consumption—be it of food, consumer goods, love, time, or money—has been a persistent theme in Sullivan's performance work. *Open Clothes* (1981) and *Civic Plots—If the Shoe Fits . . .* (1984) focused on apparel, and *Beauty* (1982) dealt with seductions. Considerations of time and place dictated the three-part work *Night Trippers* which situated participants in three distinct locales for three distinct experiences: the public baths for a recitation of folklore and old wives' tales, a church in Harlem for the reenactment of a Saturday-night card game, and an old theater for a fashion show. The peculiar seductions of place were a key element in *And He Had Six Sisters,* where Sullivan repeated the first segment of *Night Trippers,* this time in a house set in the Louisiana bayou. The six sisters groom each other and recite random folklore and in a simultaneous and obsessive crescendo that culminates in the brief monolog by the only sister who has been left out of this communal interaction. In this monolog, she asserts her

Kaylynn Sullivan in Her *And He Had Six Sisters*, April 1987
Performance at Just Above Midtown Gallery, New York.
(Photo © f-stop Fitzgerald, 1987)

Robin Kaiser and Rebecca Perrin in *And He Had Six Sisters*, April 1987
Performance at Just Above Midtown Gallery, New York.
(*Photo © f-stop Fitzgerald, 1987*)

individuality and superiority over the others because of her defiance of conformity. In *Women with Air Conditioning* and *Fandango,* Sullivan uses the metaphors of baseball and fan maneuvers to explore the miscommunication inherent in human relationships, particularly male-female ones.

More recently Sullivan has taken up the character of Carol Fugate again in *Love and Free Will,* a monolog in which Fugate reacts to an unseen interviewer who has found her after her release from prison and subsequent marriage. Sullivan focuses on yet another aspect of this woman's story: the cooperation of women in their own destruction and oppression, and their reluctance to defy the male figures in their lives. In *Half-Way to Jesus* Sullivan remembers the rantings of an old black woman hovering at death, whom she encountered while hospitalized for asthma in 1986. The often indistinguishable boundaries between the physical and the metaphysical within the reality this character was dealing with struck a responsive chord in Sullivan, who has more recently become involved in transchanneling and crystal healing. (She has come to see these as an integral part of her performance work.) These activities have also fueled her interest in locating the image of the goddess within a matrix that is integral to her own existence, rather than the usual adaptation of "foreign" or "primeval" entities that have been an important iconographic component of the women's movement in art over the last twenty or so years.

For Baltimore-based Joyce Scott, that goddess is clearly to be found in herself. Collaborating with actress Kay Lawal in the *Thunder Thigh Review,* she has extensively explored the pain and passion of being the "other," an overweight black woman in this society. Alternating the cathartic power of slapstick with gut-gripping pathos, Scott has brilliantly illuminated the shadowy self that gets lost in the flurry of consensus by which we justify and judge our lives and those about us. The review is about a positive reaffirmation of body images, and the celebration of voluptuous women who have defied the current "ideal" in our society. Apparitions of women of substance float in and out of the performance giving testimony to their rage, their indignation, and their pride and determination.

One theme explored in the *Thunder Thigh Review* is the use of food as a substitute for love and sexual satisfaction. The refrigerator in this case becomes an agent of satisfaction as well as a vehicle for temptation. A portion of the dialog here clarifies the dilemma of the heroine:

> I am different because time and nature have overwhelmed my form. I too was once thin and comely and cast a small shadow, and stepped ever so lightly. And then something happened. It started when I was a child with grandma. I remember cookies, my fingers in her pocket, and her rocking me, lulling me to sleep with him [the refrigerator] in the room. Never enough food, me pounding the corridors, eating the refuse, the discards. The feeling of dissatisfaction, I can't get none. He was always there waiting for the right time, the right place. I gave in, I came in, I tried to crawl into him. He opened wide and wrapped me up. I conceived my first child in there . . . .[17]

Rebecca Perrin and Kaylynn Sullivan in *Fandango,* April 1987
Performance at Just Above Midtown Gallery, New York.
(*Photo © f-stop Fitzgerald, 1987*)

Later a voluptuous Venus on the half shell protests that she is too important to have been birthed from a mere appendage, the cast-off genitals of a male god. A black Statue of Liberty protests that the American Dream is not for black people who were brought over to this country in bondage. One of the most moving segments in the *Thunder Thigh Review* is the wail of Satjet, a monolog by a Hottentot woman who was brought to Europe and exhibited as a curiosity because of her steatopygous physique. Her lament of the violation of her privacy (which she must endure because she is powerless and without a protector) traverses time from the slave auction block to the welfare mothers in city shelters, and eloquently captures the reality of poor and minority women in American society.

These performance works provide just one forum for Scott's political statements. She has over the years evolved into a sophisticated and pungent political artist—as demonstrated by her beadwork jewelry and sculpture—as well, dealing with themes as divergent as the Atlanta child murders, South Africa, and the crisis of black identity and existence in contemporary society.[18]

One of the most devastating commentaries on the impact of American racism on black females—specifically with regard to their physical characteristics—is Howardena Pindell's 1981 video presentation *Free, White and 21*. Pindell recounts in a hypnotizing monotone a series of events based on her experiences and those of her mother: a babysitter who scrubs the face of her mother with lye assuming that her natural pigmentation is stubborn dirt; the paternalistic attitude of white teachers towards the artist, whom they accuse of being ungrateful and unwilling to assimilate and succumb to what they thought was appropriate. As the dialog progresses, we see Pindell, wearing white pancake make-up and a blond wig, wrap and unwrap her head with white gauze. The white face is then peeled off at a dramatic moment. It is a taut, terrifying performance, gripping in its vivid and compelling emotion.

Adrian Piper's *Self-Portrait Exaggerating My Negroid Features,* and her *Political Portraits* deal with the inherent and subliminal approbation of whiteness and its proximity that is replete in the value systems of both white and black Americans. Comparably clear and powerful explanations of the physical realities of black American existence (in all its implications) are not found among the myriad works of black male artists of various aesthetic persuasions and political ideologies.

Within the last five years, there has been a marked increase in the participation of black Americans, particularly women, in performance art. Lorraine O'Grady would be gratified to know that this is not as ''exotic'' a phenomenon as it once was. Besides topical presentations, performance artists have delved into the cross-currents of the historical and cultural realities of Africans in the diaspora. Their combination of song, dance, recitation, and folk myths is seen in the work of such groups as Sweet Honey in the Rock, Urban Bush Women, and Women of the Calabash. These groups have demonstrated a self-awareness and an ability to assert their integral selves that are perhaps unparalleled in the

Kay Lawal and Joyce Scott in *Thunder Thigh Revue*, 1986
Performance.
(*Photo © Peggy Fox, 1986*)

history of the visual and performing art of black Americans. The inclusion of autobiography provides an unusually rich character to the work of these women. There is little of the distancing that characterizes even the most feminist statements in performance. There is too much urgent material that these women must get out of their systems; and too few other outlets exist that lend themselves to making the transmission of this material palpable to a more general audience. The review, *The Legend of Lily Overstreet,* toured by Rhodessa Jones (sister of post-modernist dancer Bill T. Jones) is a good example of this phenomenon.

One of the most interesting talents emerging on the performance scene is writer and scenist Lisa Jones, who in spite of her youth (she is only in her twenties) has begun to produce performance material that is incredibly cogent. Jones's troupe—the Rodeo Calconia High Fidelity Performance Theaters—consists of a number of talented women who perform vignettes that lampoon some of the sacred tenets of black mythology and deal with their often awkward interfacing with contemporary reality. Jones's point of view is that of the post-ERA, post-black liberation: she is a post-feminist black woman, and her view of the world is in no way neoconservative or reactionary. As seen in *Carmella and King Kong,* Jones comprehends the ironies and inconsistencies of the female existence in the world today. The piece was an improbable look at the post-Hollywood life of King Kong, as related by his distressed wife Carmella. We see Carmella's various attempts to deal with her spouse's neglect and infidelity, and with her own need for self-realization. Jones tackles everything from skin bleaching, sexual anomalies, contemporary sexual mores, feminism, black liberationism and the Total Woman philosophy in a barrage of dialog, music, and slide projections.[19] The work of Jones and other black women in performance have and will be important elements in achieving self-actualization of the images of all women, and particularly of those who are nonwhite. They embody in an uncanny way the prayer at the end of Ntozake Shange's *For Colored Girls Who Have Considered Suicide When the Rainbow Is Enough,* in which the ensemble describes finding god in themselves:

> i waz missing somthin
> somthin so important
> somthin promised . . .
> making me whole . . .
> all the gods comin into me
> layin me open to myself . . .
> i found god in myself
> & i loved her/i loved her fiercely.[20]

This article covers what is fast becoming just the tip of the iceberg where black American women artists and performance art are concerned. I regret not having had the opportunity to interview Sengue Nengudi and Maren Hassinger, both of whom have had a strong presence both in New York and in California;

or Robbie McCauley and Laurie Carlos, who have—along with Jessica Hagedorn—been electrifying the performance scene in New York City. Even as I prepare this for publication, I discovered more instances of one-shot video and performance works by various individuals. Thus, this may be considered just the beginning of what one hopes will be a long and fruitful dialog on black American artists in performance and video.

Notes

1. Lorraine O'Grady, "Thoughts about Myself, When Seen as a Political Performance Artist," unpublished manuscript dated January 1, 1981.

2. The presentation was given for a symposium organized in conjunction with the exhibition, "Since the Harlem Renaissance: 50 Years of Afro-American Art," held at Pennsylvania State University, October 4–6, 1985.

3. See the catalog *African Art in Motion* by Robert Ferris Thompson for further exploration of the Africa concept of performance.

4. See, Lucy Lippard, "Acting Out," in her compendium *Get the Message: A Decade for Social Change* (New York: E. P. Dutton, Inc., 1985).

5. Donald Bogle has amply explicated these black female types in his book *Toms, Coons, Mulattoes, Mammies and Bucks: An Interpretive History of Blacks in American Films* (New York: The Viking Press, 1973).

6. Joyce Scott has provided some illuminating thoughts on the dynamics of stereotypes in various societal contexts, noting that in more nonracial situations they serve as safety valves through which a given group can lampoon itself. This is distinct from the situation in a multiracial society such as the United States, where these same images are usually used to disparage a given group or groups.

7. Michele Wallace, *Black Macho and the Myth of the Superwoman* (New York: Dial Press, 1978).

8. Lucy Lippard, "I Embody," in her compendium *From The Center: Feminist Essays on Women's Art* (New York: E. P. Dutton, 1976).

9. *Adrian Piper: Reflections 1967–87.* Curated by Jane Farver, essays by Clive Phillpot and Adrian Piper (New York: The Alternative Museum, 1987).

10. Unless noted the material on Faith Ringgold, Lorraine O'Grady, Candace Hill-Montgomery, Kaylynn Sullivan, Joyce Scott, and Howardena Pindell is based on interviews, observations of performances, and informal conversations between 1985 and 1987.

11. Lowery S. Sims, "Third World Women Speak," *Women Artists News* (December 1978): 1–10.

12. Lowery S. Sims, "Race, Representation, and Appropriation," *Race and Representation: Art/Film/Video* (New York: Hunter College, 1987), p. 20.

13. Lorraine O'Grady, "Thoughts about Myself," op. cit.

14. Transcribed from notes made available to author by Lorraine O'Grady.

15. Lorraine O'Grady, unpublished statement, dated October 1984.

16. Lowery S. Sims, "Body Politics: Hannah Wilke and Kaylynn Sullivan," *Art and Ideology* (New York: The New Museum of Contemporary Art, 1984).

17. Transcription by the author from tape of performance of *Thunder Thigh Review*, Langsdale Auditorium, University of Baltimore, September 14, 1985.

18. Lowery S. Sims, ''Joyce J. Scott,'' *The Paul and Joyce Show* (Baltimore: Maryland Art Place, 1987).

19. See review of Rodeo Caldonia High Fidelity Theater by Lowery S. Sims in *High Performance* 35 (1986).

20. Ntozake Shange, *For Colored Girls Who Have Considered Suicide When the Rainbow Is Enuf* (New York; Macmillan Publishing Co., Inc., 1977), pp. 60–63.

The Last Essay on Feminist Criticism

Arlene Raven

You thought the last essay on feminist criticism had, or should have, already been written? After all, some writers on the subject of gender—and not all of them antifeminists—have named the 1980s the "postfeminist" decade.

When WITCH burned their bras at the 1968 Miss America Pageant, feminists publicly renounced longing for Cinderella in favor of her sisters—the vast sisterhood of the rest of us who, toes and heels severed, tried and failed to fit our bloodied feet into the modish shoe of cultural femininity. And in the process of trying and failing, exposed the myth.

Artists who address gender and society today are no longer compelled by the perfect feminine fit. A large body of work examines the construction of the small shoe (the social body) on the one hand, and the dismembered foot (the physical body) on the other. This work exemplifies the plurality of feminisms which exists in 1988.

But while creative analysis of man-made fabrications of gender has been hailed as the appropriate mode of feminist art for the 1980s, embracing the foot—exploring experience in the female body—has been stigmatized by being declared outmoded. One writer voiced the sentiments of numerous women and men in the arts when she observed that "suddenly nothing seemed more passé than pattern and decoration, vaginal imagery, body art, ritual and all other forms pioneered by women in response to their particular experience."[1]

"Essentialists" are assumed to have made all of the now-unfashionable art of the body during the 70s and to believe that femininity is innate (although this definition may be incomplete, since at this writing essentialism has been defined only by antiessentialists). "Post-modern deconstructionists and appropriationists" are presumed to believe that femininity is a social construction and that nothing is innate. The dichotomy put between them is fiction. Even biologically oriented

---

Parts of this article appeared in *Art Papers*, September/October 1987 and the *Village Voice*, September 1987.

"female imagery" was introduced as a self-conscious antithesis into the historical environment of phallic imagery, challenging human-made, value-laden signs, in which the social "essence" of one gender dominated the other. And even computer-generated texts embody, in their materials and message, the experience and historical consciousness of the person who created them.

Textual interpretation, employed to explode embedded conjectures about femininity, is not intrinsic to 1980s art. It has simply been put to use. Conceptual and sensual feminist perspectives coexisted in the 1960s and 1970s, and both continue to be created. Although there has been an evolution of ideas and methods over almost three decades, there is no true generation gap between the 1970s and 1980s, nor have diametrically opposed modes of artmaking characterized each period. Rather, a wrenching national reversal of circumstances since the turn of this decade and the inauguration of the Reagan administration has fueled misogynistic attitudes, frightened and discouraged women, and caused "essentialists" and "deconstructionists" to become banners of mutual attack.

Remember Georgia O'Keeffe. She inspired feminists for the greater part of the century because she pictured essential and existential femininity in a sensorial and transcendent female principle.

O'Keeffe would paint a pelvis bone. She'd render it once, twice, three times. But the pelvis itself wasn't finally what compelled her. It was the hole and what you could see through it. Seeing through the body, knowing through the bones, is a perspective, one that illuminates the reality of living matter and knowledge that the body is rooted in substance. Not only her bones, but her desert mountains, flowers, and skies, are spirited analogs for a female body made, as Susan Griffin has written, "from this earth."

O'Keeffe's centennial exhibition opened in November of 1987 at Washington's National Gallery, in a season when museums presented more female painters in one-person shows than ever before. It is the split nature of these times that, as more women gain visibility, the fullness of their visions will not be welcomed but recanted.

Envision the beginning of "second-wave" feminism, an intensely energized moment in the late 1960s, when women—teenagers, students, professionals in the arts, or housewives—sensed a change in the wind. Consciousness struck in stunning personal revelations produced by a clash of internal realities with assumptions. Once seen, this fissure broke the connection between firmly held "biological facts" and prejudice following "naturally" from them.

Painter/printmaker Ruth Weisberg had the "click!" experience when she "did an eight-foot painting of a man and woman having intercourse. The men were offended (in 1966!) that the woman was on top." [2]

Book artist and printer Susan King saw the irony of "one of my best friends telling me I shouldn't take welding, because I wasn't strong enough. So by 1970 I was ensconced in the Ceramics Department where I was lugging around 100 lb. bags of clay, and lifting 40 lb. kiln shelves."

In the larger environment of the early 1970s and emerging feminism, even women isolated from feminist activity were brought closer to their own concerns.

Performance artist Linda Montano was lonely teaching sculpture in a Catholic girls' college in Rochester, but "in that geographical, personal isolation, I was able to 'come to' performance. I presented dead chickens in a gallery. They bloated, reminded the audience of Vietnam, and I was shocked into changing from chickens to myself."

Designer Sheila Levrant de Bretteville, who would invent the first women's design program at California Institute of the Arts in 1971 "had just moved back to the United States in 1970 after working for Olivetti in Milan for two years. In Italy I had begun to look for ways to do work that was for and about people. In retrospect this process of turning away from the corporate and cultural client to the user population was a way of turning the work to include myself."

Female professionals whose self-consciousness and self-possession were flowering found expectations that they obey old female role perimeters unchanged in their workplaces.

In New York, Marcia Tucker (now director of The New Museum) began work as curator at the Whitney Museum in late 1968. "I was the first woman they had hired for this position in many years—perhaps since the days of Gertrude Vanderbilt Whitney. The first day, people mistook me for my secretary, partly because I was so young (28), partly because at that time a female curator was in itself an anomaly."

Sexism in the art world as elsewhere went hand in hand with racism and other prejudice, as it always had.

Lowery Sims, associate curator at the Metropolitan Museum of Art "was often confronted at a party or dinner with a Black maid, who was my hosts' only contact with Black people. These patrons told me they didn't think of me as Black."

Lyndon Johnson had halted bombing in Vietnam after the Tet offensive in 1968. In 1971 the draft ended and, with it, student protest subsided. Martin Luther King and Robert Kennedy had been murdered. The antiwar and civil rights movements had given way for a number of women, and they formed the core of the new feminism. But the grassroots organizing and community base of the civil rights and antiwar movements also became organizing principles of feminism.

In 1972, I attended the first East Coast conference for women in the visual arts, held at the Corcoran Gallery of Art in Washington, D.C. There I met Judy Chicago, who had taught the first women's art class at California State University, Fresno, and had inaugurated a Feminist Art Program (FAP) at the California Institute of the Arts (with Miriam Schapiro). That fall I moved to Los Angeles to work as art historian of the Feminist Art Program.

Art critic Carey Lovelace, then a student in Cal Arts' school of music, described the effect of that program: "I had little sense of political solidarity when I was 20, and struggled privately against my own ghosts, muddled ideas about (capital A) Art, and sexual identity. Meanwhile, in the hermetic white rooms of California Institute of the Arts, a historic moment was occurring. Women in the Feminist Art Programs banded together for the first time to give form to a new artistic identity, to create a nurturing environment, to point out inequities in a system everyone had taken for granted."

In Los Angeles, June Wayne taught the "Joan of Art" seminars to assist women in presenting their work professionally. Wayne, and the women who flocked to her classes, recognized that as practicing artists they had not been let in on vital information—from personal contacts to how to label slides—passed along by teachers and older or more successful colleagues to male students. Wayne's work was based on her analysis of the category "successful artist," which she had revealed as socially constructed and culturally selected as a male club rather than composed of creators of art of the highest innate value.

Wayne, de Bretteville, Weisberg, and others formed the Los Angeles Council of Women in the Arts, an organization which raised questions about who was selected for inclusion in museum exhibitions. They used statistics to reveal bias and protest inequity. But when the same women participated in the FAP's West Coast Women Artists' Conference and prepared *Womanspace,* the first West Coast women artists' exhibition space, they undertook a different task—to explore and present the art which they and other women had made.

For artists caught up in the startling insights and possibilities of feminism, being-a-woman was expressed (in much of the art on view at that time) in styles similar if not identical to those of other art. Although being-a-woman (in artmaking and the art world) was distinguished from the experience of male artists, no one claimed to know how women might behave or produce in a self-created environment.

But all during the 1970s, a contemporary tribal art emerged from the dialog of feminist groups. Within small worlds of women, identification with other women became a political concept, the basis for art/action, and a forceful vision of a future without the unwanted baggage of the antifemale mainstream. Issues raised and values held in women's communities could be asserted to challenge those in surrounding social orders. Feminist art of new or reenergized forms such as book-making, performance, video, media work, and ritual, eventually became universally understandable to the national and international tribe, its advocates and adversaries.

The Woman's Building and Feminist Studio Workshop (FSW), a cultural center and school founded by Chicago, de Bretteville, and me in Los Angeles in 1973, were the focus for sharing work and organizing with women from New York and Chicago—also centers of intensive activity—and with women working without community support. Our activities created a community which artists working in isolation were drawn to join.

Linda Montano thought that "The Woman's Building philosophy permeated the performance world. I grew, along with and with the help of women artists. The quality and quantity of support that represented the L.A. women's art scene was devotional and deep."

I remember an early private performance in which Cheri Gaulke danced for a small group huddled against the walls of her studio. She was a snake who shed her skin and became a snake goddess. She also shared some raw, violent collages which she had sewn together—photographs from pornographic magazines. I was revolted by these collages. But in the intimate trust of this group of colleagues, students, and teachers, I came to understand Gaulke's two incipient images as hallmarks of the experience of all of us which she was struggling to analyze and synthesize in her work.

Years later, when Gaulke performed *This Is My Body,* she used her own body as the ancient Serpent, a hanged witch, and Jesus Christ crucified. On the back wall of the church in which the performance took place, she surveyed historical art images, including Hugo van der Goes's *The Original Sin,* Antonio da Messina's *Crucifixion,* and Botticelli's *Pieta,* in slides. Gaulke not only represented herself and "ruined" familiar representations, but she also embodied the discourse of a self-selected feminist community.

All-female artist groups, as well as the international discourse—in print, at conferences, and in exhibitions—on which many of the assumptions about femininity were based, have been disregarded when analyzing the nature of the art produced then. "Innate" femininity said to inform female imagery, ritual, and body art was not formulated without consideration of human invention and social environment, although generalizing about women was inadequate when it obscured differences of race and class. Points of agreement between individuals and the group "women" became a new mirror for those "natives" who participated. Their configurations of intellect and perception shifted dramatically.

An economic recession and a turn from liberal principles to conservatism began at mid-decade. In 1975, unemployment rose to 8.5 percent. The Hyde Amendment, restricting federal funding for abortions and effectively putting abortion out of the reach of poor women, was introduced in 1976.

Already swimming against the "tide," two feminist publications in the arts—*Chrysalis* on the West Coast and *Heresies* in the East—were inaugurated in 1976. These publications reflected work which had been profoundly influenced by the interdisciplinary "postmodern" eclectic nature of feminist analysis, and the cross-currents of women's arts and thought in feminist enclaves. Since categories of work in the arts had been shaken and "deconstructed" by feminism, women felt freer to re-create their work. Elke Solomon, a curator of drawings at the Whitney Museum, became a full-time artist. Lucy Lippard published a novel with *Chrysalis* books. Visual artists Faith Wilding and Judy Chicago published art historical books. Historian/critic Joanna Frueh began performing.

Federal legislation which had begun to address gender inequity—guaranteeing the right to equal pay, prohibiting discrimination in educational programs receiving federal funds, and extending the jurisdiction of the Equal Employment Opportunity Commission to ban job discrimination because of sex—halted and reversed as the 1970s closed. Congress had approved the ERA and the Child Development Act authorizing federal funding for child care centers. But when Nixon won a second term, he vetoed the CDA.

Children and employment have become two major areas of conflict in the "postfeminist" era. But the issues are not new. Artists struggled to carry on creative work and activist movement work, and continue to nurture their families, since the advent of second wave feminism. Some were "doing it all" before anyone ever heard of "having it all."

Harmony Hammond worked part time for the Brooklyn Public Library as a storyteller to support herself and her daughter. "Artists, writers, and musicians went into poverty areas of Brooklyn and brought books to children in day care centers. Meanwhile I couldn't find day care for my own daughter back in Manhattan. One half of my income at the library was spent for the babysitter so that I could earn the other half."

Sheila de Bretteville gave birth to her child "after a full day of work and was working in the hospital and back in my home right after. I was able to fool myself for many years that it was indeed no trouble to do everything at once."

The collective body which had formed in the first part of the 1970s ebbed in the last years of the decade.

As Faith Wilding put it, "My life in the late 70s became increasingly solitary and hermetic, partly as a response to the political/cultural climate, economic anxiety and a sort of burnout resulting largely from the fact that it didn't seem we'd succeeded to change things in the way we'd hoped."

New West assessed the seventies in 1979 by claiming, "It was the worst of times, it was the worst of times."

Wilding wondered, "What happened to those women who came out of their home cocoon-prisons and tried to fly with their sister artists? Many were middle-aged, married, mothers. I heard rumors of husbands threatened, divorces, adultery, abandonment, alcoholism, breakdown. . . . "

Disappointment that the dreams for sweeping social changes of the sixties (which many of us harbored all through the next decade) did not materialize, was sometimes manifested as bitterness toward colleagues in the women's movement.

"A result of having a job which involved responsibility and power was" for Marcia Tucker, "the loss of friends—some of whom stated that I had suddenly become 'competitive'—and subtle abuse and ultimate abandonment in a long-term personal relationship. The worst, for me, was the lack of support from women in the art community. I still remember a meeting of women artists and critics and a handful of women like myself who worked in museums, during which I was verbally attacked in so violent a way that I experienced a profound, long-lasting sense of isolation which colored my thoughts and activities for many years."

Elke Solomon sadly acknowledged that "The women in my consciousness-raising group were ultimately not so supportive. Some have become careerists in a bad way, turned into the people that, if they were men, I wouldn't have anything to do with. Their concerns are about the self, not about the community, but in the name of the community. Was the Women's Movement of the 70s only a self-realization movement?"

Although conflict within the women's movement was sharply painful, women's disappointment with one another was a symptom and a result of persistent social problems—decline of American international leadership and national credibility, the crushing realities of imminent disasters such as Three Mile Island, inflation way out of individual control.

In 1977, the National Women's Conference in Houston and the comprehensive exhibition, *Women Artists: 1550–1950,* curated by Linda Nochlin and Ann Harris, gave feminists an opportunity to assess progress which had been made and deficiencies which still existed.

June Wayne was critical that "We are more comfortable within our ghetto than outside it. Much that is being done is no damn good, and not a word is said about that within the movement."

Ruth Weisberg charged that "Women who've done best are male-identified, affiliated with specific male artists or groups."

But painter Grace Hartigan believes that "If you're an extraordinarily gifted woman, the door is open. What women are fighting for is the right to be as mediocre as men." [3]

Confidence in national leadership had begun falling as early as 1973, when Watergate exploded and Nixon resigned. Since the important Roe vs. Wade decision secured a woman's right to abortion, women's control over their bodies continued to be hotly debated, and this legally protected control began to disintegrate as pressure from "right to life" groups (and government agencies affected by them) grew. In the 1980s, we have witnessed the defeat of the ERA and repudiation of landmark legislation of ten years ago. The Reagan presidency ended many of the social programs which had helped to build the alternative institutions which we had created. The Moral Majority (Reagan's "thunder on the right"), the Creationist movement, a fifties-style anti-Communism, the arms build-up and a new level of U.S. aggression couched in "tough retaliation" has made us wonder if two decades of humanitarian work might have been a dream. And, despite contemporary charitable activities against hunger and homelessness in which even Reagan has participated, social responsibility in the United States is a Sisyphus stone rolling down the hill of history toward a time of social, political, and economic inequity we have not known since the beginning of this century.

The most visible postmodern female artists do not describe their art as an expression of consensus, even if they seem to speak in a collective voice. And although their signature styles can be identified because they have become familiar, they are not individualistic in the ordinary sense. Conceptualists, their art is emphatically directed to the realm of the mind and the male audience, re-creating and reproducing syntheses of existing forms and subjects. Their artistic hand is an art director.

Joanna Frueh criticizes "Super-intellectualized 'feminism' of deconstruction" because it "lets some people off the hook. Such '80s feminism' is cold. But I know there are hot, passionate feminists out there. Feminism shouldn't be assimilated into the artworld. But it needs to be there, and not as a marginal voice that only complains. Money, male stardom and heroism, represent conservative values. Feminism can never, must never be conservative."

De-erotic conceptual art which cannot be separated from its patriarchal roots; and appropriation, which borrows forms, gestures, and prescribed roles, even if for critique, can reuniversalize male experience. The body is visually rendered as artifact whether an artist shows her own or another female figure. Some eschew the body altogether when working exclusively with abstract forms or text.

Even if entirely visual, forms thus conceived valorize the Word. The image may in fact be *rejected* by the word; the female body rejected in favor of a disembodied voice. And this voice is also appropriated. It is the voice without a body which first uttered the Word—the creative/accusatory God of the Hebrews. If a woman/artist speaks from the voice of this God, whose word is law but whose image can *never* be conceived or produced (much less reproduced), that woman can join her male audience, no longer implicated with her sex as occupying the body from which an image may be constructed and seen.

If you think about the eighties as the hour of "postfeminism," postmodern renunciation of the direct hand, appropriation of existing forms, and deconstruction of social fabrications become postmortem commentary on the unfashionable sensuality of feminist expression. But Simone de Beauvoir had already recognized the gains to be made by leaving the body in the 1940s. She acknowledged the centrality of the physical and sensual when musing about why she thought female artists had failed to create abstract elegance: "in compensation, their work speaks directly to the senses."

Speaking directly to the senses becomes a feminist act when the speaking voice is a trajectory away from all mediated experience, toward a more elemental self. An existential grasp of things-in-themselves beneath their manufactured representations requires seeing which opens us to the world but which is to some extent characterized by the physical oculus.

Postmodernism, in contrast, is said to be philosophically opposed to such a limitation. Michel Foucault, whose work (along with that of Lacan, Barthes, Baudrillard, and other French thinkers) has been used to interpret and validate postmodernism, does not conceive of sexuality as a given or nature as a norm. Foucault, who wrote so extensively about the revolutionary power of the body to overcome power *over* bodies, also disconnected sexuality from any natural order. With Nietzsche, he viewed nature as an invention of human subjectivity.

Of course there is an exhilarating freedom in creating the world from scratch. But there may be a limitation, at least in clarity, in any philosophy which denies biological realities when rejecting biological determinism. Arguments that there is no biologically determined femininity—which can be supported or assaulted by social ideals and practice—have been used as authentication for recent art. They represent (along with cosmetic surgery for all middle-class citizens) escapist science fictions.

Simone de Beauvoir popularized historical female consciousness as "the Other." Writers and visual artists took up otherness as a primary identification spiriting their work in the 1970s. "Self-as-other" forged a complicated, powerful female "I." Leaving the body to reverse this trajectory and escape torture cannot result in an even more primary expression of self, but only in the disappearance of the primary female voice altogether.

De Beauvoir's ideal woman was independent because she was free of biologically determined services to the species—pregnancy, lactation, menstruation. In de Beauvoir's time, an independent woman had to be postmenopausal.

But Sartrean nausea has many of us gagging again as current implications of female corporeality unfold. Woman's body is once more a battleground between self and society, when social cooperation in self-determination is endangered. Legal abortion may be withdrawn from those who need it most. Paternity dominates as a mark of lineage, while maternity could become womb rental for poor women. Rape persists. And this year Andrea Dworkin (in *Intercourse*) has made everyone angry by suggesting that within patriarchal society, socially constructed ideas about and practices based on gender are related to women's physical construction, vulnerable to internal invasion and occupation. Not a metaphor, but a concrete reality. No wonder so many women are making a philosophical exodus from their own bodies.

"Post-feminist feminists" will not analyze male power or implicate those who perpetuate inequities against women. Instead, the system stands; even female artists blame other female artists when they fail to succeed, and feminists are held responsible for right-wing backlash against feminism. The idea that patriarchal institutions must change is absent from most of today's dialogs.

Yet forms pioneered by feminists as early as the sixties are still alive and viable. Otherwise, why would artists not now associated with feminism explore decorative art, personal fantasy, biology (even male vaginal art!), environment, and ritual?

"I am amazed," Susan King wrote, "when I think back to Linda Nochlin's 'Why Have There Been No Great Women Artists?' Of course the 70s changed all of that. WE changed all of that.

A case can be made for attributing large segments of what has flowered in contemporary art to the forms and insights of the feminist art movement, appropriated without acknowledgment.

Elke Solomon is angry that "Our movement has been coopted into lip service for the culture."

Jane O'Reilly, who had written in 1970 about the "click" of seeing that what had been natural had in fact been sexist, sadly acknowledged 10 years later that there would be no liberation by next summer or even the summer after that.

"Sixteen years ago," Judy Chicago mused, "there was no such thing as a feminist artist, or feminist art, feminist art history, feminist art education. We created all that. And until our goal is reached—that is, the complete integration of women into the arts, the museums, the history books, the value structure of society, on our own terms—our job is not done. As long as our job is not done, the word "feminist" is an important word."

For composer Pauline Oliveros, "The culture of the 80s reminds me of a bunch of dinosaurs in their death throes—lumbering around, making their last gasps, shaking the earth plates with their death dance."

"In the '80s," according to Carey Lovelace, "collectors come fresh out of the business world, and dealers can never go wrong in exploiting reactionary styles that massage the beliefs of this group." "Part of the snob appeal of some powerful galleries in Los Angeles," Ruth Weisberg reflected, "is the lack of women

there. The greatest discrimination lies in the most competitive sector, the most financially and professionally rewarding areas. Today's art world, unlike the women's movement in art, promotes a disparity which is getting more extreme.''

Marcia Tucker noticed that "Increasingly, exhibition announcements don't include women; reviews and articles are still mostly about the work of men; museum shows have the same negligible proportion of men to women. People are consumed with greed, obsessed by success, preoccupied with style rather than substance in so many aspects of their lives and work. And we're living in a period when the world has gone haywire again, when the concept of morality is an 'outmoded' one, when there's one code of ethics for your life and another for your career.''

"In the art world," Judy Chicago remarked, "The Museum of Modern Art is still not called the Museum of Male Art, even though the art is male.''

The Guerrilla Girls, who take a statistical approach to inequality in the artworld, "were tired of sitting around complaining and wanted to disseminate information through guerrilla action. We didn't want to be reasonable or polite. The statistics are indisputable, and targeting prevents the people who are collectively responsible for worsening inequality in the artworld from passing the buck.''

Lucy Lippard reflected that "The Guerrilla Girls are applying basic civil rights arguments to women artists' professional situations and doing it with real flair." But "I wish there were more acknowledgment of the diversity of activist feminist art that is not just artworld-centered.''

And June Wayne said: "There is little percentage in trying to get into top dog position; one will only be allowed to smell the piss of the big dog. Who needs that?''

According to Lowery Sims, "There have been some cosmetic changes over the last sixteen years, but no substantial ones. Women are some of the strongest artists on the scene today. But they are not getting appropriate recognition in the press.''

Lucy Lippard noticed that "Feminism, and the changes it has wrought, are taken for granted by most of the younger generation—either dismissed as accomplished or dismissed as irrelevant to their lives (which of course they'll find out it isn't, but later . . .).''

"Any mention of feminist concerns to [Susan King's] women students is met with a grimace and, 'Oh, that, again?' ''

"Young women are very naive, with no sense of difficulties or process, only of the benefits. A few twenty-year-olds have been asking [Lowery Sims] about the validity of Black art. This shows me that there is a dangerous lack of historical consciousness. Black activists and feminists have not passed on the lore.''

Martha Wilson/Redy Story, performance artist and director of New York's Franklin Furnace, thinks that "Things are a little worse than they were ten years ago. But censorship can actually promote the arts, and repression allows political content to emerge. The response of women to these conditions is to do everything to circumvent the system which doesn't incorporate us."

At the same time I read Jane O'Reilly's regrets that visions of freedom had not materialized, an artist I know "tuned in" to her own visions via a nervous breakdown. Always shy, she now gives discourses on the information she's received during the past seven years. She said, "The holy grail is being turned into a styrofoam cup. We are next in line for extinction unless we get our instincts out and alive." She re-casts fairy tales in light of her lunacy. And she chides me for my fear of her mad vision.

I admit it. I think she's right.

But I struggle. Consensus of the few has not yet brought us to our senses. Can women put forth visions unmarred by primary distortions of consciousness—living in society but out of body, or in the body but shunned from culture? If women can be sensual, physical, and eternal, could biology be transformed? Could our thinking about the body also be transformed, from the dank, unruly, and natural that must be civilized, to a model of rhythms and relationships upon which a society can be built?

Notes

1. Eleanor Heartney, "How Wide Is the Gender Gap?," *ARTnews* (Summer 1987): 140.

2. All quotations unless otherwise noted are from interviews I conducted and responses to questionnaires I sent to thirty-five women who had been active in the women's movement in art of the late 1960s and 1970s, and who are still active in the arts today.

3. Grace Hartigan, quoted in Heartney, "How Wide Is the Gender Gap?," p. 141.

Contributors

Judith Barry is an artist and writer who lives and works in New York City. She has had major installations in the Museum of Modern Art and the Whitney Museum in New York City, among others. Her writing has been published in *Screen* magazine, *Wedge, Discourse, Museum Journal* and numerous other journals and periodicals. Recent biographical material can be found in *Afterimage,* October 1987, in an article entitled ''The Architecture of Representation,'' by Margaret Morse, and in *Parkett,* Fall 1987, in ''The Vampiric Text,'' by Jean Fisher.

Whitney Chadwick, Professor of Art at San Francisco State University, received her B.A. from Middlebury College in 1965 and her Ph.D. in art history from The Pennsylvania State University. The author of *Myth in Surrealist Painting, 1929–1939: Dali, Ernst and Masson* (1980) and *Women Artists and the Surrealist Movement* (1985), she has contributed articles on Surrealism and feminism to the *Art Bulletin, Artforum, Art International,* the *College Art Journal,* and the *Woman's Art Journal.* She is currently preparing a book on women artists and the politics of representation.

Carol Duncan has been teaching art history and related interdisciplinary courses for more than 15 years at Ramapo College in New Jersey, where she is Professor of Art History. She frequently guest-lectures at universities and colleges across the country and in Europe. Her scholarly and critical writings have dealt with European and American art and art institutions from the eighteenth century to the present. Her research centers on the ideological meanings of art within its social and cultural context.

Sandy Flitterman-Lewis is Assistant Professor in the English department at Rutgers University where she teaches courses in literature, film, and women's studies. She was one of four founding editors of *Camera Obscura: A Journal of Feminism and Film Theory,* and has written for numerous publications, including *Women and Film, Screen, Wide Angle, Literature and Psychology,* and *Enclitic,* among others. Her work is anthologized in four collections: *Theories of Authorship,*

Regarding Television, Channels of Discourse, and *Dada and Surrealist Film.* Her book on French women directors, *To Desire Differently: Feminism and the French Cinema,* is forthcoming from the University of Illinois Press.

Joanna Frueh earned her B.A. from Sarah Lawrence College and her M.A. and Ph.D. from the University of Chicago. She has written extensively on contemporary art and women artists and her publications include articles in *Artforum, Art in America, Art Journal, Arts Magazine,* the *Feminist Art Journal,* and the *New Art Examiner,* for which she is a contributing editor. Frueh is also a performance artist who has presented work nationally. She has taught at Oberlin College, the University of Arizona and the University of Missouri at St. Louis.

Shifra Goldman is an art historian based in Los Angeles. She has authored *Contemporary Mexican Painting in a Time of Change* (1981), co-authored with Tomás Ybarra-Frausto *Arte Chicano: A Comprehensive Annotated Bibliography of Chicano Art, 1965–1981* (1985), and has published dozens of articles on modern Latin American art in the U.S., Latin America, and Europe.

Maryse Holder was born in France in 1941. At 21 she became a United States citizen. Holder graduated from Brooklyn College and worked on a Ph.D. at Cornell University and later at City University in New York. She taught in the City University system and placed her film and art criticism in feminist publications. Holder's book *Give Sorrow Words: Maryse Holder's Letters from Mexico* (1979) contains letters from her trips to Mexico in 1976 and 1977. She was murdered in Mexico City in September 1977.

Cassandra L. Langer was born in Woodridge, New York, educated at the University of Miami, Harvard, Columbia, and New York Universities. She has been a Smithsonian post-doctoral fellow at the National Museum of American Art. She has taught art history and criticism at Florida International University and was most recently Associate Professor and Chair of the art history department at the University of South Carolina, Columbia. A veteran art critic for more than fifteen years, her article credits include *Arts, Art Criticism,* the *College Art Journal, American Artist Magazine, Art Papers,* the *Women's Art Journal, Women Artists News* and the *International Journal of Women's Studies.* She is currently finishing a monograph on John F. Kensett (1816–1872) for Cambridge University Press, working on a bibliography of feminist art criticism for G. K. Hall, and writing a novel.

Teresa de Lauretis, Professor of the History of Consciousness at the University of California, Santa Cruz, is the author of *Alice Doesn't: Feminism, Semiotics, Cinema,* the editor of *Feminist Studies/Critical Studies,* and the coeditor (with Stephen Heath) of *The Cinematic Apparatus.* She is also the general editor of the series "Theories of Representation and Difference" for Indiana University Press. Her most recent book is *Technologies of Gender: Essays on Theory, Film, and Fiction.*

Gloria Feman Orenstein is Professor of Women's Studies and Comparative Literature at the University of Southern California. She has authored *The Theatre of the Marvelous: Surrealism and the Contemporary Stage* and many articles on the women of Surrealism and contemporary women writers and artists. She was co-creator of the Women's Salon for Literature in New York (1975–1985). Her continued research on the reemergence of the Goddess in art and literature in the work of contemporary women will be published in her next book, *A Gynecentric Vision: From the Occultation to the Reflowering of the Goddess in Art and Literature by Contemporary Women.*

Arlene Raven lectures widely and writes for journals that include the *Village Voice, Arts Magazine,* the *New Art Examiner, High Performance,* and the *Women's Review of Books.* She is also a writer for Harry N. Abrams. Her selected essays were recently published as *Crossing Over: Feminism and Art of Social Concern* (UMI Research Press, 1988). Raven is currently on the faculty of The New School for Social Research. She was founder of the Women's Caucus for Art, the Los Angeles Woman's Building, and *Chrysalis* magazine. Recipient of numerous grants and awards, including 2 NEA art critics fellowships and an honorary Doctor of Humanities degree from Hood College, she has curated exhibitions for a number of institutions, including the Baltimore Museum of Art and the Long Beach Museum of Art. Raven studied at Hood College, George Washington University, and Johns Hopkins University, and holds an M.F.A. in painting, and M.A. and Ph.D. degrees in art history.

Moira Roth, now Trefethen Professor of Art History, Mills College, Oakland (previously she taught at the University of California, San Diego) is a modernist art historian and critic. She studied at the London School of Economics and Washington Square College, New York University, and received her Ph.D. at the University of California, Berkeley. She has written extensively on performance art, women's art, and contemporary art generally. Her writings include "The Aesthetic of Indifference" (*Artforum,* November 1977), "Visions and Re-Visions" (*Arforum,* November 1980), *The Amazing Decade: Women and Performance Art in America, 1970–1980* (1983, editor and contributor), and a forthcoming article, "Suzanne Lacy: Social Reformer and Witch (*Drama Review*).

Lowery Stokes Sims earned her B.A. in art history from Queens College, where she was elected to Phi Beta Kappa, and her M.A. in art history from Johns Hopkins University. She is currently pursuing her doctoral studies at the Graduate Center of the City University of New York. Sims has been on the staff of the

Metropolitan Museum of Arts since 1972, and is currently Associate Curator in the Department of Twentieth-Century Art. She has served on panels for the Department of Cultural Affairs of the City of New York, the New York State Council on the Arts, and the National Endowment for the Arts and the Humanities. She also has served as guest curator at the Queens Museum, the Studio Museum, Pratt Institute, the California Museum of Afro-American History and Culture, and the New Museum. She has lectured at the A.I.R. Gallery in New York, the Detroit Institute of Art, Vassar College, and Princeton University, and has written extensively on contemporary artists, with a special interest in Afro-American artists.

Lise Vogel has a doctorate in art history from Harvard University and one in sociology from Brandeis University. Active in the women's movement and the left since the 1960s, she currently lives in New York City and teaches sociology at Rider College. Her recent publications are in the areas of feminist theory, women's history, and gender policy. Forthcoming is a book, *Pregnancy at Work: The Debate over Special Treatment,* to be published by Rutgers University Press.

Index